OC 18

The
TRACK
in the
FOREST

The *CREATION of a* LEGENDARY
1968 US OLYMPIC TEAM

BOB BURNS

CHICAGO
REVIEW
PRESS

Copyright © 2019 by Bob Burns
All rights reserved
First edition
Published by Chicago Review Press Incorporated
814 North Franklin Street
Chicago, Illinois 60610
ISBN 978-0-89733-937-7

Library of Congress Cataloging-in-Publication Data

Names: Burns, Bob, 1957– author.
Title: The track in the forest : the creation of a legendary 1968 US Olympic
   Team / Bob Burns.
Description: First edition. | Chicago, Illinois : Chicago Review Press,
   [2019] | Includes bibliographical references and index.
Identifiers: LCCN 2018010532 (print) | LCCN 2018022236 (ebook) | ISBN
   9780897339384 (adobe pdf) | ISBN 9781641600804 (epub) | ISBN
   9781641600811 (kindle) | ISBN 9780897339377 (cloth)
Subjects: LCSH: Track and field athletes—United States—History—20th
   century. | Olympic Games (19th : 1968 : Mexico City, Mexico)
Classification: LCC GV1060.6 (ebook) | LCC GV1060.6 .B87 2019 (print)
   | DDC 796.420922 [B] —dc23
LC record available at https://lccn.loc.gov/2018010532

Typesetting: Nord Compo
Map design: Chris Erichsen

For images on pages 81, 88, 135, and 161, every effort has been made to contact
the copyright holders. The editors would welcome information concerning any
inadvertent errors or omissions.

Printed in the United States of America
5 4 3 2 1

To my dad, John Burns, for (among other things) taking me
to my first track meet—the Echo Summit Olympic trials

I can still taste the air. In the morning it was like a fresh glass of spring water.

—Larry James, world-record holder
in the 400 meters, on Echo Summit

CONTENTS

Key Figures ix

Map xi

Prologue: Return to the Summit xiii

1   Into the Great Unknown 1

2   Echo Summit 9

3   The Mastermind 24

4   The Resisters 31

5   The Boycott Campaign 39

6   The Innovator 48

7   The Cruelest Month 57

8   Aftershocks 61

9   Bumpy Road to Summit 74

10   Magic Mountain 86

11   Melting Pot 96

12   Take Your Marks 116

13   Out of This World 133

14   Highs and Lows 153

15   Interlude 164

16   Mexico City 172

17   Legacies 196

Epilogue: Distant Echoes 217

Acknowledgments. 225
Notes. 227
Bibliography 237
Index 241

KEY FIGURES

Bob Beamon—Onetime juvenile delinquent who soared above and beyond the turmoil of 1968 to set a world record for the ages.

Ralph Boston—Venerable long jumper whose last shot at Olympic glory ran headfirst into racial politics—and Beamon's otherworldly talent.

Bill Bowerman—Oregon coach and future Nike cofounder who oversaw the high-altitude training camp and final trials at Echo Summit.

John Carlos—Brash sprinter from Harlem who found his stride with the Speed City group in San Jose.

Harold Connolly—Politically active hammer thrower who stood up for his black teammates.

Olga Connolly—Wife of Harold who like other women had to compete in separate Olympic trials.

Willie Davenport—First African American to compete in both the Summer and Winter Olympics.

Harry Edwards—Controversial sociology professor whose glowering face and incendiary words roiled the sports world in 1968.

Lee Evans—Ferocious competitor whose support of the Olympic Project for Human Rights caused him great angst in Mexico City.

Tom Farrell—Army runner and 1964 Olympian who participated in the 1967 trial run at Echo Summit.

Dick Fosbury—Lanky upstart from Oregon who revolutionized the high jump with his blithe Fosbury Flop.

Larry James—The Mighty Burner's meteoric arrival in 1968 pushed Evans and the 400-meter dash to greater heights.

Payton Jordan—White-haired head coach from Stanford who gradually won the trust of the entire US Olympic team.

Walt Little—Ex-sportswriter whose big dreams and friendship with Jordan helped make Echo Summit possible.

Randy Matson—Shot-putter considered the surest gold-medal winner in US men's track.

Billy Mills—Native American hero of the Tokyo Olympics seeking one last run for glory.

Al Oerter—Discus legend known for his unanny ability to peak for the Olympic Games.

Dave Patrick—Villanova miler whose Olympic hopes came to a devastating end at Echo Summit.

Mel Pender—Sprinter who was brought home from Vietnam to try out for second Olympic team.

Bob Rice—US Forest Service district ranger who permitted the track in the forest to be built.

Jim Ryun—Seemingly unbeatable middle-distance star who couldn't outrace effects of altitude.

Bob Seagren—Southern California star who broke the world record in pole vault at Echo Summit.

Jay Silvester—Oerter's archrival who resented politics interfering with his Olympic preparations.

Tommie Smith—Incomparable sprinter at the center of the black boycott movement in 1968.

Bill Toomey—Decathlon standout who embraced training conditions and nightlife at Tahoe.

Tom Waddell—Army medic who made the Olympic team after refusing to serve in Vietnam and who later founded the Gay Olympics.

Stan Wright—Black sprint coach whose outspoken opposition to the Olympic boycott put him in the cross fire.

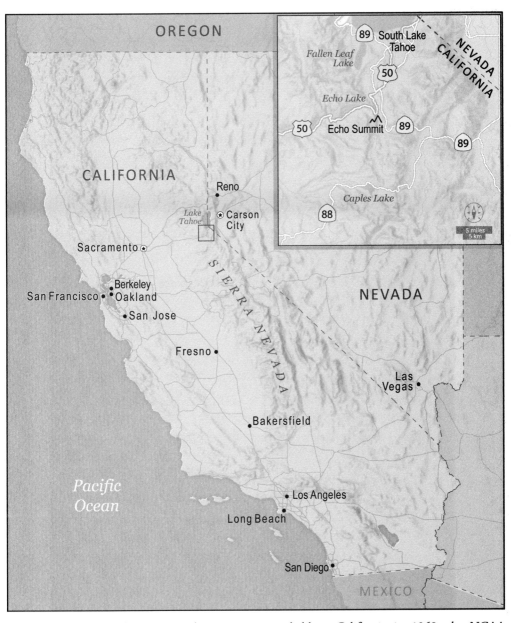

The four biggest track meets in the country were held in California in 1968: the NCAA Championships (Berkeley), AAU Championships (Sacramento), semifinal Olympic trials (Los Angeles), and final Olympic trials (Echo Summit above South Lake Tahoe).

PROLOGUE

RETURN TO THE SUMMIT

FOR MOST TOUR buses lumbering southeast on US Highway 50, Echo Summit is nothing more than a roadside sign—a welcome reminder that the blue waters and green gaming tables of Lake Tahoe beckon just around the bend. As it was a century and a half earlier for fortune seekers racing to the Comstock silver mines, the mountain pass near the California-Nevada border remains more of an obstacle than a destination.

Except for one summer morning in 2014, when Forest Service personnel directed a black coach off the busy highway for a special tribute at the summit. A group of well-preserved men in their sixties and seventies, some accompanied by wives and grandchildren, emerged from the front door of the bus into the alpine sun. The bonhomie and banter brought to mind a class reunion, which in fact it was—a reunion of one of the greatest classes of Olympic athletes assembled in any sport.

In the thin and highly politicized air of the 1968 Olympic Games in Mexico City, the US men's track and field team won twelve gold medals and set six world records. The team featured such towering figures as Al Oerter, Bob Beamon, Lee Evans, Willie Davenport, Randy Matson, Ralph Boston, Jim Ryun, Bill Toomey, Jim Hines, and Dick Fosbury.

It was a track team for the ages, but it was more than that. The threat of an Olympic boycott by black athletes generated an inordinate amount of media coverage in the months leading up to the Mexico City Games, and the clenched-fist salute on the medal podium by sprinters Tommie Smith and John Carlos remains one of the most immutable images from the turbulent 1960s.

The exploits of the 1968 US Olympic team were etched in stone long ago. But it wasn't until the tour bus arrived at the Sierra Nevada pass overlooking Lake Tahoe that Echo Summit's part in shaping that legend was carved into granite.

To commemorate the selection of Echo Summit as a California Historic Landmark, the Forest Service office in Placerville organized a "Return to the Summit" celebration in June 2014. A brass marker, set in an enormous granite boulder and surrounded by splotches of lichen, greeted the men who made it happen:

SITE OF ECHO SUMMIT

IN 1968, ECHO SUMMIT SERVED AS A HIGH-ALTITUDE TRAINING CENTER AND SITE OF THE U.S. OLYMPIC MEN'S TRACK AND FIELD TRIALS. FOUR WORLD RECORDS WERE SHATTERED HERE ON THE TRACK CARVED OUT OF THE ELDORADO NATIONAL FOREST. THE U.S. TEAM SELECTED FOR THE 1968 OLYMPIC GAMES IN MEXICO CITY WAS CELEBRATED WORLDWIDE FOR ITS ATHLETIC DOMINANCE AND DEEP COMMITMENT TO RACIAL EQUALITY.

The pilgrims stretched their legs following the ninety-minute drive from Sacramento. High jumpers Ed Caruthers and Reynaldo Brown, tall and regal, stuck close together. Ed Burke, the evergreen hammer thrower who was setting age-group records four decades after making his second Olympic team at Echo Summit, had aged as well as any ponderosa pine. Distance runner Tracy Smith and racewalker Larry Young looked as if they could hike the entire Pacific Crest Trail, which passes within feet of the boulder. Geoff Vanderstock, the hurdler who broke one of the four world records set at Echo Summit, got reacquainted with his great rival, Ron Whitney. It was Vanderstock's first trip back to Echo Summit since 1968.

"I barely recognized the place until I walked around," Vanderstock said later. "I had forgotten that they took the track down the hill afterward. They did it for a good reason, but I kind of wish they had left it where it was."

Indeed, the 400-meter oval left Echo Summit almost as quickly as the departing Olympians in September 1968. Once the snow melted that winter, the pink-colored surface was uprooted and trucked down the hill, where it was reinstalled at South Tahoe Intermediate School.

One thing that hadn't changed since 1968 was the verbosity of Mel Pender, the 5-foot, 5-inch sprinter with the blinding start. Looking preposterously fit for a man of seventy-six, Pender still resembled the kid brother insistent on being heard as well as seen.

"Hey short stack, shut up," Pender was told as the Olympians assembled for a group shot. "You sound like a machine gun—rat-a-tat-tap. Do you ever stop talking?"

"This is a movie," Pender replied. "We got to be talking, right?"

Caruthers, a foot taller than Pender and considerably less voluble, won an epic high jump competition at Echo Summit before claiming an Olympic silver medal in Mexico City. Caruthers enjoyed his Echo Summit experience so much he took his family on vacations to Lake Tahoe for years afterward.

(Left to right) Larry Young, Norm Tate, Reynaldo Brown, Ed Caruthers, Ed Burke, and Tommie Smith (partially obscured) gather at the historical landmark plaque. *The USDA Forest Service*

"Oh, my lord, this is better than I thought it would be," Caruthers said. "When I think of what this team accomplished, and that I was a part of it . . . I couldn't be any happier or prouder. You couldn't ask for a better spot to hold a track meet."

In September 1967, after surveying other sites in Arizona and Colorado, the US Olympic Committee (USOC) selected Echo Summit as a high-altitude training center and site of the final US trials primarily because its 7,382-foot elevation was nearly identical to Mexico City's. The training camp opened in July 1968, and most of the hundred-plus Olympic contenders spent six to eight weeks living, training, and competing on the mountain. Many were housed in trailers set up on the other side of Highway 50.

The Forest Service agreed to the track's construction but insisted that the setting be left as undisturbed as possible. Hundreds of ponderosa pines rose from the infield. Runners disappeared from sight

The view of the track from the adjacent ski hill in 1968 was anything but ordinary. *Photo by Steve Murdock, courtesy of* Track and Field News

Geoff Vanderstock returned to the scene of his world record in the intermediate hurdles for the first time at the Echo Summit reunion. *The USDA Forest Service*

on the curves and backstretch. Javelins came flying out of the trees. The site didn't have much room for spectator seating, but fans improvised, climbing atop boulders to get the best view of the high jump competition.

In the final of the 200-meter dash, for instance, the spectators sitting in the modest bleachers set up along the finish line had no inkling of who was winning for several suspenseful seconds. John Carlos came flying out of the trees with a big lead over Smith and maintained his advantage to the finish, breaking the world record with a spectacular clocking of 19.92 seconds.

In his 2014 return to the summit, Smith spoke of seeing another world record being set, not from the perspective of a runner-up but as a spectator.

"I remember watching Bob Seagren jump his height in the pole vault," Smith said. "We were watching from the stands, and it looked like he was falling out of the trees."

Norm Tate, who qualified for the US Olympic team in the triple jump at Echo Summit, still had a bounce in his step at the reunion, mugging for a photo with the Smokey the Bear mascot the Forest Service enlisted for the event. Vanderstock didn't just forget that the track had been shipped down the hill—"I'd forgotten how funny Norm Tate is," he said.

In 1968, Tate was put in charge of helping athletes find part-time jobs in South Lake Tahoe during their stays at Echo Summit. He also participated in futile attempts to pool money and make a killing at the casinos.

"We were celebrities for eight weeks, and we played it like we were," Tate said. "We were friends, and we're still friends—laughing, drinking, having a good time."

Bill Toomey, the 1968 decathlon champion, drove up from his home on Lake Tahoe's north shore to join his fellow Olympians. Toomey remembered the time on the mountain as "psychological warfare amidst the tranquility," with so many competitors living in such close proximity for ten weeks, knowing that only the top three in each event would move on to Mexico City.

But Toomey remembered the overall experience with mischievous glee.

"It was sort of like Mount Olympus," Toomey said. "You imagined Zeus looking down, commenting to the gods and goddesses, saying, 'This is the way I intended it.' Then Bacchus smiled and said, 'Yeah, and they get to go to Tahoe at night.'"

With his penchant for thunderbolts, a wrathful Zeus would have had a field day in 1968. There have been few years like it, and with the eleventh-hour exception of the spacecraft Apollo 8 orbiting the moon on Christmas Day, 1968 is mostly remembered for the calamities unleashed, one after the other.

The Tet Offensive in late January turned millions of Americans against the Vietnam War while hammering the final nail in the coffin of Lyndon Johnson's presidency. The rioting that followed the April assassination of Martin Luther King Jr. left more than one hundred US cities in flames. Students at Columbia University in New York seized several campus buildings for a week. Robert F. Kennedy was gunned down in California, nine weeks after King's murder.

All year long, students across the world took to the streets, from Paris to Mexico City to Berkeley. Images of police officers pummeling antiwar protesters at the Democratic National Convention in Chicago were beamed around the world. The optimism engendered by the Prague Spring was crushed by Soviet tanks in August. Days before Olympians from around the world arrived, Mexican police opened fire on protesting students. The Mexico City Olympics were the "Problem Games" before they even started, and the pejorative stuck.

"Nineteen sixty-eight was a perverse genius of a year: a masterpiece of shatterings," wrote essayist Lance Morrow. "The printer's ink from the papers that announced it all would smudge and smudge the fingers: history every day dirtied the hands."

In the United States, barrels of printer's ink were spilled on race relations and the Vietnam War. More than sixteen thousand US soldiers died in Vietnam in 1968, the deadliest year of the war for American service members. A number of the postcollegiate athletes at Echo Summit were competing for the US Army or one of the other service branches, partly for the training opportunities, partly to avoid being sent to Vietnam. Of the dozen Olympians attending the Forest Service celebration, two had served in the army while at Echo Summit—Pender and distance runner Tracy Smith.

Pender joined the army at age seventeen and served two tours of duty in Vietnam, the first stint in 1967. "They pulled me out of Vietnam so I could train for the Olympics," Pender said, but he was ordered by the army brass to not even think about joining his black teammates in any protests or demonstrations. Tracy Smith dropped out of Oregon State in 1967 to focus exclusively on the Olympics. Since that meant giving up his college draft deferment, he kept his running career on track by enlisting. The army brass allowed PFC Smith to live and train with his world-renowned coach in Santa Monica, California.

"Basically, we just trained," Smith said. "I went to the PX for food and to pick up my paycheck. I had a job in the bowling alley, dusting off the balls. I'm kind of ashamed of it, really. I'm sure some of the guys I went through basic training with were killed in Vietnam."

Race, not war, is the issue most associated with the 1968 Olympic men's track team. Beginning in late 1967 and continuing through the winter and spring of 1968, Tommie Smith and Lee Evans were the most prominent athletes supporting the Olympic Project for Human Rights (OPHR). Harry Edwards, a sociology professor at San Jose State, was the media-savvy face of the group advocating a black boycott of the Mexico City Olympics. Those lending varying degrees of support to the OPHR cause included Martin Luther King Jr., Muhammad Ali, and Jackie Robinson. But many more were against the idea, from Olympic icon Jesse Owens to the International Olympic Committee's (IOC) autocratic leader, Avery Brundage. Edwards, Smith, and Evans received hate letters and death threats throughout the Olympic year.

Before arriving at Echo Summit, the black athletes contending for spots on the Olympic team had decided against a boycott. The occasional journalist would drive up from the San Francisco Bay Area or Reno to see if the controversy still had any legs, but for the most part, Echo Summit became an alpine refuge. Without television sets in the trailers and cabins, the battles raging at sea level seemed more than 7,300 feet away.

———————

Befitting an organization accustomed to setting up large camps for fire-fighters on a moment's notice, the Forest Service organized a first-class reunion. A crowd of about two hundred took their seats beneath a tent set up in front of a small stage. From four rustic poles flew flags of the United States, California, the Forest Service, and the 1968 Olympic team. A light breeze rippled through the trees, the air as pure as "a fresh glass of spring water," as one Olympian described it years before.

Elected officials from El Dorado County and the city of South Lake Tahoe made brief remarks, as did representatives from the California Office of Historic Preservation and USA Track & Field. Walt Little III represented his late father, a South Lake Tahoe sports editor and recreation director who came up with the idea of holding the meet at Echo Summit and pursued it relentlessly. Speaking on behalf of the Olympians were Tommie Smith and John Carlos.

John Carlos speaking at the Echo Summit reunion in 2014. *The USDA Forest Service*

What a difference a few decades can make. It would have been unimaginable to think that a US governmental agency would have chosen to honor the black sprinters in 1968 or the years immediately following, when much of the American public viewed Smith and Carlos as angry militants.

But this was 2014, not 1968, and the Forest Service, in springing for the celebration, was more interested in the social significance of the Echo Summit trials than in the world records broken on the track in the forest. Smith, Carlos, and Tate participated the day before the reunion in a question-and-answer session with a group of Forest Service employees in a Placerville movie theater, following a showing of the documentary film *Fists of Freedom.*

"It's important that today we acknowledge this significant part of civil rights history, as well as the records that were set here," Forest Supervisor Laurence Crabtree said in his remarks. "Their athleticism allowed for world attention, and they had the courage to direct that attention to a much a larger issue."

Tommie Smith standing in front of the California Historical Landmark plaque at Echo Summit. *The USDA Forest Service*

Sporting a silver beard and gold earring, Carlos was mellower than the brash twenty-three-year-old who shattered the 20-second barrier at Echo Summit, but he still exuded some of his old swagger.

"Mr. Smith and I were vilified back then," Carlos said. "Now, they call us heroes. Someone even went so far as to call Tommie Smith and John Carlos patriots. Let me tell you: all of the people on this team were patriots."

Carlos expressed regret that the Echo Summit trials were an all-male affair. The women vying for spots on the 1968 Olympic track team weren't allowed anywhere near Lake Tahoe. Their trials were held at sea level, in Walnut, California, and the women were allotted just two weeks of altitude training in Los Alamos, New Mexico. In the same vein, one of the enduring criticisms of the OPHR is that it refused to reach out to female athletes such as sprinter Wyomia Tyus and long jumper Willye White.

"It's a shame that the women who represented this nation didn't have the opportunity to experience this beauty and love," Carlos said.

With his wife, Delois, taking photos with her iPad, Smith kept his remarks light.

"I'm thankful that the National Forest people found it in their hearts to chop down some trees," Smith said. "I kind of miss that track. It was one time in our lives that we were pretty, wasn't it? To return to where our legacy began, it's amazing. We're still standing. We're on this side of the grass. It's a blessing."

Austin Angell, a longtime South Lake Tahoe resident who assisted Little in his efforts to secure the Olympic trials and attended each day of the 1968 trials, surprised the Olympians by presenting each of them with small pieces of the original Echo Summit track. When the Tartan surface was removed from its second home at the intermediate school in 2007 because of age, Angell wisely saved some of it for posterity.

Following speeches and photos, Smith, Carlos, and others walked across the parking lot to figure out where the 200-meter starting line had been. "Don't ask me to jog," Smith said. "We're at altitude." Although

South Lake Tahoe track enthusiast Austin Angell (holding box) presents Mel Pender, Ron Whitney, and Norm Tate with pieces of the Echo Summit track in 2014. *The USDA Forest Service*

Vanderstock and Smith lamented the historic track's absence, perhaps it was fitting that they had to reimagine it after so many years. The track in the forest, and the time spent getting ready for the Olympics on the mountaintop, felt like a fantasy in 1968, and it still does today.

"This is a living organism for us," Carlos said. "I remember the snow falling out of the sky, the cold days, the sunny days in our hearts. We had a chance to bond, to fall in love with one another, as well as be very competitive with one another. South Lake Tahoe will be with us for eons, long after we're dead and gone."

In one of the most divisive, disturbing years in American history, Echo Summit offered a remarkable group of men shelter from the storm. This is the story of their journey to and from the summit.

1

INTO THE GREAT
UNKNOWN

UNBEKNOWNST TO ANYONE at the time, the first step toward building a track in the California forest was taken five years earlier in Baden-Baden, a tony West German spa town nestled in the foothills of the Black Forest near the French border.

Baden is German for spa, and the town assumed its curiously hyphenated double name between the world wars to differentiate it from other baths and spas across the European continent. But the locale gained fame centuries before. The Roman emperor Caracalla enjoyed its curative waters in the third century, and it remained a favorite vacation spot for European monarchs and artists through the twentieth century.

The well-heeled members of the IOC made their own pilgrimage in 1963, when they gathered in Baden-Baden to select the host city for the 1968 Olympics—or the XIX Olympics, as the IOC referred to them in a nod to Caracalla and Roman numeration. Joining the IOC in Baden-Baden were representatives of four cities making their final pitches for the 1968 Olympics: Detroit, Buenos Aires, Lyon, and Mexico City.

Detroit, the city that gave rise to the auto industry and the Motown sound, was widely viewed as the favorite. "It looks more and more as if the United States is going to get the games," said Douglas Roby, president of the USOC.

Mexico City's delegation was the first to arrive in Baden-Baden, four days before the final vote. The Mexicans emphasized their rich history, bringing with them a huge statue of the Aztec god Quetzalcoatl. With Cold War tensions at their height, Mexico's representatives appealed to the bloc of voters loyal to the Soviet Union by stressing their country's neutral political position. When the vote was taken on October 16, 1963, Mexico City prevailed on the first ballot, receiving thirty of the fifty-eight votes cast.

The big news was that for the first time, the Olympics would be held at high altitude. The majority of IOC voters were unconcerned that Mexico City's elevation of 7,350 feet was nearly a mile and a half higher than any previous Summer Olympic site. Mexican officials defused the altitude issue by downplaying the effect the thin air would have on the health of the visiting athletes. They cited numerous studies alleging that a short period of acclimatization would guarantee a level playing field. A member of the Mexican delegation, Dr. Eduardo Hay, tried to turn the altitude question around by attributing Mexico City's refreshing climate to its elevation. The IOC's Detroit-born president, Avery Brundage, defended the selection of Mexico City by saying, "The Olympics belong to all the world, not the part of it at sea level."

With the 1968 Olympics still five years out, concern about Mexico City's altitude was relatively muted in the aftermath of the IOC vote. *Sports Illustrated* asked in late 1963, "How will the altitude affect the performance of Olympic athletes? In a city where the big nightclubs provide oxygen tanks for exhausted twisters, and in which hangovers seem endless, this is a question worth asking. The answer is that the effect will be more than somewhat but not necessarily drastic."

Even today, there's no surefire way to measure the effect altitude will have on an individual pushing the limits of endurance. But it's not as if scientists and coaches were completely ignorant in the 1960s about what it meant to compete in an oxygen-starved environment, either. Two of the world's most prominent exercise physiologists—Per-Olaf Astrand of Sweden and Bruno Balke of Germany—conducted pioneering research on the effects of altitude in the years immediately following World War II and continued their work through the Mexico City Olympics.

Astrand tested Swedish cross-country skiers at the 1960 Winter Olympics in Squaw Valley, California, forty-three miles north of Echo Summit near Lake Tahoe's north shore. Astrand's studies at Squaw Valley led to the following conclusion: "At higher altitudes pathological ECG [electrocardiography] has been found to occur during heavy muscular work, so also heart failure." After receiving his PhD in physical performance capacity from the University of Berlin in 1945, Balke worked for the US Air Force School of Aviation Medicine in San Antonio. Astrand and Balke mentored Jack Daniels, a two-time US Olympian in the modern pentathlon who conducted studies of his own at Echo Summit.

Growing interest in mountaineering in the late nineteenth and early twentieth centuries prompted the first studies on altitude's effect on humans engaged in feats of physical endurance. Two years after the first ascent of the world's highest mountain by Edmund Hillary and Tenzing Norgay—with the assistance of oxygen kits—Mexico City played host to the 1955 Pan American Games. Billed the "Olympics of the Western Hemisphere," the Pan Am Games included the first major international track and field competition conducted at high altitude. Granted, 7,350 feet is a far cry from Everest's 29,029 feet, but Hillary and Norgay weren't racing the clock, and they weren't world-class runners, either. (Not until 1978 would Everest be climbed without the aid of supplemental oxygen.) Memories of the 1955 Pan American Games provided ammunition for skeptics who said the IOC never should have awarded the Olympics to Mexico City.

News reports from the 1955 Pan American Games noted the number of runners who collapsed following their races, accompanied by dramatic photos of the fallen hooked up to oxygen devices. Guatemalan officials shared their oxygen with other teams, including the United States. *Sports Illustrated* wrote, "Well-conditioned men from the lowlands dropped like flies. The games became a battle against altitude, and the only effective weapons were tanks of oxygen."

After being taken off the field on a stretcher following his victory in the 400-meter hurdles, Josh Culbreath said, "My throat felt on fire down to my stomach." The distance races were won in slow times, but the experience of US sprinter Lou Jones at the 1955 Pan American Games provided a glimpse of the pros and cons of competing at high altitude. Jones, a twenty-three-year-old army private, won the 400 meters in Mexico City in the world-record time of 45.4 seconds. His clocking shaved a half second off the previous mark, the biggest improvement on the 400-meter record in more than twenty years. Jones collapsed after crossing the finish line and didn't know he had set a world record until he regained consciousness several minutes later. Overall, however, the Pan Am Games were seen as a success and probably helped more than harmed Mexico City's Olympic bid eight years later.

Any criticism of the vote in Baden-Baden was muted as the 1964 Tokyo Olympics drew nearer. Less than two decades after the country had been devastated by firebombing in World War II, the Japanese government and organizers received universal plaudits for their rebuilt city and terrific facilities. Highlights of the Tokyo Olympics included historic wins by US distance runners Bob Schul and Billy Mills in the two longest races on the track. Mills, a twenty-six-year-old first lieutenant in the marines who had grown up an orphan on the Pine Ridge Indian Reservation in South Dakota, sprinted past the world-record holder from Australia, Ron Clarke, and Mohamed Gammoudi of Tunisia in the final homestretch of the 10,000 meters. (Four years later, Clarke and Gammoudi would be two of the central figures of the Mexico City Games, and Mills would be involved in a controversy at Echo Summit that possibly cost him a spot on what would have been his second Olympic team.)

As the track world caught its breath following the excitement of Tokyo, coaches, administrators, and athletes began turning their attention to Mexico City. The Soviet Union announced in 1965 that it had convened scientists and coaches to study acclimatization and complete a preliminary survey of high-altitude training camps for the athletes it would send to Mexico City in 1968. In March 1966, the USOC cosponsored an "International Symposium on the Effects of Altitude on Physical Performance" in the mile-high city of Albuquerque, New Mexico. In his summary of the conference, Balke, the German-born physiologist, said scientists and coaches needed to take the lead in recommending to their country's administrators what specific steps needed to be taken to give their athletes the best chance of success in Mexico City's thin air. The Albuquerque symposium determined that the shortest period of pre-Olympic altitude training would be three weeks, and that the length would possibly be extended to six weeks, in contravention of the IOC's rule limiting the amount of time lowland athletes be allowed to train at altitude camps.

Mexico City organizers held "pre-Olympic" events in 1965, 1966, and 1967, more to allow scientists and physicians to conduct research than to hold full-scale competitions. The 1965 gathering, known unofficially as the "Little Olympics," drew two hundred athletes from seventeen countries. Spectators were amused to see athletes donning special masks and having their blood taken before and after races. "We know that a respiratory thermostat in the body will readjust itself to the altitude in time," said Dr. Daniel Hanley of the US medical squad in Mexico City. "The problem is to find out how long this readjustment will take."

The most closely watched race at the Little Olympics pitted the inimitable Clarke, who had followed his Tokyo disappointment with a spree of record-setting performances, against Gammoudi and Mills. The race was even slower than expected. Gammoudi won in 14 minutes, 40.6 seconds, 1 minute and 15 seconds off Clarke's world record of 13:25.6. Clarke was second, and Mills struggled home fifth in 15:10.2. "There is this awful sensation of breathing deeply and not being able to pull enough air into your lungs," Mills said. "I hate to lose a race, but this was for the doctors."

The US medical team agreed that athletes in the explosive events—the jumps, sprints, and hurdles—could arrive a day or two before competing at altitude and perform without any adverse effects. "You begin to acclimate by first burning off the excess bicarbonate in your system," Dr. Hanley said. "Then you start building more blood cells and hemoglobin, the oxygen-carrying factor in red blood cells." Hanley recommended that the USOC assemble a group of physicians and coaches to come up with a workable acclimatization program sometime in 1966. But high-altitude training camps would not fully replicate the stress of Olympic competition, Hanley warned.

The mixed results of the Little Olympics did little to quell the controversy over the selection of Mexico City. One of the most prominent critics was Dr. Roger Bannister, the Englishman who in 1954 became the first person to run a mile in less than four minutes. He would go on to become a respected neurologist. Bannister took to the pages of the *New York Times* to communicate his worries.

"The astonishing choice of Mexico City for the next Olympic games in 1968 has introduced a new program in distance training," Bannister wrote. "At 7,000 feet there is nearly 25 percent less oxygen in the atmosphere, and as we have seen, performance is limited by the transport of oxygen. I do not agree with the remark attributed to the Finnish coach Onin Niakanen that 'there will be those that will die,' but altitude could be the critical additional factor leading to collapse under special circumstances."

Bannister warned that African runners who had lived and trained at altitude their entire lives would have an unfair advantage in Mexico City. Bannister would be proven correct two years later, but the African wave that washed over the Mexico City distance races in 1968 had been building for several years. Holding the Olympics at high altitude unleashed the first torrent.

Abebe Bikila, a palace guard for Ethiopian emperor Haile Selassie, won the marathon at the 1960 Olympics, running in his bare feet over the cobbled streets of Rome. Bikila successfully defended his Olympic marathon championship in Tokyo, where his compatriot Mamo Wolde finished fourth behind Mills, Gammoudi, and Clarke in the 10,000 meters. A Kenyan by the name of Kipchoge Keino had shown promise in finishing fifth in the Tokyo 5,000 meters. But it wasn't until 1966 that Bannister and others began seeing the runners from the mountains of East Africa as a threat to the world order.

Clarke had taken distance running into uncharted territory in 1965, setting twelve world records in forty-four days. The high point came in Oslo, Norway, where on July 14 Clarke took 35 seconds off his world-record mark in the 10,000 meters by clocking 27:39.4. The fast-improving Keino became the first African runner to set a world record on the track in November 1965, clocking 13:24.2 for 5,000 meters, but Clarke reclaimed the record the following July in a sensational 13:16.6. The 1966 British Empire and Commonwealth Games in Kingston, Jamaica, presented Clarke with an opportunity to add a major title to his record collection.

There was plenty of oxygen available in the coastal city of Kingston, but it was of the hot and leaden variety. With its British roots, the Commonwealth Games conducted races at yards rather than meters, so

Clarke's first chance for gold came in the 6-mile run on the first day of the track schedule. He talked before the race of wanting to leave something in the tank for his matchup with Keino two days later in the 3-mile. But Naftali Temu, a twenty-two-year-old army private from the hills outside Nairobi, handled Clarke's surging tactics and left the record holder a well-beaten second. Temu ran the last mile in 4:17. Clarke had to settle for a second silver medal in the 3-mile, being outkicked by Keino in the final straight.

"It's hard to run against those blokes," Clarke groaned after the 6-mile. "They train and live up in those high altitudes, and even someone you've never heard of can beat you."

In his *Times* article, which appeared several weeks after the watershed Commonwealth Games, Bannister argued that living and training at altitude helps runners develop adaptive responses to the lack of oxygen, which translates into greater efficiency.

"Already several countries, with Mexico City particularly in mind, have established permanent training camps at high altitudes," Bannister wrote. "How far have we come from true sport? It would indeed be laughable if it were not so tragic. A pious rule from the International Olympic Committee limiting the length of altitude training to four weeks in the three months preceding the Olympic Games is a tacit admission of the blunder of holding the games at such an altitude and a recognition of the way in which athletes of the future will train."

The Soviet Union built training facilities in Kazakhstan and Armenia, each at sites above 10,000 feet. The French government did the same at Font-Romeu in the Pyrenees, extending an invitation to Clarke to train there free of charge in 1968. Japanese distance runners trained at Mount Norikura. With a sudden sense of urgency, the USOC turned its altitude decision-making over to Oregon coach Bill Bowerman.

Bowerman is best known today for coaching a charismatic runner named Steve Prefontaine and for cofounding the Nike shoe colossus with Phil Knight in the early 1970s. But Bowerman, an Oregon native who fought with the Tenth Mountain Division in World War II, was well established by the mid-1960s as one of the most innovative, successful track coaches in the United States. His teams at the University of Oregon won National Collegiate Athletic Association (NCAA) Championships in 1962, 1964, and 1965, and Bowerman's advocacy of jogging's health benefits triggered a running boom in Eugene and across the country.

Bowerman's outspokenness and sometimes prickly personality often put him at odds with officials from the Amateur Athletic Union (AAU) and USOC. When collegiate track coaches advocated breaking free of the AAU's draconian control of their sport, Bowerman played a leading role. But time was short, and few questioned his credentials, ingenuity, and energy when it came to the mountainous task of preparing Americans for Mexico City's high altitude.

"We had to learn how to train at altitude and learn it fast," said Hilmer Lodge, chairman of the USOC's track and field committee at the time. "We also had to find a place for our Olympic Trials. If there was somebody better than Bill at interfacing between athletes, coaches, and doctors, he didn't raise his hand."

"I think it was one of those things that no one knew enough about to object to me taking it on," Bowerman said. "The track coaches' association had already resolved to study altitude, so when the Olympic track and field committee met, they said, 'Bowerman, you're the one with the Tenth Mountain Division patch on your briefcase. You're our Olympic high-altitude training coordinator.'"

As Bowerman went to work north of the border, Mexican officials smugly sounded as if they had put the altitude controversy behind them. Yet the Mexicans raised a few eyebrows when they moved the Olympic equestrian competition to Oaxtepec, a tourist town with an elevation 3,000 feet lower than Mexico City.

"Horses are inclined to go on well beyond the prudent level of effort," said one member of the International Equestrian Federation. Another equestrian explained, "They do not have the common sense that humans do."

2

ECHO SUMMIT

BILL BOWERMAN ASSEMBLED a list of college towns, ski areas, and alpine retreats for possible locations to hold a high-altitude training camp that would acclimate Olympic hopefuls to the thin air of Mexico City. The highest point east of the Mississippi River is Mount Mitchell, a 6,684-foot peak in North Carolina, so the search was limited to the western United States. When the hunt began in early 1967, the most logical sites were thought to be located in Colorado, New Mexico, and Arizona.

Walt Little Jr., the recreation director of the newly incorporated city of South Lake Tahoe, got wind of the search through a longtime friend, Stanford track coach Payton Jordan. Little's surname never described his imagination or ambitions. Several years earlier, he went to Washington, DC, to meet with Bob Mathias, the Olympic decathlon champion who represented California's San Joaquin Valley in Congress. Little was keen on enlisting support to make Squaw Valley, site of the 1960 Winter Olympics, a year-round training center for Olympic hopefuls. Mathias heard him out before saying he didn't think the plan was realistic. When Little learned that the USOC needed a mountainous site to prepare athletes for the Mexico City Games, he started thinking big again. When he shared the idea with Jim Jones, South Tahoe High School's track coach, Jones asked where the track would be located.

"I don't know, but we'll figure it out," Jones remembers Little saying.

Little had attended Santa Monica Junior College in Southern California with Jordan, and they'd stayed in touch over the years. Jordan coached against Bowerman in the powerful Pacific-8 Conference and agreed to help Little pitch South Lake Tahoe as a possible site. City manager John Williams saw the possibilities and offered his full support.

Stanford track coach Payton Jordan supported longtime friend Walt Little's
quest to bring the high-altitude training camp and trials to South Lake Tahoe.
Stanford athletics

"Walt had a dream that maybe this would be a place we might want
to come," Jordan said. "He was the inspiration."

While the apple fell quite a ways from the tree, Little did inherit some
of the politicking and networking skills of his charismatic father. Walt
Little Sr. was an attorney and longtime California legislator who served as
Speaker of the State Assembly—the second-most powerful political position in the state behind the governor—in 1933. The elder Little was an
influential member of the Colorado River Commission in the mid-1920s
that determined how the hydroelectric benefits of Boulder Dam would be
divided among Nevada, California, and Arizona. Walt Sr. defended the

Inyo County residents who had been charged with dynamiting the Los Angeles Aqueduct in 1927. The case attracted national attention, and all charges against the accused were dismissed. When he retired from politics, Walt Sr. became an executive with Union Pacific Railroad.

The elder Little's legislative district included Hollywood, so it wasn't unusual to have movie stars drop by the family home in Santa Monica. One memorable dinner included Audie Murphy, the World War II hero and actor, and Jack Dempsey, the great heavyweight boxer. The Speaker's three children, Walt Jr., Richard, and Barbara, were primarily raised by nannies. Richard became a successful lobbyist, and Barbara married a US steel executive.

Walt Jr. took a different path—an interesting one, but one hardly lined with riches. His two surviving sons, Walt III and Bill, remember their parents being forced to give up their South Lake Tahoe home following the 1968 Olympic trials after they dipped too far into their own pockets to help feed the athletes.

"Dad was kind of the black sheep of the family," Walt Little III said. "He became a newspaperman."

Walt Jr. was a marine serving in the Aleutian Islands during World War II when his wife, Vivian, gave birth to their first child. The telegram sent to Alaska was supposed to read, "Vivian has just given birth to a beautiful tow-headed baby boy," but it instead came out "a beautiful two-headed baby boy." The puckish father telegrammed back, "In that case, we can always put him in the circus."

As sports editor of the *Bakersfield Californian* in the 1950s, Little used his connections to bring Mae West to the opening day celebration of a new Little League park. Little wasn't a glib speaker and was hardly a dashing figure, but people liked him, and he shot for the stars. "We'd shake our heads and say, 'Who *don't* you know?'" Walt III said. "It seemed like he knew everybody."

Little left Bakersfield for another newspaper job in Boise, Idaho, but that gig didn't work out, so he returned to California to become editor of the *Lake Tahoe News*. South Lake Tahoe at the time bore little resemblance to the winter and summer destination that today attracts more than one million tourists a year. When the Little family arrived in

1958, there was just one stoplight on Tahoe's south shore. South Lake Tahoe didn't become an incorporated city until 1965. Its population in 1968 was about twelve thousand.

The overwhelming beauty of Lake Tahoe had been extolled for the better part of a century, conveyed more through words and photographs than actual visitors. The second-deepest lake in the United States received its first national plug with the publishing of Mark Twain's *Roughing It* in 1872. Twain visited when it was still known as Lake Bigler. The secessionist views of California governor John Bigler during the Civil War prompted an unofficial name change. In the language of the Washoe Tribe that populated its shores, Tahoe translates to "big waters." (Oddly, the name change wasn't signed into law until 1945.)

It's hard to tell where truth ends and fiction begins in *Roughing It*, such as when Twain describes the forest fire he inadvertently set on the lake's northeast shore. But his first impression captures what it must have been like to see Tahoe in its unspoiled glory:

> At last the lake burst upon us—a noble sheet of blue water lifted six thousand three hundred feet above the level of the sea, and walled in by a rim of snow-clad mountain peaks that towered aloft full three thousand feet higher still! It was a vast oval, and one would have to use up eighty of a hundred good miles in traveling around it. As it lay there with the shadows of the mountains brilliantly photographed upon its still surface I thought it must be surely the fairest picture the whole earth affords.

Twain's lone visit to Tahoe occurred in mid-September 1861—the same time of year that the Echo Summit trials were held 107 years later. It's one of the best times of year to visit.

———————

The USOC track and field committee followed Bowerman's recommendation in selecting four sites to host high-altitude training and testing in 1967 in what amounted to a trial run to determine where the 1968 camp would be held. South Lake Tahoe (6,237 feet) made the cut along with Alamosa, Colorado (7,544 feet); Los Alamos, New Mexico (7,350 feet); and Flagstaff, Arizona (6,909 feet).

Bowerman selected four college coaches to supervise the training at each site. Ralph Higgins of Oklahoma State oversaw the group at Alamosa. Arizona coach Carl Cooper was assigned to Los Alamos, and Montana coach Harley Lewis led the contingent in Flagstaff. Bob Tracy, the track coach at St. Cloud State in Minnesota, directed the camp in South Lake Tahoe.

Eight to ten runners—guinea pigs, in a sense—were assigned to each of the four altitude sites. Jim Ryun, the world-record holder in the 1,500 meters and the mile, went to Alamosa. The Flagstaff group included Steve Stageberg, a talented young distance runner from Georgetown, and Larry Wieczorek, a miler from Iowa. Bowerman directed most of the Oregon-based runners to Los Alamos, the birthplace of the atomic bomb.

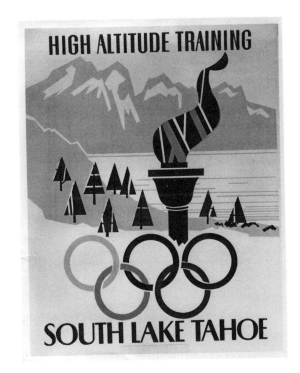

A reproduction of a poster promoting the high-altitude center.
Courtesy of City of South Lake Tahoe

Joining Tracy in South Lake Tahoe in August 1967 was a group that included Tom Farrell, a 1964 Olympian in the 800 meters, and Preston Davis, a nationally ranked miler from Texas. Each of the coaches at the four sites had a medical staff that poked and prodded the athletes each day, conducting hemoglobin tests, measuring heart rates, and performing a myriad of other assessments.

Farrell had qualified for the US Olympic team in 1964 as a twenty-year-old sophomore at St. John's University in New York. He exceeded all expectations in Tokyo by placing fifth in the 800-meter final in 1:46.6, more than four seconds faster than his best entering the Olympic year. Farrell showed his Tokyo performance wasn't a fluke by ranking fourth in the world in both 1965 and 1966. In late 1966, after graduating from St. John's and getting married, he was drafted into the army.

"There's a guy called Uncle Sam who said, 'I've got you for two years,'" Farrell said. "I wanted to keep training after I graduated, and I figured if I made the 1968 Olympic team, fine. If not, I'd be done with my two years and get out of the army."

Farrell was stationed at Fort MacArthur near Los Angeles, where he trained with a number of other Olympic hopefuls, including Davis, Tracy Smith, and Tom Von Ruden. "It was kind of like what the Russians did," Farrell said. "I got paid and was training with some of the best runners in the United States. It was tremendous."

Out of the blue, an even better training situation presented itself to Farrell and Davis in the summer of 1967. "A message came that said they were looking for a couple of guys to go to a place called South Lake Tahoe to train for a month," Farrell said. "Who's going to turn down a month at Tahoe when you're in the army? It was the most wonderful place in the world to be at the time."

When Farrell and Davis got off the plane in Reno, a Rolls-Royce was idling at the curb.

"I'll bet that's for us," Farrell said to Davis, aware that casino magnate Bill Harrah, a deep-pocketed supporter of South Lake Tahoe's Olympic effort, owned a rare collection of classic automobiles. "Sure enough, we were driven to Lake Tahoe in one of Bill Harrah's Rolls-Royces," Farrell said.

Most of the runners sent to the altitude test sites in 1967 competed at distances of at least 1,500 meters. Physiologists were uncertain how altitude would affect the 800 meters, with its emphasis on both speed and endurance. "The 800 was on the border as to whether altitude helped or not," Farrell said. "I personally think I could have run faster at sea level."

Tracy, the St. Cloud coach overseeing the Tahoe trial run, had his nine athletes train at surrounding sites, including Heavenly Valley, a ski resort straddling the California-Nevada state line. Heavenly Valley owner Bill Killebrew arranged for the runners to train at elevations ranging from 8,300 to 9,000 feet. University of Nevada track coach Dick Dankworth laid out a circular mile track at 9,000 feet, where the fastest any of them could initially run was 6 minutes, 30 seconds—more than two minutes slower than the norm. Other workouts were held at South Tahoe Intermediate School, which eventually became the permanent home of the Echo Summit track.

The California and Nevada governors, Ronald Reagan and Paul Laxalt, each pitched Tahoe's virtues in laudatory letters to the USOC. But Little knew there was one problem that had to be ironed out for his city to have any shot at being awarded the 1968 altitude camp and final trials.

"Frankly, we are not in first place among the four cities under consideration," Little said at a community meeting in early August. Little noted South Lake Tahoe's elevation is nearly 1,000 feet below that of Mexico City, and 700 to 1,100 feet lower than the elevations of Flagstaff, Los Alamos, and Alamosa. The difference was substantial in terms of acclimating the athletes to the conditions they'd face in Mexico City.

The implication was that Little would have to scour the peaks rising above Tahoe to compete on a level footing with the other sites. Killebrew had offered the use of Heavenly Valley, but it wasn't realistic to build a track on such a steep mountain. Little pumped up the local business community by saying the city would reap an economic benefit of $250,000 by hosting the six-week camp in 1968. "This doesn't include the millions of dollars' worth of publicity via newspapers, radio and television," he added optimistically.

The selection committee listed its criteria in the following order: altitude, adequate training, housing and meals, keeping the daily cost of hosting each athlete at less than $12.50, recreational opportunities, and community interest.

With the USOC's track and field committee set to select the winner in September 1967, Tracy and Little searched high and wide for a location with the requisite elevation. Afterward, Little credited his son Bill for coming up with the winning ticket.

Bill had a winter job working at Echo Summit Ski Area, ten miles south of the lake along Highway 50. Originally called Nebelhorn after a 7,297-foot peak in the Allgäu Alps of Germany, the modest ski hill consisted of two rope tows and one chairlift. "Why can't they put a track in the parking lot at Echo Summit?" Bill asked his father.

Tracy and Walt Little drove up Meyers Grade and saw from their altimeter that Echo Summit's elevation was 7,382 feet—32 feet higher than Mexico City. Little and Tracy felt like miners who'd struck a hidden vein.

Permission would be needed from the US Forest Service and from the owner of the ski area, but South Lake Tahoe suddenly had an option that met the most important of the USOC committee's priorities. On his final visit to South Lake Tahoe prior to the September 12 vote by the USOC track committee in Chicago, Bowerman took note of the elevation sign at Echo Summit.

"It was not a secret that Bill Bowerman upgraded South Tahoe considerably following his second visit to the area," the *Tahoe Daily Tribune* reported. "He was high in his praise of the initiative shown by John Williams, Walt Little and Bob Tracy. Bowerman was impressed with the potential of training the various event selectees at altitudes from 6,229 feet to 8,300 feet and most particularly at 7,382 feet. The latter elevation is only a few feet off Mexico City's elevation."

One of the three hundred thousand participants in the epic migration known as the California gold rush was a young lawyer from Ohio named John Calhoun "Cockeye" Johnson. Johnson arrived in Placerville, or "Hangtown," as it was known in those days, in July 1849. Eighteen months earlier, James Marshall launched the gold rush by striking gold nine miles northeast of Placerville on the south fork of the American River. The lure of gold is what brought Johnson west, but once his crossed eyes saw the lush meadows and wooded hills just east of Placerville, Cockeye filed a claim on what became the first cultivated farm in El Dorado County.

During the peak years of the gold rush—1849 to 1852—most emigrants crossed the Sierra Nevada through Carson Pass, located about 25 miles south of Echo Summit. John C. Fremont and Kit Carson first crossed the 8,574-foot pass on their way to Sutter's Fort in Sacramento in the winter of 1844, and while Carson Pass proved passable for the wagons during the gold rush, the subsequent discovery of silver in the Nevada Territory led to a search for an easier, faster route.

After serving as adjutant in the state militia during the El Dorado Indian War of 1850–51, Johnson went to work. Accompanied by Fall Leaf of the Delaware Tribe, Johnson blazed a trail that took fifty miles off the established Carson River route and crossed the Sierra at a more navigable elevation. Johnson's Cutoff started in Carson Valley and climbed over Spooner Summit, but rather than descending directly to Lake Tahoe, the cutoff followed a ridge leading to the current site of Meyers. The route then ascended today's Echo Summit before locating the south fork of the American River and continuing along to Placerville.

Johnson's Cutoff was discovered too late for most of the gold seekers, but it was the main route for Californians traveling to the Comstock mines following the discovery of silver near Virginia City in 1859. From Yank's Station in present-day Meyers, Pony Express riders (and their horses) galloped over the summit en route to their final stop in Sacramento. And four years before the advent of the Pony Express, John "Snowshoe" Thompson began a decade's worth of solitary trips in which he carried the mail over Echo Summit on skis.

The completion of the transcontinental railroad in 1869 steered most east–west travel over the Sierra away from Johnson's Cutoff, leaving the road in disrepair for the remainder of the nineteenth century. The current name of Echo Summit wasn't applied until the late 1800s. Previous names included Johnson's Hill, Johnson Pass, Mickey Free Point, Nevett's

Pass, Osgood's Summit, and Big Hill Summit. Mickey Free deserves a brief aside, if only because he was such an abominable character. He robbed and killed solitary miners before the law caught up with him in 1855. His hanging in Coloma reportedly drew a crowd of six thousand.

The construction of the first transcontinental road for automobiles, the Lincoln Highway, took two routes over the Sierra—one over Donner Pass, the other over Echo Summit. Highway 50, as it became known following World War II, is mostly a two-lane road from the point it crosses the American River until it reaches Meyers. Free-for-alls ensue as impatient drivers accelerate madly in the one passing lane heading west atop Echo Summit following the climb up Meyers Grade.

Keeping Highway 50 plowed and open in the winter months is paramount for the Lake Tahoe ski resorts and casinos. The California Department of Transportation built a maintenance yard at Echo Summit to keep the traffic flowing year-round—a decision that greatly added to the distinctive atmosphere of the 1968 Olympic trials.

The four coaches on the 1967 altitude search committee—Cooper, Higgins, Lewis, and Tracy—submitted detailed reports to Bowerman at the conclusion of the training sessions. Lewis, the Montana coach, reflected a half century later on the process that put the 1968 US Olympic trials on the summit overlooking Lake Tahoe.

"Bill was a very strong-minded individual," Lewis said. "He was committed to making sure the athletes had the proper housing, meals, and medical attention. When he and I talked by phone, he said, 'South Lake Tahoe has a group of people who really want to do this and will commit the resources to do it right.'

"None of us wanted to divide the team," Lewis said, referring to the men, not the women. "There was a strong feeling that we wanted to develop some camaraderie heading to Mexico City. It came down to who was willing to put up the money and build the facilities."

Williams, the South Lake Tahoe city manager, outlined the estimated costs to his city council in 1967. Construction of an all-weather track would cost $143,000. An additional $53,000 was budgeted for housing costs. Food and other miscellaneous expenses would run about $65,000. Williams told the council that the all-weather track could be removed and relocated to either the high school or the intermediate school in South Lake Tahoe. He also informed the council that the final selection meet for the US Olympic men's track and field team would be held at the conclusion of the training camp, sometime in September 1968.

With the anticipated financial assistance from the USOC, Williams said the net cost to the city would fall somewhere between $120,000 and $160,000. The expense would be covered by a hotel tax. With the full-throated support of the local business community, the council quickly signed off on the bid.

The USOC's track and field committee met on September 11, 1967, in Chicago. Joining Little and Williams in Chicago was South Lake Tahoe city councilman Gene Marshall; Bob Hampton of Dillingham Corporation, a development company with business interests on the South Shore; Bob Keys from Governor Reagan's office; and Bill Schroeder, founder of the Helms Athletic Foundation in Los Angeles and a highly regarded figure in Olympic circles.

The forty-three members of the committee followed Bowerman's recommendation in selecting South Lake Tahoe over the other three contenders. The high-altitude committee used a 100-point scale in grading the sites. Echo Summit received 85 points, followed by Alamosa (72), Los Alamos (70), and Flagstaff (55).

At the same USOC meeting in Chicago, the committee named Payton Jordan head coach of the 1968 US Olympic men's track team. Bowerman would be in charge of the high-altitude camp that preceded the trials, a setup that led to some confusion about who was in charge.

Lewis said the support of the local business community was the decisive factor in selecting South Lake Tahoe as the host city. Whether he was being facetious or not, Farrell believes he and Davis played key roles.

"Preston and I were kind of responsible for them selecting Lake Tahoe," Farrell said. "We got to eat in all the restaurants and gave the place rave reviews. . . . I think I deserve some of the credit."

Echo Summit is part of the Eldorado National Forest. As to why the name of the national forest is one word and the county name is two, legend has it that a clerk once mistakenly placed a small *d* after *El*, and the Forest Service supervisor fancied the differentiation. *Eldorado* the forest remained.

The Forest Service owns approximately half the land in the Lake Tahoe basin and three-fourths of the watershed feeding the lake, including streams flowing from the Echo Summit area. Government control of so much land didn't exactly endear the rangers in their quasi-military uniforms to the progrowth South Shore movers and shakers of the 1960s. For instance, when the casino owners in Stateline were prohibited from building any structure higher than the tallest tree on their property, Bill Harrah simply purchased additional acreage up the mountain, where the trees were taller. His hotel got built.

When Bob Rice was hired as district ranger of the Lake Valley Ranger District in the mid-1960s, the career forester saw a need to mend fences with the antifederalist crowd. "Most foresters were more comfortable talking to trees," Rice said. "I mean, the symbol on our badge is a tree. But we were starting to get a tremendous number of people visiting the South Shore. It was important to get the whole community involved in the decision-making process."

An opportunity presented itself when Williams, South Lake Tahoe's city manager, approached Rice about finding a location that met the USOC's demands.

"Bob, we've got to have this facility at 7,400 feet," Williams said. "Are you interested?"

"What does it mean?" Rice asked.

"It means putting in an oval track," Williams said.

It helped that two of the Forest Service decision-makers had an affinity for track and field. Rice's father had been an outstanding runner in Wisconsin, and Doug Leisz, the supervisor of the Eldorado National Forest and Rice's boss, had run the quarter-mile in high school.

"I had strong feelings about trying to make it work," Leisz said. "It wasn't without objections in the Forest Service. Some people thought it

District Ranger Bob Rice of the US Forest Service signed off on construction of a track in the Eldorado National Forest. *Courtesy of Bob Rice*

would compromise the site. We could have said no, but a lot of us were athletic and ardent skiers. We took the attitude of 'Let's try to find a way to do it.' There are times when you need to think outside the box. It was in the public interest."

Rice was in charge of drawing up the permit that allowed organizers to lay a 400-meter track in the forest. Preparation of the site began in November 1967. The trees that Rice agreed to have cut down were ground up on-site. Trees inside the track along the backstretch were trimmed to make sure that limbs wouldn't fall on the competitors. Many of the granite boulders were left untouched—one of which would provide good viewing for an epic high jump competition.

The California Department of Transportation, or Caltrans, agreed to convert its Kingvale maintenance facility, located directly across Highway 50, into a temporary mountaintop village for athlete housing. Some of the athletes would stay in houses used by highway crews in the winter;

large house trailers would accommodate the rest. Athletes who preferred to stay in the communities of Meyers or Tahoe Paradise at the base of the summit would be housed in hotels or rental homes and be transported up the mountain each day to train at 7,382 feet.

As the track was being installed in the spring of 1968, Reagan issued a press release complimenting South Lake Tahoe officials for their initiative in selling the USOC on the site at Echo Summit. Reagan noted in the release that no state funds were required for the project, calling it "an example of outstanding cooperation between federal, state and municipal agencies."

———————

The setting may have been on the primitive side, but the track itself was cutting-edge modern. 3M, the Minnesota-based company at the forefront of the revolution in track surfaces, sold four Tartan tracks to Mexico City organizers, including the surface to be used in the Olympic Stadium for track and field competition. The composition of Echo Summit's track would be identical to the one in Mexico City, except it would have six lanes rather than eight on the curves because of space constraints.

The West Coast manager for 3M was Bill Nieder, the 1960 Olympic gold medalist in the shot put. "We had to shovel snow to put the track in," said Nieder, who supervised the installation. "It was cold up there."

Before getting into the track business, 3M produced such products as grinding wheels, waterproof sandpaper, and Scotch tape. The first Tartan surfaces were installed at horse racing tracks in Florida, but the polyurethane surface proved too abrasive when horses and jockeys fell. Tartan didn't work for greyhound racing, either. "They ran fast on it—too fast," Nieder said. "They couldn't make the curve."

Humans encountered no such problems. Unlike clay or cinders, Tartan provided excellent footing in good and bad weather. Urethane is mixed together to form a substance resembling the eraser on a pencil, in Nieder's description. The substance is then ground up and sprayed with pebbles that provide traction.

"Tartan is extremely fast because it's resilient," Nieder said. "Every step is going forward, not going backward or sideways. That was a fast track up at Echo Summit. They wouldn't have set all those world records if it wasn't."

3

THE MASTERMIND

As LATE SUMMER descended on Lake Tahoe following the Chicago announcement, clouds began to form two hundred miles to the east. The storm front gathering in San Jose soon released thunderclaps that shook the Olympic landscape of 1968.

The rainmakers were the incendiary athlete-turned-activist Harry Edwards and three African American track greats who would soon lord over the Echo Summit proceedings—Tommie Smith, Lee Evans, and, later, John Carlos.

Edwards met Smith and Evans in the mid-1960s at what was then known as San Jose State College. The city of San Jose was known in track circles as "Speed City" for the record-setting group of sprinters that track coach Lloyd "Bud" Winter assembled at the city's state college. The school gained a different sort of notoriety beginning in the fall of 1967. Edwards, Smith, and Evans became the central figures in the Olympic Project for Human Rights (OPHR), the group advocating a boycott by black athletes of the 1968 Summer Olympics in Mexico City to protest racial segregation and discrimination in the United States and around the world.

Edwards was the lightning rod whose commanding physical presence and verbal skills mesmerized the media for the better part of a year. As a *New York Times* profile of Edwards put it, "He is surely a colorful phrase maker. . . . But unlike most Black Power leaders, diamond-hard glints of humor occasionally escape from Edwards' otherwise splenetic rhetoric."

While Edwards dominated the media spotlight, Smith and Evans were gifted sprinters who appeared willing to make the ultimate athletic sacrifice—to give up their Olympic dreams for the greater cause of human rights and racial equality.

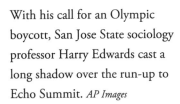

With his call for an Olympic boycott, San Jose State sociology professor Harry Edwards cast a long shadow over the run-up to Echo Summit. *AP Images*

"We had to take some kind of a stand," Evans said. "It's like the James Brown song: 'Say it loud, I'm black and I'm proud.'"

No one spoke louder or more forcefully in 1968 about racism in sports than Edwards. A 6-foot-8, 250-pound giant of a man, just a couple of years removed from an accomplished athletic career of his own, he had played basketball and thrown the discus at San Jose State in the early 1960s before earning a Woodrow Wilson Fellowship to Cornell University, where he began work on his doctorate in the nascent field of sports sociology. When Edwards returned to San Jose State in 1966 as an associate professor of sociology, he urged the black athletes on campus to assert their rights. Edwards gained national attention when he organized a campus-wide protest that forced the cancellation of San Jose State's season-opening football game in 1967.

The fuse was lit. Smith and Evans were awed by Edwards's eloquence, and they agreed with much of what he was saying. Smith recalls meeting Edwards for the first time and asking himself, "This is a very smart person; what is he doing playing basketball?" Smith continued, "My being a listener appealed to him and fit his personality. Harry Edwards is very verbal, still is very verbal, and he loves to be heard."

While in Tokyo for the World University Games in September 1967, Smith told a Japanese reporter that black athletes in the United States were considering a boycott of the Mexico City Olympics. Smith's comments created a firestorm of criticism back home. Smith received one letter that said:

DEAR TRAITOR,

You are not only a disgrace to your College, your Country . . . but to yourself! Please don't try to win a place on the Olympic Team. I'd rather have our Country finish last, without you, than first with you.

Another letter, from a US serviceman stationed in Yokohama, Japan, was even nastier.

You don't know me and I don't know you, however I have heard that you are a fast nigger. You said off the track you are just another nigger. Well, I have seen your picture and there is no argument from me on this matter. . . . Now call all your niggers together, plan your action (heroic type) and go out and snatch an elderly white lady's purse, or perhaps break a window out of an old man's shop. You know do something real brave something you and only you niggers are capable of doing.

On October 7, 1967, shortly after returning from Japan, Smith met with Edwards and several other activists at Edwards's home in San Jose. From that small gathering came the naming of the Olympic Project for Human Rights and the first substantive talk of a black boycott. Edwards decided to launch the rebellion in late November at the Black Youth Conference in Los Angeles.

From that point on, the run-up to Mexico City was dominated by the outsized presence of Harry Edwards and the question of what following he did or didn't have among the top US black athletes. Convincing athletes to give up their Olympic dreams would prove to be a futile quest, but Edwards mined the controversy for all it was worth, creating the mood to "do something" that ultimately led Smith and John Carlos to raise their fists on the victory stand in Mexico City.

Harry Edwards was a man-child of seventeen when he caught a westbound train out of East St. Louis, Illinois, for the promised land of California in 1959. The three-day journey gave him ample time to think about the sordid world he was leaving behind.

"The one thing I went over and over in my mind was that I'm never going back to East St. Louis unless I have everything that I'm leaving for," Edwards said. "A degree, an athletic career—I was driven. If I had been on a jet, I probably never would have done it. But three days on a train, you've got a whole bunch of time to get it in order. I made up my mind. I knew I could do better.

"I had to get out. I was too volatile in terms of the way I reacted to injustices. I'd have been dead if I stayed. No doubt about it. I'd have been dead."

Edwards grew up alongside seven brothers and sisters in a shotgun shack without indoor plumbing or hot water. His father, also named Harry, was an ex-con with a third-grade education. His mother deserted the family when Harry was nine years old.

"Looking back on it, the thing that amazes me is that my parents were able to do as well as they did," Edwards said. "I don't think I could have done it. My father literally went into poor health trying to prove that a black ex-convict in a substantially racist society could support a wife and eight children on $65 a week. He was an angry man. It got to the place he had a permanent scowl on his face."

In the wake of the US Supreme Court's *Brown v. Board of Education* decision in 1954, Edwards was one of the first black students to enroll at East Side High School. Edwards remembers being told on his first day of high school English to sit in the back of the classroom, ostensibly because the other students wouldn't be able to see over his huge frame.

"What I learned in the English class was minimal," Edwards said. "And it wasn't just the teacher's fault. It was mine too. I mean, I had no idea how to deal with these people."

A black attorney in East St. Louis named Frank Summers believed in Edwards enough to advance him $500 to leave the ghetto and go west. Edwards planned to play football at the University of Southern California (USC), only to learn on arrival that he'd need to pass a college admissions exam. "I could barely read, much less pass," Edwards said. "There was absolutely no way that I would have been able to pass it. So I went to Fresno City College instead, which was a feeder college for USC."

Edwards set a national junior-college record in the discus throw while at Fresno City College. He discovered that he enjoyed reading and going to class. When it came time to transfer to a four-year school, Edwards chose San Jose State College, where he received a combined basketball-track scholarship.

At San Jose State, Edwards threw the discus 179 feet—a school record—but quit the team because of a falling out with track coach Bud Winter, the same man Smith and Evans came to revere for his color blindness. Edwards had no such issues on the basketball court, other than a penchant for fouling out of games. San Jose State's basketball coach was Stu Inman, who later became general manager of the National Basketball Association's Portland Trail Blazers. "Harry was never an overly gifted kid, but he could clearly help you win games," Inman said. "He wanted structure, and he always wanted to know the purpose of everything we did."

In 1960, the Spartans played a couple of early-season games in St. Louis. Edwards was on the freshman team at the time and didn't make the trip. Wanting to get a better sense of Edwards's background and meet his father, Inman made a side trip to East St. Louis. "I had heard of East St. Louis and knew it was a tough area," Inman said. "But I hadn't ever really been in a slum area before."

Rain and snow were falling when Inman knocked on the door. He remembers wondering how long it had been since the two little girls watching television in the front room had eaten. Edwards's father was asleep on a bed without sheets. The elder Harry got up from bed and engaged Inman in an interesting conversation about union rights.

"It was an eye-opener for me," Inman said. "All of the stories Harry told me came alive. You could sense why kids wanted to get out."

Edwards would later boast that his aggression on the basketball court earned him invitations to try out for two professional football teams, the Minnesota Vikings and the San Diego Chargers. "I broke some noses, I put some people in the hospital," he said. "I loved contact. I once got called for a foul on the center tip, it was that bad."

That's not how his teammates remember him. They recall an athlete who cared more about acquiring an education than about using college athletics as a stepping-stone to the pros.

"He was one of the hardest-working people I've ever seen in college, both on the court and with the books," Ron Labetich said. "I remember we had a game one night in San Francisco, and there was one light on in the whole bus coming home. It was Harry, studying."

S. T. Saffold and Edwards were the only black players on the 1964 San Jose State basketball team. "Harry Edwards was very instrumental in getting us to think of ourselves as something other than athletes," Saffold said. "He told us to make sure that we were close enough to graduating when our athletic eligibility was up that we'd be able to finish our degrees."

As an undergraduate Edwards had taken note of the injustices he and other black athletes experienced in San Jose—the inability to find student housing, blatant racism in the school's fraternity system, professors who didn't view athletes as students. But it was the time Edwards spent at Cornell that opened his eyes to the possibilities of a new course of academic study.

"When I indicated that I wanted to write my dissertation on race and sport," Edwards said, "the basic disposition was, 'What's to be told? Sport is the citadel of interracial harmony and brotherhood.' I don't know why I saw the connection when other people denied it even existed. What led Sigmund Freud to talk about the ego? It was something he saw. This was something I saw."

Edwards in particular studied the intersection of sports and politics at the Olympic Games. He was especially interested in the story behind the marathon at the 1936 Olympics in Berlin, when two Korean runners were forced to compete for Japan, which occupied Korea from 1910 until 1945. Sohn Kee-chung and Nam Seung-yong, the gold and bronze medalists, were forced to adopt Japanese names and bear the indignity of hearing the Japanese national anthem played at their medal ceremony.

"The winner was given a small oak tree, and he used it to block the rising sun on his jersey," Edwards said. "The third-place finisher bowed his head and kept his hands down at his side. At those same Olympics, [IOC president] Avery Brundage prevented two US Jewish athletes from competing because he didn't want to offend Hitler's sensibilities. Then the US and Soviet athletes became foot soldiers in the titanic struggle of the Cold War.

"So when people said in 1967 and 1968 that the Olympics were above politics, I knew better."

4

THE RESISTERS

Tommie Smith was an unlikely candidate to become a legendary symbol of resistance. Harry Edwards and S. T. Saffold were at the San Jose airport on an August day in 1963 to welcome a painfully shy track and basketball recruit. It was the first time the incoming freshman had flown on an airplane, and his appearance—jeans too short for his absurdly long legs, torn-up sneakers, ears jutting out from a closely shorn head—caused Edwards to burst out laughing.

Tommie Smith was born in Clarksville, Texas, on D-day—June 6, 1944, when Allied troops crossed the English Channel and turned the tide of World War II. Smith was one of twelve children in a sharecropping family. Two other children died in infancy. The Smiths moved to California's Central Valley when Tommie was six years old. To pay for the bus ride west, the family spent two and a half years working in a labor camp in Stratford, California, a small agricultural town south of Fresno.

Shortly after arriving in California, Smith and his father were riding a bus that transported workers from the camp to the fields. The principal of Stratford Elementary School climbed aboard and informed the parents that their kids were required by California law to attend school. James Richard Smith argued with the principal for several minutes before relenting.

Smith repeated second grade when he mistakenly walked into the wrong classroom on the first day of classes at an elementary school in the neighboring town of Lemoore. He was too shy to point out the mistake. While he had a hard time adjusting to sitting in the same classroom as white students, it was in Lemoore that Smith began demonstrating the athletic prowess that put him on the single-prop plane to San Jose. When

31

a coach noticed his speed on the playground and suggested he run track, Smith went home and asked his father if that would be OK.

James Richard Smith saw sports as a waste of time that could be better used working, but he agreed to let his son run—with one condition. "If you run and get second place, you'll have to go back in the field with the rest of us next Saturday." The son took the message to heart, and seldom lost a race, ever.

"One of my best friends was Elmer Thomas, a kid from the Indian reservation," Smith said. "We were the two best athletes in school, but nobody wanted to have anything to do with us because of our clothes and the fact that we were poor. In the fields, some of the white folks didn't treat us as well as they treated the others. But I didn't notice it. It wasn't until I got to San Jose and began getting educated that I saw the bigger picture."

At Lemoore High School, Smith played wide receiver on the football team, set scoring records on the basketball court, and displayed a world of talent on the track. In one meet, he long jumped 24 feet, 2 inches, breaking a record set by Rafer Johnson, the Kingsburg native who won an Olympic gold medal in the decathlon at the 1960 Olympics. Smith clocked 47.3 in the 440-yard dash as a senior, a time that would attract college recruiters today. He narrowed his choice of college scholarship offers down to USC and San Jose State, opting for the less glamorous of the two because San Jose was close to Oakland, where his brother and sister lived. "And it was just far enough away so that I wouldn't have to go home and work in the fields every weekend," Smith said.

But when he arrived at the San Jose airport, Edwards and Saffold gave him a warning. "They told me that San Jose State was not a socially equitable place," Smith said. "They also mentioned that there were more black athletes than there were black women on campus."

Smith entered San Jose State on a combined football-basketball-track scholarship, though he didn't play a down of college football. After leading the freshman basketball team in scoring and rebounding, Smith concentrated on track the remainder of his college career. "I went to college to play basketball, but I found out the court was too short," Smith said. "Same with the 100 meters."

Edwards had quit the track team several years earlier after getting into a shouting match with Winter in the coach's office. By contrast, Smith and Evans loved the folksy white coach who never pressured them to subjugate their political interests. Plus, Winter understood the science of sprinting like few others. Winter taught navy pilots relaxation techniques during World War II and preached the same precepts to his sprinters at San Jose State. Winter's sprinters were known for their high knee lifts and long strides, and the world had never seen a sprinter lift his knees like Smith, whose stride measured nearly nine feet.

"I went to San Jose State to get an education," Smith said. "I ran track because I was good at it and I was treated well. Bud talked to me as if I was a human being. He let me be who I was."

To avoid being shipped off to Vietnam, Smith joined the ROTC. He discovered that he actually liked the drills, the uniform, and the discipline. "I loved the military process," Smith said. "I wanted to be either a police officer, a military man, or a teacher. The protest destroyed the first one for me."

By the spring of his sophomore year in 1965, Smith had emerged as one of the world's best sprinters. That coming-out year on the track coincided with a growing sense of racial awareness. He and Saffold had spent many evenings listening to Edwards hold forth on the slights black athletes experienced on a daily basis.

Smith's first step toward the victory-stand protest in Mexico City took place on March 13, 1965. A largely black group of students planned to march sixty miles from San Jose to San Francisco to show their solidarity with the civil rights protests taking place in the American South. Smith wanted to participate, but he had a track meet that day. Conscious of his duty to Winter and his track teammates, Smith decided to run in the meet and catch up with the marchers later that evening.

Winter had arranged for two finish lines to be set up at the end of the day's featured race, the 220-yard dash on a straightaway. One set of timers would be positioned at 200 meters, another at 220 yards, about 4 feet farther up the track. These distances are no longer contested on a straightaway, only around a curve, but at the time, the straightaway "furlong" was the track-and-field equivalent of a high-fueled dragster race—straight, fast, and furious. The world record in 1965 for 220 yards on a straightaway was 20 seconds flat, set by Dave Sime in 1956.

Smith had already won the 100-yard dash and run legs on two relays when he settled his long legs into the starting blocks at the far end of San Jose State's cinder track. He tried to erase the march from his mind.

He streaked down the cinder track faster than he'd ever run before, tying the world record of 20.0 at both distances. It was the beginning of an unparalleled three-year run in which Smith would hold eleven world records simultaneously.

After accepting congratulations from Winter, Smith caught a ride up the peninsula in Art Simburg's Volkswagen. Simburg, a white student who wrote for the San Jose State newspaper and enjoyed hanging out with Smith and other black athletes, later landed a job with the shoe manufacturer Puma and would play a controversial role in the "shoe wars" in South Lake Tahoe and Mexico City.

Simburg and Smith joined the marchers that evening in Sunnyvale and walked the remaining forty miles to San Francisco the following day. As they set off, one of the organizers informed the hundred or so marchers that they had a distinguished guest—a San Jose State student who had tied a world record at a track meet the day before.

Saffold roomed with Smith for four years in San Jose. When they moved out of the dormitories, they shared an apartment a block from campus, for which they paid seventy-five dollars per month. Smith's bed folded out of a closet. Saffold slept in the dinette. Saffold noticed that his friend was steadily becoming more aware of the world around him. "The San Francisco march—I think it grew from there with Tommie," Saffold said.

A year later, Smith set four more world records. On May 7, 1966, in San Jose, he clocked a shocking 19.5 for the straightaway 200 meters and 220 yards, taking a full half-second off the mark he tied the year before. On June 11 in Sacramento, Smith clocked 20.0 for 220 yards around a curve, two-tenths faster than Henry Carr's world-record mark. Lee Evans, then a freshman at San Jose City College, finished a full second behind Smith but still broke the national junior-college record.

It would be hard to imagine two great sprinters more dissimilar in style, form, and temperament than Tommie Smith and Lee Evans. Smith ran with elegance and grace. The sunglasses he wore in races added to his aura. Evans was known as "the Tasmanian devil" for the fury he brought to his races—shoulders rolling, face contorted in pain, weaving from one side of his lane to the other. Running never looked easy with Evans.

But Smith and Evans shared a number of qualities, the foremost being a capacity for hard work born in the grape and cotton fields of California's Central Valley. Judge and Pearlie Mae Evans shared Smith's sharecropping roots. They came to California from Louisiana, first settling in Madera, fifty-five miles north of Lemoore. Smith is sure he and Evans crossed paths long before they put Speed City on the map.

"I think we saw each other in the grape fields, though Lee and I didn't know it at the time," Smith said.

Evans remembers working the fields every summer until he was sixteen years old—"every summer, all summer, ten to twelve hours in the cotton field and grape patch. The guys at the scale cheated you and called you 'nigger.' After doing that kind of work, track seemed easy."

The family later moved to San Jose, where Evans made a name for himself as a quarter-miler at Overfelt High School. His best high school time of 46.9 was the second fastest in the nation in 1965, trailing only his future Olympic teammate, Ron Freeman of New Jersey. Evans was recruited by several top college programs, including Oregon and Southern University, a historically black college in Baton Rouge, Louisiana. Southern was coached by Dick Hill, who had coached the 1964 Olympic 100-meter champion Bob Hayes while at Florida A&M. Hill told Evans that other California kids had adapted well to attending school in the Deep South. But Evans's parents painted Louisiana as a fearful place. "Jim Crow down there," Judge Evans told his son. Oregon coach Bill Bowerman tried to sell Evans on the fact that he'd coached Otis Davis to victory in the 400 meters at the 1960 Olympics, but Evans was used to having his mother attend all his meets, and she wouldn't be able to do that if he went to Oregon.

Already married with a young child, Evans decided to stay close to home. He enrolled at San Jose City College with the intention of getting his grades up and transferring to San Jose State. Evans burst onto the national and international scene like a meteor as a college freshman in 1966, lowering his best to 45.2, winning the 1966 AAU national title in New York, and finishing the season ranked first in the world by *Track & Field News*.

Smith took Evans under his wing when he transferred to San Jose State in the fall of 1966. "Evans, these are the classes you have to take to graduate," Smith told him. "Make sure you take them all."

Evans and Smith raced three times over 200 meters in 1967, Evans winning once. Track fans longed for a 400-meter showdown—Smith had run a number of tantalizing relay legs—but Winter kept his stars apart until May 20, 1967, the final home meet of Smith's college career.

"I knew Bud was setting up something," Smith said. "I never understood why he wouldn't run me against Lee in the 400. But we had an all-comers meet coming up and Bud said, 'Tom-Tom, I'm going to put you in the same race.'"

Winter expected at least one of them to break Adolph Plummer's four-year-old world record of 44.9 for 440 yards. Smith tried to tamp down the prerace hype, even suggesting to Evans that they intentionally cross the finish line together.

"There were a lot of folks at the meet, people on top of buildings, people in trees, everywhere," Smith said. "I talked to Lee before and said, 'Let's run something like a 45.3 and finish in a dead heat.' Lee didn't say anything in response. I thought that was strange. Then the race started and all I saw was heels and elbows. Lee tricked me, and I decided I'd go after him. It was speed against power."

With four thousand fans on hand to watch the long-awaited showdown, Evans went out fast in lane four and led by two-tenths of a second at the halfway point. Smith, assigned the more favorable third lane, kept Evans within his sights and took the lead coming off the final curve. Smith broke the world records for 400 meters (44.5) and 440 yards (44.8). Evans finished a half second behind. He would never get a second shot at Smith over one lap.

"Lee would have won against anybody else," Winter said. "It's just that he ran up against someone who may be superhuman."

With Smith returning to his preferred 200 meters, Evans defended his AAU title by the slimmest of margins over a nineteen-year-old upstart named Vince Matthews. Evans lowered his personal best to 44.9 in winning the Pan American Games in Winnipeg, again edging out Matthews. In the *Track & Field News* world rankings for 1967, US quarter-milers claimed seven of the top ten spots, with Evans, Matthews, and Smith ranking first, second, and third.

The magazine noted that Smith was unquestionably the world's best but that he hadn't run enough races to justify the top spot. With Smith expressing no desire to abandon the 200, Evans entered 1968 as the consensus 400-meter favorite for Mexico City.

Evans had grown increasingly aware of a world beyond track through his travels with the national team and his association with Smith and Edwards at San Jose State. A marginal student in high school, Evans began applying what he read in college to racial dynamics he'd never really considered before. "Reading the autobiography of Malcolm X really opened my eyes and reminded me of the things my father told me about growing up in the Jim Crow South. Malcolm said, 'Don't sit on the sidelines.' I began realizing that if everyone sits on the sidelines, we'll never end segregation."

John Carlos arrived in San Jose with the subtlety of a frontier sheriff busting through the doors of a saloon. If anyone thought he'd be content to quietly blend into the Speed City background, they hadn't done their homework. Carlos was brash, boisterous, arrogant, moody, and funny, a "kaleidoscope," in the words of his new coach, Bud Winter. Carlos had almost nothing in common with Smith aside from the color of their skin and an ability to run like the wind.

"The difference between Smith and Carlos was like the difference between Lemoore, California, and Harlem, New York," long jumper Ralph Boston said.

One year after graduating from a trade school in New York City, Carlos accepted a scholarship to run track at East Texas State. With his wife and baby daughter in tow, Carlos learned quickly that his kind wasn't particularly welcomed in Commerce, Texas. He fought with the track coach and took his family back to New York after one stormy year in the Lone Star State.

Harry Edwards sought out Carlos in New York and suggested that he transfer to San Jose State. Carlos took him up on it. While he wasn't eligible to compete for the Spartans in 1968, he joined a training group that included not only Smith and Evans but also national-class sprinters Ronnie Ray Smith, Billy Gaines, Kirk Clayton, and Jerry Williams. Carlos would have to take practice more seriously than he had at East Texas State to stand out in such fast company. He was up for the challenge, and it wasn't like he was starting from scratch. Carlos finished the 1967 season ranked third in the world in the 200 meters.

Carlos wasn't as politically inclined as Smith and Evans, but he had several months to get up to speed. When *Track & Field News* surveyed a number of top black athletes in late 1967 for their thoughts about the proposed boycott, Carlos sounded moderately receptive.

"The motives behind the boycott are all right," Carlos said. "Today's Negro is using his own mind and realizes he's being mistreated. If enough athletes boycott it can be effective. After all, boycotting is a lot better than going out in the streets and rioting."

All the way through Echo Summit, Smith and Evans were considered the most political of the black Olympians. Carlos was seen as less serious, a late arrival to the cause. That would change in Mexico City, where the most lasting statement would be made by Smith and Carlos.

5

THE BOYCOTT CAMPAIGN

IN 1967, WHEN Harry Edwards was teaching a "Racial Minorities" course in the school's sociology department, San Jose State's student body of twenty-three thousand contained one hundred black people at the most. The vast majority were athletes on scholarship. Black students were barred from joining fraternities and sororities, steered into nonacademic courses, and denied access to off-campus housing, among other injustices.

Older and more emboldened than he'd been a few years before as an undergraduate, Harry Edwards formed the United Black Students for Action in September 1967. The group issued a list of demands to the school's administration that included the end of racial discrimination in student housing. When administrators ignored their requests, Edwards and his followers threatened to prevent San Jose State's opening football game of the 1967 season from being played.

Fearing violence from what Edwards ominously referred to as "outside agitators," San Jose State president Robert Clark canceled the football game against the University of Texas at El Paso and acceded to many of the black group's demands. Clark's decision drew condemnation from Ronald Reagan, who had won the California governorship in 1966 by promising to crack down on campus unrest. Flushed with victory, Edwards turned his sights to one of sport's most sacred cows—the Olympic Games.

The Los Angeles Black Youth Conference was scheduled for Thanksgiving weekend at the Second Baptist Church. Edwards used the conference to announce the Olympic Project for Human Rights and make the case for a black boycott of the Mexico City Olympics. Lee Evans and Tommie Smith were in the audience, as were Lew Alcindor, the All-American center on UCLA's basketball team; high hurdler Ron Copeland; and Otis Burrell, a world-ranked high jumper.

Edwards forbade white journalists from covering the workshop. Outside the church, a fight erupted between Communists and Black Power followers of Ron Karenga, the founder of Kwanzaa, the pan-African holiday.

The meeting ran two and a half hours. Near the end, Edwards asked the attendees what they wanted to do. "Boycott!" the group responded in acclamation. The Olympic boycott was tied to a promise to not take part in any event that included South Africans and Rhodesians and to stay away from any events connected with the New York Athletic Club (NYAC), the exclusive private social and sports club that allegedly discriminated against black people and Jews.

As they prepared to head back to San Jose, Smith said to Evans, "All I hope is that this does some good, that it doesn't create any chaos."

When he returned to San Jose following the Los Angeles conference, Edwards met with Louis Lomax, a prominent black journalist. They drew up a list of demands to be presented at a December 15 meeting in New York. They'd invite two of the most prominent civil rights leaders in the country—Martin Luther King Jr., president of the Southern Christian Leadership Conference, and Floyd McKissick, director of the Congress of Racial Equality (CORE). Lomax also recommended that Edwards shuck the coat and tie and dress in "pseudo-revolutionary rags"—dark glasses, black jacket, beads, and work boots. Amp up the rhetoric while you're at it, Lomax advised.

"As it became crystal clear that the name of the game was keeping the media's attention on the movement, one had to go right up to the edge of civility," Edwards said. "I did everything I could to speak uncompromisingly, militantly, because the white media ate it up."

Edwards made for good copy. He referred to the president as "Lynchin' Baines Johnson." Reagan was "a petrified pig, unfit to govern." He told one interviewer, "The crackers are losing all over. In Vietnam, Thailand, Laos, Bolivia, all over. The third-world power—black, red, yellow, brown—is taking the white man apart in chunks. We must get the cracker off our backs by Olympic boycott, by out-and-out revolution, by whatever means."

On his office wall at San Jose State, Edwards posted pictures of boycott critics Jesse Owens and Willie Mays, labeling them as "Traitor (Negro) of the Week."

King and McKissick were at his side at the Americana Hotel in New York when Edwards announced the demands that needed to be met to avoid a black boycott of the Mexico City Olympics:

• Restoration of Muhammad Ali's title and right to box in this country.
• Removal of the anti-Semitic and anti-black personality Avery Brundage from his post as Chairman of the International Olympic Committee.
• Curtailment of participation of all-white teams and individuals from the Union of South Africa and Southern Rhodesia in all United States and Olympic athletic events.
• The addition of at least two black coaches to the men's track and field coaching staff appointed to coach the 1968 United States Olympic team. (Stanley V. Wright is a member of the coaching team but he is a devout Negro and therefore is unacceptable.)
• The appointment of at least two black people to policy-making positions in the United States Olympic Committee.
• The complete desegregation of the bigot-dominated and racist New York Athletic Club.

The OPHR manifesto impugned one of the most prominent black track coaches in the country. And Stan Wright, an early critic of the boycott idea, wasn't the type to let being referred to as an "unacceptable devout Negro" wash off his back.

"Harry Edwards called me an Uncle Tom and a handkerchief head," Wright said years later. "I'm a lot of things, but I'm not an Uncle Tom. I've been run out of Louisiana, locked up in Mississippi. I have never given up my personal honor to racism."

From 1951 to 1967 at Texas Southern University, a historically black school in Houston, Wright's teams won eleven conference titles and a pair of National Association of Intercollegiate Athletics (NAIA) championships. (Black colleges competed under the NAIA banner.) In 1962, when Texas Southern became the first black school to participate in the prestigious Texas Relays, the Flying Tigers won all five relay races in meet-record times. By the end of the day, the predominantly white crowd in Austin was cheering lustily for the small-school speedsters.

Four years later, Wright became the first black person to be named head coach of a US national track team. His greatest athlete at Texas Southern was Jim Hines, whom Wright recruited out of Oakland, California. Hines was ranked first in the world in the 100 meters in 1967.

"Stan was a great coach. He treated the whole team as family," Hines said. "The man in no way is an Uncle Tom. I can vouch for him 200 percent."

Wright had tried to recruit Edwards to Texas Southern to throw the discus, believing he had great potential. It would be another eight years before their paths would cross again, and neither made much of an effort to understand the other's views. Wright opposed an Olympic boycott and didn't hesitate to say so. He wrote a letter to *Sports Illustrated* that included the following salvo:

> *In my humble opinion, the Black Power does not truly represent the 21,508,000 Negroes in this country. It does not even represent 5% of the Negroes. I am certain that the movement leaders are not sincere in their beliefs when it is a known fact that they agitate and provoke other people to destruction while they flee the consequences. . . . I say to Tommie [Smith] and the others, we as Negroes do have grievances, but we do not need spokesmen who are poisonous propagandists and who capitalize on our real grievances for their own personal gains.*

Wright was particularly sensitive to any accusation that he'd been named to the Olympic coaching staff as a token, compliant Negro. For Ralph Boston, the world's top-ranked long jumper, one of the most unfortunate consequences of the OPHR was its denunciation of Stan Wright.

"I never forgot the beating Stan took in 1968," Boston said. "Harry Edwards wasn't even there in Mexico City. A lot of us noticed that.

Tommie, Carlos, and Lee asked the same thing: 'Where's Harry?' Stan Wright was there, from the start to the finish."

Wright had been the US relay coach when Evans and Smith teamed with Robert Frey and Theron Lewis in 1966 to become the first 4 x 400 relay team to break three minutes. That same year, Wright admonished Evans when the young runner asked who Ho Chi Minh was. Read the newspaper and learn what's going on in the world, Wright said.

At the height of the boycott controversy in 1968, Evans tried to express his conflicted feelings in a letter to Wright. "Coach, Tom and I dig you, and wouldn't want any harm to come to you," Evans wrote. "The Black people on the West Coast, as you must know by now, are a little different in ways such as preparing for a revolution and things like that."

Evans unwittingly touched on what would become one of the most pervasive criticisms of the OPHR—that Harry Edwards never reached out beyond his San Jose circle.

"Harry Edwards never met with any of the East Coast guys," said triple jumper Norm Tate, a 1966 graduate of North Carolina Central, a historically black university in Durham. "We were being asked to participate in something we knew nothing about. We didn't meet as a group until after the team was assembled. The thing that bothered us more than anything else was that the majority of decisions were being made with very little input."

OPHR and Edwards would also be criticized for not inviting black women into their club. The point seldom came up in 1968, but Edwards later rebutted the sexism charge by claiming that most of the black women competing for Olympic berths in 1968 attended historically black colleges. "Black schools told them if you're the least bit associated with OPHR, you'll be kicked out of school, because we wouldn't be able to keep getting money from our legislators," Edwards said.

Tennessee State University was Nashville's answer to Speed City, and the coach of the vaunted Tigerbelles, Ed Temple, was their Bud Winter. The comparison, in fact, might be a disservice to Tennessee State and Temple.

The school was established in 1912 as the Tennessee Agricultural & Industrial State Normal School for Negroes. By 1968, the year in which the school was renamed Tennessee State, Temple had built one of the greatest dynasties in the history of women's athletics.

At the 1956 and 1960 Olympics, the US teams in the 4 x 100 relay were composed solely of Tigerbelles, the most famous being Wilma Rudolph. At the Tokyo Olympics in 1964, Tennessee State teammates Wyomia Tyus and Edith McGuire finished one-two in the women's 100 meters. Two of Temple's athletes—Tyus and Madeline Manning in the 800 meters—were expected to contend for gold medals in Mexico City.

When Edwards tried to organize a black boycott, Tyus was sympathetic to the cause. Temple didn't think a boycott would serve the athletes' interests but didn't try to influence Tyus one way or the other.

"You've been educated, you've been around the world, you know how the game works," Temple told her. "Make sure you think things through. But you need to make the team before you can boycott anything."

Two of the OPHR demands—the expulsion of South Africa and the removal of Avery Brundage as IOC president—proved popular with many US athletes, white and black. And a third target—the NYAC—would soon find itself in the crosshairs as well.

The Olympic participation of South Africa became a lightning rod in the late 1950s and early 1960s as decolonized African nations began competing in the Olympics for the first time. Apartheid had been the South African government's official policy since 1948, but Brundage and the IOC viewed it as an internal matter.

In 1962, Jan de Klerk, South Africa's minister of home affairs, announced a ban on South Africans competing in mixed-race events at home and abroad. In 1963—at the same Baden-Baden session where Mexico City was awarded the 1968 Olympics—the IOC suspended South Africa. The sports-mad country on Africa's southern tip stayed home from the 1964 Olympics in Tokyo.

With the United States having its own history of apartheid, the South African issue resonated. But Brundage and the IOC, resentful of any notion that their quadrennial festival was sullied by politics, encouraged South Africa to apply for readmission after the Tokyo Olympics.

In September 1967, the IOC sent a delegation to see firsthand whether South Africa had made the changes needed to comply with the Olympic Charter's antidiscrimination wording. South African officials assured their IOC visitors that a single team composed of whites and nonwhites would travel together to Mexico City, wear the same uniform, and compete under the same flag.

The IOC summary of its fact-finding mission, which wasn't made public until mid-February, recommended readmitting South Africa to the Olympics.

———

Edwards delivered one of his most biting lines when he spoke about the "anti-Semitic and anti-black personality" Avery Brundage, who ruled the Olympic kingdom with an iron hand. "Avery Brundage was to this movement what Bull Connor was to the civil rights movement," Edwards said.

As the commissioner of public safety in Birmingham, Alabama, Connor became a symbol of white racism when he unleashed police attack dogs and fire hoses on black protesters, including many children, in 1963. Brundage never did anything as racially egregious as Connor, but there was enough in his background to give Edwards and other black people reason to question his motives.

Brundage, who made a fortune in the construction business, owned Montecito Country Club, which didn't admit black people as members. He referred to US black athletes such as Tommie Smith and John Carlos not by their names but as "boys." He didn't have a problem with German filmmaker Leni Riefenstahl including swastikas and Nazi salutes in her film of the 1936 Olympics in Berlin, but he expunged any mention or visual evidence of the Black Power protests from both the IOC's official film and the USOC's report of the Mexico City Games.

"A racist down to his toes," Lee Evans said. A white teammate on the 1968 US Olympic team, Marty Liquori, concurred. "Avery Brundage was a brutal, racist pig," Liquori said.

In *The Games Must Go On*, a 1984 biography of Brundage, author Allen Guttmann offered a more nuanced picture, noting that Brundage welcomed African nations into the Olympic fold and was critical of how apartheid discriminated against black South African athletes.

The anti-Semitic charge was harder to wash away. As president of what was then known as the American Olympic Committee, Brundage single-handedly fought off the cacophony calling for the United States to boycott the 1936 Olympics rather than provide legitimacy to Adolf Hitler's Nazi regime. He impugned the motives of those who supported a Berlin boycott by saying, "Many of the individuals and organizations active in the present campaign to boycott the Olympics have Communist antecedents. Radicals and communists must keep their hands off American sport."

While the Berlin Olympics are remembered for the brilliant performances of Jesse Owens and his black teammates, two Jewish sprinters, Marty Glickman and Sam Stoller, were controversially left off the US sprint relay team. Brundage bristled at suggestions that Glickman and Stoller were sacrificed to appease Hitler and his sinister propaganda chief, Joseph Goebbels.

"An erroneous report was circulated that two athletes had been dropped from the American relay team because of their religion," Brundage wrote in a post-Olympic report. "This is absurd."

To his supporters, Brundage was a steely leader who oversaw the massive growth of the Olympic movement while remaining true to the nineteenth-century ideals espoused by the founder of the modern Games, Baron Pierre de Coubertin. To Harry Edwards, Brundage was an octogenarian Bull Connor—a foil too good to be true.

In 1868, the NYAC staged North America's first indoor track and field meet. Dozens of athletes affiliated with the NYAC won Olympic gold medals in the club's first century, including Ray Ewry, the great turn-of-the-century jumper, and Al Oerter, the Long Island native who won Olympic discus titles in 1956, 1960, and 1964. To celebrate its centennial in 1968, the NYAC invited the cream of US Olympic hopefuls and a

Soviet delegation to its February 16 indoor meet at the newly renovated Madison Square Garden.

Edwards had other plans, and for one night, at least, the OPHR united the track community behind a common cause.

While the NYAC remained an all-male club until 1989, the club came under fire in the early 1960s for membership policies that excluded black people and Jews. The OPHR boycott of the NYAC meet in 1968 didn't pry open the doors of the archetypal old boys' club, but it certainly put Edwards in the national spotlight. Dozens of black athletes withdrew from the meet, as did Villanova, Georgetown, and a number of other college teams. All of New York's parochial and public high schools pulled out, as did the small Soviet delegation.

"We thought the New York AC was doing itself an injustice by not letting Negroes in the organization," explained Villanova captain Dave Patrick. "We also thought that we have such a great team feeling that we didn't want to take a chance and try to split any views. We function as a team, and we should go or not go as a team. We decided not to go."

Edwards vowed to surround Madison Square Garden with thousands of picketers the night of the meet. At a premeet press conference in which he refused to respond to any questioner who used the term "Negro," Edwards said any black athlete who crossed the picket line could find himself in trouble.

The threats worked. Fewer than ten black athletes competed as Edwards and a crowd of fifteen hundred to two thousand protesters surrounded Madison Square Garden. A scuffle between police and activists resulted in several people being taken to St. Vincent's Hospital with minor cuts and bruises.

"I really respect the guys who stayed out of the meet," said Richmond Flowers, a white hurdler from the University of Tennessee. "I only wish there were some way to moderate this."

That week in mid-February represented the high-water mark for the Olympic Project for Human Rights. Two days before the NYAC meet, the IOC voted to readmit South Africa to the Olympic Games.

"This new issue will force the black man to fight," Edwards said of South Africa's readmission. "Let Whitey run his own Olympics."

6

THE INNOVATOR

WHILE MUCH OF the attention leading up to Echo Summit centered on San Jose, a gangly high jumper was fomenting an altogether different revolution a few hundred miles north in Oregon. In the Olympic-year spotlight, Dick Fosbury turned one of the most elemental athletic pursuits—seeing how high you can jump off the ground—on its ear. Today, every world-class high jumper, male and female, uses what's still known as the Fosbury Flop, but in 1968, when the conventional technique was the straddle, springing over the bar backward was blasphemous, innovative, delightful, ridiculous, or all of the above.

Fosbury's highest jump entering the Olympic year was 6 feet, 10¾ inches. He won the Pacific-8 Conference title and placed fifth in the 1967 NCAA Outdoor Championships as an Oregon State sophomore, but he wasn't ranked among the top ten jumpers in the country at the end of the year.

"We thought he was a crackpot," said Ed Caruthers, a 1964 Olympian who ranked first in the world in 1967.

To be considered a serious contender for a berth on the US Olympic team in those days, 7 feet was considered the point of entry in the high jump. Fosbury didn't have to wait long for opportunities to join the 7-foot club. Meet promoters on the winter indoor circuit were aware of the spell Fosbury's flop cast on spectators attending the 1967 NCAA meet in Provo, Utah. The crackpot could help them sell tickets, so invitations swamped the mailbox of Fosbury's coach at Oregon State, Berny Wagner.

"I had never jumped indoors before, and all of a sudden I was jumping every weekend," Fosbury said.

Twenty-six days into the new year, at the Athens Invitational indoor meet in Oakland, California, Fosbury cleared 7 feet for the first time. "First you try to jump five feet, then six feet, then seven feet," Fosbury said. "It was a big deal for me. It put me on the cover of *Track & Field News.*"

Fosbury cleared 7 feet or higher in his next five meets, improving his personal best to 7-1¼ in Louisville and winning the NCAA indoor title in Detroit. Curious spectators ignored everything else going on when Fosbury began his prejump ritual of rocking back and forth on his heels, clenching and unclenching his hands. With his long, ungainly stride, the 6-foot-4, 185-pound Oregon State junior ran straight at the bar before swinging slightly to the left, similar to the approach taken by straddle jumpers. Any similarity ended abruptly at takeoff.

While most straddle jumpers took off on their left foot, Fosbury planted his right, or outside foot, for the launch. He then turned his back to the crossbar and glanced over his shoulder to determine the precise moment to kick his legs into the air. He landed in the pit on

Dick Fosbury cleared a meet-record 7-2¼ to win the 1968 national collegiate outdoor title in Berkeley, California. *AP Images*

what looked to be his neck but was actually his upper back. He tumbled head over heels back to his feet and exited the pit to the sound of cheers and laughter.

The 1960s were a decade of seismic changes in track and field. The introduction of fiberglass poles in 1961 led to a spate of record setting, adding nearly two feet to the world record in seven years. The 1968 Olympics in Mexico City were the first to be held on an all-weather Tartan track. The cutthroat competition between Adidas and Puma led to greatly improved shoe design—and illegal payoffs for the Olympic contenders wearing them. And while Mexico City was the first Olympics to feature drug and sex testing, steroid use went undetected and grew in popularity, particularly in the throwing events.

Those improvements originated in laboratories. The Fosbury Flop stands alone for its individual genius. The only comparable development came when shot-putter Parry O'Brien introduced the glide technique in the early 1950s, when he turned his back on the throwing area and executed a 180-degree spin before releasing the shot. But O'Brien's glide has been largely supplanted by the 360-degree spin rotational discus style used by most top putters today.

Fosbury's spectacular improvement in 1968 prompted a legion of young high jumpers to follow suit. Eight years later, all three medalists at the Montreal Olympics would be floppers, including Dwight Stones, the first flopper to set a world record.

As for Fosbury's lasting fame, it certainly didn't hurt that a sportswriter at the *Medford Mail-Tribune* gave the new style a catchy, alliterative name.

"We're lucky Dick's last name wasn't Smith," Stones said.

The Fosbury Flop it remains, a half century after its incubation.

"I liked the contradiction in the name: a flop could be a success," Fosbury said. "It was descriptive, it was alliterative, and it fit."

The Fosbury Flop's inventor grew up in Medford, a community of twenty-nine thousand located twenty-seven miles north of the California border in the Rogue River valley. Dick's father was a sales manager for a trucking company, his mother a secretary. Their son first tried the high jump in the fifth grade. He gravitated toward the antiquated scissors style, in which the jumper throws first the inside leg and then the outside leg over the bar in a scissoring motion. It's a natural way to jump—like a kid jumping over a fence—but the body's center of gravity is too high to make it efficient. Through middle school and into high school, coaches tried to steer the tall, skinny kid toward the straddle style that Charlie Dumas employed to become the first man to clear 7 feet in 1956. Straddle jumpers took off on the inside leg and rotated the torso over the bar. The king of the straddle was Valeriy Brumel, the Soviet master who set six world records in the early 1960s, topping out at 7-5¾ in 1963.

Coincidentally, 1963 proved to be a pivotal year in Fosbury's life. He was a rail-thin sophomore at Medford High School, and he had switched back to the scissors after failing to find any kind of groove with the straddle. His personal best was a middling 5 feet, 4 inches.

"The scissors style is simply running at the bar and hurdling it sitting up," Fosbury said. "It was easy but limited, and no one else was doing it at the time. So I was the worst guy in our school, the worst guy in the conference, and probably the worst in the state of Oregon. It was really frustrating."

Fosbury's sophomore season was winding down, and he was desperate to make a contribution. His mind was wired for problem-solving—he'd earn a degree in civil engineering at Oregon State. But he also had energy to burn and the desire to earn a varsity letter. With his physique, the high jump seemed to be his best bet. He'd sat on the bench in basketball and knew he was in over his head as a defensive lineman when he lost three teeth and suffered a concussion trying to tackle teammate Bill Enyart in football practice. "Earthquake" Enyart would go on to earn All-America honors as a 235-pound running back at Oregon State.

"I was really stubborn," Fosbury said. "I wanted to be on the track team."

At a late-season meet that spring in Grants Pass, thirty-five miles northwest of Medford, Fosbury suddenly figured out that if he moved his shoulders back when he jumped, he'd be able to lift his hips high enough to clear the bar. In one afternoon, he improved his best by six inches and invented a new style of high jumping.

"I finished the day clearing 5-10, and I was laying flat on my back instead of sitting on the bar," Fosbury said. "The other coaches went through the rulebook to see if this was a legal technique. Everything was fine. That was really the first day. That was the revolution. That day convinced me that I had something."

As he refined his technique in high school, Fosbury continued improving, eventually clearing 6-7 to win the Oregon state championship as a senior. Bill Bowerman, the acclaimed University of Oregon coach who'd also grown up in Medford, sent Fosbury a telegram inviting him to visit the Oregon campus in Eugene. Fosbury informed Bowerman that he wanted to major in engineering, a major Oregon didn't offer, and that he'd already accepted a scholarship to Oregon State. Bowerman wished him the best.

Wagner, the coach at Oregon State, was known for developing top-notch high jumpers. When Fosbury arrived on the Corvallis campus in the fall of 1965, Wagner tried to switch the freshman's style back to the straddle. Wagner considered the flop a "shortcut to mediocrity."

"Berny tried to change him, but he couldn't do it," said John Chaplin, an Oregon State assistant at the time who later gained fame for coaching a succession of record-setting Kenyan distance runners at Washington State. "The only reason Berny let Fosbury do the flop is that he had two other good high jumpers. Berny figured what the hell, let him do it."

Wagner grew intrigued by the flop, which Fosbury continued to use in competition. One summer day following Fosbury's freshman year in 1966, Wagner took some film of him flopping. In plaid Bermuda shorts, Fosbury cleared 6-6 by a good half foot. "That was when I first thought he was going to be a high jumper," Wagner said.

Just because Fosbury's invention was deemed legal didn't make it less lethal, according to a smattering of doctors, coaches, and parents who railed against the technique in the wake of Fosbury's meteoric Olympic season. Dr. J. T. O'Hanlan wrote an article for the *Virginia Medical Monthly* in which he said the technique was safe for Fosbury, who benefited from landing in special foam-cushioned pits such as "an expensive air-filled bladder, peculiar to the Olympics." But youngsters experimenting with the flop could sustain severe vertebral damage, O'Hanlan warned.

The Virginia doctor was overly alarmist, largely because of a misunderstanding that floppers land on their necks. Fosbury landed on his back and shoulders. But O'Hanlan had a valid point about the danger of flopping into sawdust and sand pits.

"They sounded the alarm to make sure the facilities were safe," Fosbury said of the doctors' warnings. "I completely missed the pit one time in high school. I floated past the pit and landed on the grass, thank God. It knocked the wind out of me, but I was OK."

To accommodate Fosbury, the coaches at Medford High School cobbled together a makeshift pit of scrap foam, cotton, and rags, bound together by netting. But the pits at out-of-town meets were sawdust. "I flopped into sawdust a lot of times," Fosbury said. "You had to have the proper equipment, i.e., a pitchfork. The jumpers would use the pitchfork to fluff up the pit where we landed. I took care of that myself."

As for the chicken-or-the-egg question of which came first, the flop or foam pits, the answer is the flop. But the corresponding development of foam-rubber landing pits accelerated the revolution. At Echo Summit and in Mexico City, the pits were much smaller than they are today, but they did provide Fosbury with a soft, cushioned landing.

––––––––––

Not to ruin a great story, but Fosbury wasn't actually the first flopper. Bruce Quande was.

While browsing through microfilm at the *Missoulian* in the late 1990s, a sportswriter at the paper, Rial Cummings, noticed a picture of a high jumper flying over the bar on his back. The photo was dated May 24, 1963, and the athlete was Quande, a senior at Flathead High School in Kalispell, Montana. Cummings contacted Quande, a businessman in Missoula, and learned that he began experimenting with the flop in 1961. Quande told Cummings that his highest clearance in high school was 6-2, albeit in practice.

Quande gave up the sport after one college season at St. Olaf in Minnesota, where he raised his best to 6-3. He wanted to devote more time to his studies, and a doctor told him he risked permanent injury to his neck and shoulders if he kept jumping into sawdust pits.

In an interesting twist, Quande did join some buddies in attending the Echo Summit trials while he was serving in the army in 1968.

"I wasn't there for the high jump, so I didn't see Fosbury jump," Quande said. "I did play flag football with John Carlos, Charlie Greene and Larry Questad, though."

Long before Quande's story surfaced, Debbie Brill's tale was common knowledge in the track world. Like Fosbury and Quande, Brill was a free spirit from the Pacific Northwest—in her case, small towns in the Canadian forests east of Vancouver, British Columbia. Unlike Fosbury and Quande, Brill had a long career, ranking among the world's top ten on twelve occasions from 1970 to 1985. She was the world's top-ranked female jumper in 1979 and set a Canadian record of 6-6 that remained unmatched nearly four decades later. In 2004, Brill set a world age-group record by bending her fifty-one-year-old body over the bar at 5-3.

In her autobiography, *Jump*, Brill explains: "High jumping has always been the easiest, most natural thing for me. It was like running through the mountain meadows my father took me to whenever he had some free time."

In 1966, with no knowledge of Fosbury or his embryonic flop, Brill switched from the scissors to a technique her coach christened the "Brill Bend." It wasn't until she attended a meet in Vancouver in 1967 that she first saw Fosbury jump. Her friends ran up to her excitedly and said, "There's someone else who jumps just like you!"

When she first showed an interest in the event, Brill's father found some fishnets and stuffed them with foam rubber from a secondhand furniture store, giving her a safe place to land.

"Fosbury and I were the first to exploit the new jumping conditions," Brill wrote in her book. "Why us? It was perhaps significant that we were both North American. The Eastern countries were already deep into the science of sport, with heavily regimented coaching. I don't think individual instinct flourishes in that kind of atmosphere."

The Mexico City Olympics came too soon for Brill, who was six years younger than Fosbury. In 1969, she became the first North American woman to jump 6 feet, a height she'd continue clearing for nearly twenty more years.

"The backwards style was just so simple to do," Brill said. "It was perfectly natural for all of us."

To the track world of 1968, jumping over the bar backward was anything but natural. It was the creation of a goofy outlier. In a few short years, the advantages became increasingly apparent, and cushier landing pits provided additional impetus. The Russians and other Eastern Bloc countries overcame their initial skepticism to embrace the flop.

When he emerged on the national and world scene in 1968, Fosbury predicted that future floppers would refine his style and make it much more efficient. What amazes Stones is how well Fosbury's intuitive style has held up over the decades.

"Dick's form, even to this day, is among the best ever," said Stones, a master technician who set three world outdoor records in the mid-1970s and retired with a best jump of 7-8. "I never could understand what he was doing with his arms, holding one up and one down, but it still squared him up over the bar. His form was a thing of beauty. When I set my first world record in 1973, someone asked me if I was going to rename the Fosbury Flop. I responded, 'Are you crazy? I didn't invent it.'"

Stones did develop his own theory on why Fosbury, of all people, came up with a new way of doing things.

"He's an engineer, and that played no small part in him coming up with it," Stones said. "Physics is all about the laws of motion. Dick understood it intuitively. He's also a very creative guy—an artist, a painter. He's a wonderful mix of right and left brain. It makes sense that a guy like that would revolutionize track and field."

The racial turbulence of 1968 didn't have much effect on the revolutionary high jumper.

"I supported the black movement, I was opposed to the war, I was a typical late-sixties college kid," Fosbury said. "But while I thought the Olympic Project for Human Rights was important, it didn't really affect me because they weren't asking any of the white guys to boycott."

Plus, he had a lot going on. In the fall of 1967, Fosbury was placed on academic probation, costing him his student deferment. He took the bus to Portland in December for his draft physical. Fosbury made sure to mention that he'd hurt his back in high school while manning a chainsaw for his job in park maintenance. An osteopath noticed something amiss on Fosbury's X-ray. He was told to go back to school and that they'd get back to him.

"My father was a marine, my grandfather was a marine, but they didn't pressure me," Fosbury said. "I really didn't want to go. I wore the uniform at the Olympic Games."

Two weeks after winning the NCAA indoor title, Fosbury received a notice telling him he was unfit to serve. But he was a college junior without a major after getting booted out of the school of engineering.

"Taking classes in physics, calculus, and differential equations while being gone every weekend and getting a social education on top of everything else—I had just turned twenty-one—my schoolwork suffered," he recalled. "Others could handle it. Dick Fosbury could not."

Four years after Mexico City, Fosbury would receive his degree in civil engineering from Oregon State. Of course, that was long after he'd used both sides of his brain to engineer a high jumping revolution.

"It was completely fate," Fosbury said of his discovery. "There's no rationalization for it. Part of it is drive. I wanted to stay on the team. I was highly motivated. So I figured it out on my own."

7

THE CRUELEST MONTH

FOR ALL BUT two minutes of his nationally televised address from the Oval Office on March 31, 1968, President Lyndon Baines Johnson spoke exclusively of the "long and bloody war" that had turned what might have been one of the most consequential presidencies in history into one of the most reviled.

Johnson expressed hope that a bombing halt would compel the North Vietnamese to consider a peaceful settlement of the war that had killed nearly five thousand US soldiers in the first three months of 1968. Not until the tail end of his half-hour talk did Johnson drop the real bombshell.

"I shall not seek, and I will not accept, the nomination of my party for another term as your president," he said.

Editorial writers and foreign leaders immediately lauded Johnson's statesmanship. His approval ratings soared. Four days after the announcement, on April 4, Johnson attended the installation of Terence Cooke as archbishop of New York in St. Patrick's Cathedral. Several thousand people respectfully applauded the president as he and his daughter Luci took their seats. In his sermon, Archbishop Cooke said, "Mr. President, our hearts, our hopes, our continued prayers, are with you."

Recalling the cathedral visit in his memoirs, Johnson wrote, "The world that day seemed to me a pretty good place."

Eleven hundred miles away, in Memphis, Tennessee, Rev. Martin Luther King Jr. had his own problems to worry about. A week earlier, King had visited Memphis to demonstrate his support for striking garbage workers.

The March 28 march on Beale Street descended into an orgy of window breaking and tear gas. A policeman shot and killed a black teenager. As the march spiraled out of control, King, the apostle of nonviolence, broke off from the group and went to a riverfront hotel. He watched on television as Memphis mayor Henry Loeb criticized the march's leaders and announced that three thousand soldiers of the National Guard would take control of the situation.

King awoke the next morning to scalding criticism. The *Memphis Commercial Appeal* called him "Chicken á la King." A headline in the *Dallas Morning News* called him "the headline-hunting priest of nonviolent violence." Senator Robert Byrd of West Virginia castigated King as "a man who gets other people into trouble and then takes off like a scared rabbit."

The *New York Times* called the Memphis march "a powerful embarrassment to Dr. King" and urged him to call off his planned Poor People's Campaign march on Washington, DC.

Many frustrated black people had already tuned out King's gospel of nonviolence. King himself feared in the spring of 1968 that his time had passed. Nonetheless, he insisted on returning to Memphis for a second march. On April 3, the Nobel laureate checked into the Lorraine Motel. That evening, King addressed a rally of three thousand supporters at Mason Temple. He cited the book of Exodus and mentioned the bomb threat that delayed his flight that morning.

"We've got some difficult days ahead," King said. "But it doesn't really matter to me now. Because I've been to the mountaintop. And I don't mind. Like anybody, I would like to live a long life. Longevity has its place. But I'm not concerned with that now. I just want to do God's will. And He's allowed me to go up to the mountain, and I've looked over, and I've seen the Promised Land.

"I may not get there with you. But I want you to know tonight that we as a people will get to the Promised Land. So I'm happy tonight. I'm not worried about anything. I'm not fearing any man. Mine eyes have seen the glory of the coming of the Lord."

Less than twenty-four hours later, King was pronounced dead in a Memphis hospital, the victim of an assassin's bullet. "America is shocked and saddened by the brutal slaying tonight of Dr. Martin Luther King," Johnson said in his second nationally televised address of the past five days. "I ask every citizen to reject the blind violence that has struck Dr. King, who lived by nonviolence."

Johnson realized that any momentum gained by his refusal to run for reelection had gone up in smoke with the murder in Memphis.

Rioting broke out within twenty blocks of the White House that evening. The rage spread west, north, and south, turning dozens of cities across the country into war zones by the following afternoon. Johnson told one of his aides that if he were a black man living in Harlem, he'd be joining in the rioting.

Floyd McKissick, the national CORE chairman, gravely pronounced King's dream dead when he spoke to reporters covering the postassassination rioting in Washington, DC. "King was the last prince of nonviolence," McKissick said. "Nonviolence is now a dead philosophy, and it was not the black people that killed it. It was the white people that killed nonviolence."

McKissick and King had stood behind Harry Edwards when he announced the OPHR's demands at the Americana Hotel in late 1967. "No one looking at the six demands can ignore the truth in them," King had said in his brief remarks at the press conference. King would say little if anything more about the Olympics publicly in the last four months of his life, but his words of support in New York were gold currency to Edwards's cause.

As Edwards wrote in his autobiography, "Dr. King's assassination and the 'days or rage and rivers of fire' that followed momentarily enhanced the legitimacy of the Olympic Project for Human Rights as one of the few unconventional routes of nonviolent Black protest remaining."

When the track circuit moved to California shortly after King's assassination, Edwards issued a statement saying the goals of the OPHR were "to be carried out as solemn memorials to the late Dr. Martin Luther

King, Jr., in recognition of the unselfish sacrifices of him and his family toward the realization of freedom, justice, and equality for all mankind."

The track season would continue uninterrupted. But for many athletes, King's death was the earthquake that shook hardest beneath their feet. "If you weren't aware before, you became aware then," Lee Evans said of the months leading up to Echo Summit. "Martin Luther King was a man of nonviolence, and he was gunned down in hatred."

8

AFTERSHOCKS

In the wake of the King assassination, Tennessee governor Buford Ellington ordered four thousand members of the Tennessee National Guard to Nashville, where snipers were firing on police officers from rooftops. Long jumper Ralph Boston was living in Nashville at the time, working at his alma mater, Tennessee State. Boston was preparing for his third and final Olympics in the long jump after winning a gold medal in 1960 and a silver medal in 1964.

Boston's regal bearing and winning personality made him one of the most respected figures in the sport, not just in the United States but around the world. His decade-long rivalry and friendship with Soviet long jumper Igor Ter-Ovanesyan lent a human face to Cold War propaganda. When one of the demands set forth by Harry Edwards and the OPHR was that a black man be appointed to the USOC, Lee Evans and Tommie Smith recommended Boston to fill that position.

Boston had grown up in Laurel, Mississippi, a textile town of twenty-five thousand, the youngest in a family of ten children. "Nothing happens in Laurel but morning, noon, and night," Boston said. "I did a lot of hunting and fishing." With the major universities south of the Mason-Dixon Line closed off to black athletes in the late 1950s, Boston enrolled at Tennessee State, where he quickly developed into one of the nation's top long jumpers. In 1960, the twenty-one-year-old broke the world record set by Jesse Owens twenty-five years earlier. Boston would set six world outdoor records over the course of his career, the most in the event's history.

Boston made it clear early on that he wouldn't consider boycotting the Mexico City Games. "It doesn't make any sense," he said. Edwards and some of the more militant athletes criticized the previously unassailable veteran for being out of the touch with the times. But King's assassination prompted Boston to reexamine his feelings about going to Mexico City.

"For the first time since the talks about the boycott began," Boston told *Sports Illustrated* a couple of weeks after King's assassination,

> I feel that I really have a valid reason to boycott. I sat and thought about it and I see that if I go to Mexico City and represent the United States I would be representing people like the one who killed Dr. King. And there are more people like that going around. I feel that I shouldn't represent people like that.
>
> It makes you think Stokely Carmichael and Rap Brown are right. All my life I felt that violence wasn't the way to deal with the problem. How do you keep feeling this way when things like that keep coming? How?

No sooner had his comments been published than Boston began receiving hate mail. "I've still got the letters," Boston said nearly fifty years later. "I got hate mail and I wasn't even a staunch supporter of the boycott. Can you believe that? But I've seen the hate mail Tommie [Smith] and John [Carlos] got. Theirs was much worse."

President Johnson had declared Sunday, April 7, a national day of mourning. He ordered that all US flags be flown at half-mast in honor of the slain civil rights leader. With Major League Baseball scheduled to begin its season that weekend, Commissioner William Eckert left it up to individual teams to decide whether to play their season openers as scheduled. Several teams opted to postpone their openers, but when the Houston Astros went ahead with plans to play their April 8 game against the Pittsburgh Pirates, Pittsburgh's all-star outfielder, Roberto Clemente, refused to play on the day of King's memorial service. When other black players, including Bob Gibson, the ace pitcher for the St. Louis Cardinals, said they wouldn't play any games until after King's funeral, Eckert's office relented and postponed all season openers until April 10.

On the day King was killed, Stan Wright arrived in Austin, Texas. Wright, the only black member of the US Olympic track coaching staff, was serving as the honorary meet referee of the Texas Relays. University of Texas football coach and athletic director Darrell Royal broke the news of King's assassination to Wright in a phone call. Royal asked Wright whether he thought the meet should be canceled.

Wright told Royal that he thought the meet should proceed as scheduled, as long as the visiting teams felt right about competing. The stadium flag flew at half-mast as spectators and athletes observed a moment of silence in King's honor.

A reporter asked Wright what effect he thought the proposed OPHR boycott would have on the Olympic trials. "I am not a hero like Martin Luther King, but I know I have a responsibility to the country and to the Olympic Committee," Wright said.

Villanova was scheduled to face the University of Tennessee in a dual meet on Saturday, April 6, in Knoxville. Many of the black athletes on Villanova's team were uncomfortable about venturing into the belly of the beast, so to speak, particularly just two days after King's assassination.

Earlier in the year, with Harry Edwards exerting pressure on East Coast college teams to join in the OPHR's boycott of the NYAC indoor meet, Villanova coach James "Jumbo" Elliott instructed his captain, Dave Patrick, to call the team together and decide collectively what they wanted to do. The Wildcats voted unanimously to boycott the NYAC meet.

Elliott again left the decision about whether to compete in the Tennessee meet up to the team. Patrick took another vote. This time the team was split, with a narrow majority choosing to compete. Sophomore quarter-miler Larry James was uncomfortable with the decision, but he was just a sophomore, so he went along with it.

"The black athletes were torn," James said. "The seniors wanted to run. Rather than hold the team hostage, we went."

One of the spectators at the 1967 AAU Championships in Bakersfield was a Villanova freshman who, like most first-year collegians in that era, was ineligible to compete at the varsity level in conference or national meets.

"I remember sitting high in the stands, watching the finals of the 440," James said. "Lee Evans and Vince Matthews battled it out, but I could see a gap between them and the other guys. I sort of saw myself in that gap. That vision carried me to the next season."

Raised by a single mother in White Plains, New Jersey, James competed mostly in the hurdles and triple jump in high school, "an all-around guy" more than a star, as he put it. Track gave him a sense of belonging. "I stuttered as a youngster," he said. "Track was compatible to my makeup. It helped me connect with other people. You score points, you're valuable to the team. You make a contribution, people don't care if you stutter."

The Olympic year was less than a month old when James announced his arrival. He won the 500-yard run at the Millrose Games, the most prestigious meet on the indoor circuit. After winning the Millrose 600, Evans tracked down Elliott to ask the coach what event James would be running outdoors. Elliott smiled, said nothing, and walked away.

James was nicknamed "the Mighty Burner" by his Villanova teammates. At the IC4A Indoor Championships, the Burner handled Dave Hemery, a highly regarded Englishman running for Boston University. Next up was the NCAA Indoor Championships at Cobo Arena in Detroit, where James clocked the fastest time ever for 440 yards on a 160-yard track: 47 seconds flat. When James anchored Villanova's mile relay to victory, clinching the NCAA indoor team title for the Wildcats, Elliott told his sophomore meteor what he had kept hidden from Evans.

"Forget about the hurdles," Elliott said. "You're a quarter-miler."

The meet between Villanova and Tennessee was billed as a "North vs. South" summit meeting by the Tennessee newspapers. The *Knoxville News-Sentinel* ran daily stories for a full week leading up to the meet.

Elliott had been Villanova's coach in 1935, working for a pittance while running a multimillion-dollar construction company in Philadelphia.

Don Bragg (pole vault), Charlie Jenkins (400 meters), and Ron Delany (1,500 meters) all won Olympic championships under Elliott's tutelage. Having just won the NCAA indoor team title, Elliott's 1968 group was shaping up to be one of the best of his long tenure.

Since taking Tennessee's coaching job in 1963, Chuck Rohe had established the Volunteers as the premier program in the Southeastern Conference. Rohe's prize catch was a two-sport sensation with a name and personal story straight out of a TV script: Richmond Flowers Jr. In the hothouse racial climate of US track and field in 1968, Flowers occupied a unique position. He was a white man winning races in an event dominated by black men, and his family history gave him credibility on matters of race.

Flowers grew up in Dothan, a southeastern Alabama city of about thirty thousand located near the Florida and Georgia state lines. His family moved to the state capital of Montgomery when his father, Richmond Flowers Sr., was elected Alabama attorney general in 1962. The elder Flowers ran on the same segregationist Democratic ticket as governor-elect George Wallace, but the two men were soon at odds.

Wallace was a racial agitator who famously declared on assuming the governorship in 1963, "Segregation now, segregation tomorrow, segregation forever!" Flowers had defended segregation in his campaign, but he was much more moderate than the firebrand governor, and the attorney general believed in the rule of law.

When Wallace symbolically tried to block black students from enrolling at the University of Alabama before acceding to the federal marshals escorting Vivian Malone and James Hood through a side door into the administration building, Flowers publicly criticized the governor for his cheap stunt. The rift grew when Flowers began prosecuting members of the Ku Klux Klan.

Richmond Jr., flat-footed and asthmatic as a youngster, blossomed athletically at Montgomery's Lanier High School. By the time he was a senior, Flowers was not only a terrific football player but also one of the fastest high school high hurdlers in the country.

It was an article of faith in Alabama that the best homegrown football players play for Paul "Bear" Bryant at the state's flagship university in

Tuscaloosa. But Flowers, like his father, had an independent streak. He was deeply affected by the booing his father received when he attended one of his son's track meets in Montgomery.

On a recruiting trip to Knoxville, Tennessee track coach Chuck Rohe showed Flowers where the new track stadium would be built, complete with one of the first Tartan surfaces in the country. Tennessee football coach Doug Dickey told the blue-chip recruit that he could sit out the 1967 football season if he felt it would help him qualify for the 1968 Olympics in the hurdles.

Despite a last-ditch pitch from Bryant, Flowers stunned his home state by signing a letter of intent with Tennessee. When an Alabama sportswriter asked him how he could pass up the experience of playing for Bear Bryant, Flowers responded cheekily, "I think it would be a greater experience to beat him."

Flowers lived up to the hype in Knoxville, ranking fourth in the world in the high hurdles in 1967. That fall, he earned All-America honors as a flanker on the Tennessee football team that went 9-2-1 and was named national champion in one poll. The national attention Flowers received in those heady days was partly a result of his father's feud with Wallace, but it also came from being a white running back and hurdler. There was no denying his athletic ability as talk turned to his chances of winning an Olympic medal in Mexico City.

At the 1968 NCAA Indoor Championships in Detroit, Flowers edged another two-sport star, Earl McCullouch of USC, to win the 55-meter high hurdles. Erv Hall of Villanova finished third, and the rematch between Flowers and Hall figured to be one of the highlights of the April 6 dual meet in Knoxville.

When Harry Edwards orchestrated a black boycott of the NYAC, Flowers expressed sympathy to the cause but chose to compete. The white hurdler did, however, have a problem with the way he felt Edwards was strong-arming others to join his cause.

"I learned from experience that bigots are sorry excuses for human beings," Flowers would say. "I also learned that they come in two colors. Harry Edwards and his group may have had an excuse for being racist, but they were still racists.

"I was very much aware of racism. We had crosses burned in our yard when I was growing up. I didn't have a guilty conscience."

————————

Larry James's reservations about competing in Knoxville only multiplied when he heard that news of King's killing had elicited a standing ovation in the Tennessee student center. Neither the *Knoxville News-Sentinel* nor the University of Tennessee student newspaper, the *UT Daily Beacon*, mentioned the alleged student union incident in their coverage of the King assassination. While Memphis remained on razor's edge, with National Guard troops patrolling the streets, and while snipers shot at police on the Tennessee A&I campus in Nashville, Knoxville remained peaceful.

On the day of the Tennessee-Villanova meet, in an edition filled with uniformly sorrowful coverage of the tragedy, the *Daily Beacon* ran several letters under the headline "Sick U.S. Society Needs Examining." A business major named Julia Eastman wrote in one of those letters:

> *American Nobel Peace Prize winner Dr. Martin Luther King was killed Thursday night. His sin? He was a Negro.*
>
> *I was sitting in my room when a friend entered and said, before his death, "I hope he dies."*
>
> *I was deeply shocked and I couldn't quite believe I had heard her correctly. "He started all the violence and riots. He deserved it," my friend said.*
>
> *And this was the Christian point of view I heard around me. Girls laughed and clapped. King was dead.*

While jogging outside the hotel on the morning of the meet, James encountered the most overtly racist act of his life. "A Volkswagen drove by. It was packed, I recall," he said. "The guys yelled out the window,

'Run, nigger, run!' I'm jogging and I come to dead halt. I couldn't believe what I'd just heard. One part of me said, 'I'm going back to the hotel and not run.' But another part of me said, 'Go out and make a statement.'"

When the Villanova team bus pulled up to the stadium an hour and a half before the 1:30 PM start, James looked at the crowd milling about, smiled at Dave Patrick, and said, "I'm not going to be the first one off this bus."

"Larry had a sense of humor, even at a time like that," Patrick said.

———————

The crowd that turned out on a seventy-degree afternoon took both teams by surprise. More than ninety-five hundred spectators filled the grandstands and spilled out onto the hills along each curve. While Villanova had the edge in star power and pedigree, the dual-meet format played to Tennessee's strength of having a well-rounded team across all seventeen events.

As expected, Villanova dominated the running events, but Tennessee's superiority in the field events gave the Volunteers the team win, 77 points to Villanova's 67. Flowers was Tennessee's high-point man, winning the 120-yard high hurdles, anchoring the 440-yard relay team to victory, and placing second and third in the 100- and 220-yard dashes. In the high hurdles, Flowers and another Olympic hopeful, Villanova junior Erv Hall, ran stride for stride before Flowers opened a small gap coming off the final barrier, clocking 13.5 to Hall's 13.6. Hall did manage to beat Flowers in both of the sprints that afternoon.

The Knoxville result that sent shock waves across the track world came in the 440-yard dash. James rocketed around the track in 45.2 seconds, the third-fastest time in history, and equivalent to a 44.9 for the Olympic distance of 400 meters. Hardee McAlhaney broke the Tennessee record—one of seven school marks set by the Volunteers that afternoon—but still finished nearly a second behind in 46.1.

"I don't think I ever ran against a more ferocious competitor," said McAlhaney, a quarter-miler from segregated South Carolina who had never raced against a black athlete until he arrived in Knoxville. "Larry was all business on the track. He never boasted about anything."

James was catching his breath when Patrick, the Villanova captain, practically bowled him over in excitement.

"Burner, you know what this means?" Patrick shouted. "You're up there! You're bona fide!"

For all the pain it caused him, the trip to Knoxville was worth it. With a shove from the racists in the Volkswagen, Larry James was headed toward the mountaintop.

The University of Texas at El Paso competed in the Texas Relays the weekend following King's assassination, but the black athletes on the team didn't feel right about it. On returning to El Paso, they ran into Harry Edwards, who happened to be on campus to give a lecture. The UTEP black athletes briefly met with Edwards, though they insisted afterward that he had nothing to do with the decision they soon made among themselves.

A topsy-turvy season track season at UTEP was about to get even more chaotic. In February, several of its black athletes, including standout long jumper Bob Beamon, broke the picket line at the NYAC indoor meet in New York. While their decision to compete in New York drew the ire of Edwards and other OPHR supporters, they were praised in El Paso for their defiance of the racial rabble-rousers. In March, the Miners finished a strong fifth in the team race at the NCAA Indoor Championships in Detroit behind Beamon's individual wins in the long triple jumps. In the NCAA long jump, Beamon flew 27 feet, 2¾ inches, a new indoor world record.

Chastened by their NYAC experience, the racial climate on their own campus, and the assassination of the nation's leading civil rights leader, nine black members of the UTEP track team voted to boycott an Easter weekend meet in Provo, Utah, against Utah State and Brigham Young University. UTEP track coach Wayne Vandenburg told the athletes they'd be kicked off the team if they went through with it. Eight of them, including Beamon, held firm.

"There were about a dozen reasons," said UTEP runner Dave Morgan. "The Mormons teach that Negroes are descended from the devil. As a reason for the track team's boycott, it may sound like a small thing to a white person, but who the hell wants to go up there and run your tail off in front of a bunch of spectators who think you've got horns? And it was Easter week, and it seemed to us that there was an obvious connection between the martyrdom of Jesus and the martyrdom of Dr. King. To a white it might be nothing; to us it had great significance."

UTEP had been known as Texas Western until the school changed its name in 1967. In 1966, Texas Western made sports history by upsetting Kentucky in the final of the NCAA basketball tournament with an all-black starting lineup. But that groundbreaking accomplishment didn't erase the fact that the black students were treated as second-class citizens on the El Paso campus. In 1968 there were fewer than 250 black students in a student body of 10,000. Black athletes were discouraged from dating white women, and some members of the athletic department's coaching staff had a habit of referring to black athletes as "niggers."

In a 1968 series titled "The Black Athlete—A Shameful Story," *Sports Illustrated* devoted one of the articles to the racial problems at UTEP. Beamon and other black athletes at UTEP painted a sordid picture of the inequities they put up with every day at a university eager to reap the benefits of their physical talents without caring much about their education and social lives.

"If a Negro looks for help he doesn't find it," Beamon said. "I have a four-year-old car that needs $300 of repairs. I don't know where I'm gonna get the money to fix it. If I were the *white* long-jump champion that car would be fixed like magic."

El Paso was a world removed from the impoverished South Jamaica section of Queens where Beamon grew up. He never met his father, and his mother died when he was eleven months old. His late mother's husband—Beamon's stepfather—was an abusive ex-con. Bob was drinking regularly by age twelve, shoplifting and dealing drugs by thirteen. Teachers wrote him off as incorrigible. Nurses wrote in his school medical file that the troubled teen stuck pins in himself.

"No one knew what to do with me," Beamon said. "They all predicted I would be in prison by the time I was fourteen."

Rather than be sent to a reformatory school, Beamon enrolled in P.S. 622 on Fifty-Second Street in Manhattan, where students were frisked for weapons and drugs each morning. He later transferred to Jamaica High School, an academically rigorous school with a largely Jewish enrollment. Jamaica's dean of boys and track coach was Larry Ellis, a Bronx native and first cousin of Stan Wright, the 1968 Olympic assistant coach. (Ellis would later serve as the head men's coach of the 1984 US Olympic team.)

"I thought Jamaica High would give Bob the opportunity he wanted to better himself," Ellis said. "Selfishly, I wanted a boy with that kind of ability on our track team."

Beamon thrived at Jamaica High School, guided by both Ellis and the school's basketball coach, Hilty Shapiro. At 6 feet 3 and 150 pounds, Beamon was never a particularly skilled basketball player, but his leaping ability was off the charts. He averaged 15 points and 14 rebounds a game for the Jamaica varsity in the 1964–65 season. That spring, his track potential became crystal clear: Beamon had the longest mark of any high school student in the country in the triple jump (50 feet, 3¾ inches) and the second-best mark in the long jump (25-3½).

Graduating 1,093rd in a class of 1,182 at Jamaica High School left Beamon leery of accepting a scholarship to a major university such as Southern California, the most powerful collegiate team in the country. He chose to attend North Carolina A&T, a predominantly black school in Greensboro. Before the integration of southern athletic programs in the late 1960s and early '70s, many top athletes chose the same route. The 1968 US Olympic men's team was stocked with athletes who attended historically black colleges: Boston, Jim Hines, Willie Davenport, Vince Matthews, Norm Tate, Leon Coleman, Charles Mays, and Art Walker.

It didn't take long for Beamon to realize he'd made a mistake in selecting North Carolina A&T. He wasn't expected to go to class, and he didn't, for the most part. His US ranking in the long jump improved one spot from 1965, from sixth to fifth, but when Ellis called in the fall of 1967 to let him know that Vandenburg would offer him a full scholarship if he'd transfer to UTEP, Beamon jumped at the chance.

As a transfer student, Beamon was ineligible to compete for the Miners in 1967, but the change did wonders for his jumping. Beamon jumped a lifetime-best 26-11½ to win the 1967 AAU indoor title and finished the outdoor season ranked fourth in the world. Though his technique was still raw when compared to that of Boston or Ter-Ovanesyan, Beamon entered the Olympic season as a legitimate gold-medal threat. An unbeaten indoor season, capped by his record leap at the NCAA indoor meet, raised his stock even higher.

When the nine black athletes went to Vandenburg's apartment to tell the coach they wouldn't compete in the April 13 meet against BYU and Utah State, Vandenburg told them if they didn't compete, they'd be kicked off the team and would lose their scholarships. Beamon and the others continued to practice with the team during the week, giving Vandenburg hope that they'd changed their minds, but eight of the nine stayed behind when the team left for Provo on Friday.

Beamon wasn't the ringleader of the BYU boycott, but his willingness to go along with Morgan and the others indicated a growing social awareness.

In a paper he wrote for an English class in the spring of 1968, Beamon weighed the pros and cons of an Olympic boycott. He started the essay by recounting the contents of a racist letter he'd received from someone in Colorado Springs.

"You fellows should consider yourself lucky that blacks are accepted to compete against other races," the Coloradan wrote Beamon. "Who do you think you are, just because you can run? So can a rabbit! This country got along very well for many, many years without black people and will continue to do so long after you have faded into nothingness. Don't overrate yourself."

Beamon then wrote in his essay, "What can the black athlete do when attitudes like that are so widespread? He wants to protest, to show that he, too, is a human being with the same kind of feelings as his white brother. It is because of just such people as the writer of that letter than Professor Edwards' boycott movement came about."

Ultimately, Beamon concluded that he could bring more renown to his race by winning an Olympic gold medal than he could by not participating.

"The years go fast, especially for an athlete whose time of glory is brief," he wrote. "He cannot afford to wait for another four years and the next Olympics to roll around. His time to bear the torch is now—or not at all."

The aftershocks of King's murder were felt in Lausanne, Switzerland, where the executive board of the IOC voted on April 21 to reverse its ruling on South Africa. Two months after accepting the apartheid regime back into the Olympic movement, the IOC board bowed to international pressure and rescinded the invitation. South Africa would not return to the Olympic fold until 1992.

Thirty-nine nations, including thirty-two from Africa, had vowed to boycott the Mexico City Games if South Africa was allowed to participate. The Soviet Union had sent out signals that it, too, would stay away if the IOC didn't reconsider, and South Africa's exclusion was part of the list of demands drawn up north of the Mexican border by Harry Edwards and the Olympic Project for Human Rights.

"We did not want that chap from California coming down to Mexico City and setting off riots," one IOC member said after the ban was reinstituted.

9

BUMPY ROAD TO SUMMIT

ASSUMING THERE WOULDN'T be a black boycott, US hopes for the Mexico City Olympics were sky high as construction began on the Echo Summit track in the spring of 1968. In the 1967 world rankings published by *Track & Field News*, ten Americans were ranked number one: Jim Hines (100 meters), Tommie Smith (200), Lee Evans (400), Jim Ryun (1,500), Willie Davenport (110 high hurdles), Ron Whitney (400 hurdles), Ed Caruthers (high jump), Paul Wilson (pole vault), Ralph Boston (long jump), and Randy Matson (shot put).

It was probably a stretch to think the US men would match the twelve gold medals they'd won at the 1964 Tokyo Olympics, since that total included out-of-the-ordinary wins in the 5,000 and 10,000 meters by Bob Schul and Billy Mills. Schul and Mills were attempting comebacks in 1968, but most experts figured the distance races in Mexico City would pit altitude-raised Africans against Ron Clarke, the world-record holder from Australia. Regardless, Mexico's northern neighbor had its usual embarrassment of riches, on both the track and field.

The 400 meters had long been one of the strongest American events, and the early-season exploits of Larry James caught the attention of Evans out in San Jose. Three weeks after his breakout run in Knoxville, James went even faster, anchoring Villanova to victory in the mile relay at the Penn Relays with a 43.9-second lap, the fastest quarter-mile relay split in history. Three weeks later, Villanova traveled west to compete in the West Coast Relays, a Fresno fixture that drew large, enthusiastic contingents of black fans. The atmosphere was particularly charged in 1968, as a crowd of fourteen thousand turned out to watch Evans, the homegrown hero, go up against James in the mile relay. Villanova led San Jose State by about 3 yards when James received the baton for the anchor leg. James held that margin down the backstretch and final curve before Evans powered past to finish 5 yards clear of his newest rival. Winters clocked Evans in 44.5, James in 45.5. Joyous teammates and fans put Evans on their shoulders and paraded him back and forth across the infield. To this day, Evans considers the race in Fresno the highlight of his career.

"If I feel bad about myself, I think about that race, and I feel better," Evans said.

Beginning with the West Coast Relays and continuing through Echo Summit in September, California would be the epicenter of the track world. At the Modesto Relays in late May, Jay Silvester set the first world record of the season in an Olympic event, throwing the discus 218 feet, 3½ inches. The intense Utahn had been one of the world's top throwers for nearly a decade and believed 1968 would be the year in which he'd finally climb out of Al Oerter's shadow. Silvester had finished fourth at the 1964 Olympics in Tokyo, where Oerter won his third straight gold medal. Silvester won his first 1968 matchup with Oerter at the West Coast Relays decisively, and his record-setting throw in Modesto was more than 10 feet farther than Oerter's lifetime best. "To get the record back after losing it once makes you feel young again," Silvester said.

––––––––––––

The spotlight then shifted to Edwards Stadium in Berkeley for the first major outdoor meet of the season, the NCAA Championships. While Cal was known for its liberal politics and student activism—Ronald Reagan began his campaign for governor in 1966 by vowing to "clean up the mess in Berkeley"—it was the university's athletic department that found itself mired in racial controversy in early 1968. Along with the University of Washington and the University of Texas at El Paso, Cal was one of three schools "white-listed" by Harry Edwards and the OPHR for their alleged mistreatment of black athletes. The center on Cal's basketball team, Bob Presley, had been kicked off the squad by coach Rene Herrerias for insubordination. Presley claimed that the coach didn't like the length of his Afro hairstyle. While Presley was quickly accepted back on the team, a newly formed group called the Black Athletes of the University of California, along with Edwards, raised a major stink, and Herrerias and athletic director Pete Newell wound up resigning their positions.

The NCAA Championships took place one week after the assassination of Robert F. Kennedy in Los Angeles. Kennedy had finished speaking to supporters on the evening of June 5 following his hard-fought win in the state's Democratic presidential primary when a twenty-four-year-old Palestinian shot him twice in the hotel kitchen. Helping wrest the gun from Sirhan Sirhan was Rafer Johnson, the former Olympic decathlon champion—the same Rafer Johnson who had drawn Edwards's ire for speaking out against the black boycott. If there was an irony in Johnson's actions speaking louder than words, Edwards seemed to miss it.

Perhaps the country was too numb to respond to RFK's assassination with the same outrage that had accompanied King's murder two months earlier. There weren't any riots, and few sporting events were postponed. Enthusiastic crowds turned out in beautiful weather the next weekend to watch the cream of collegiate track and field. The top six Americans in each NCAA event would qualify for the first Olympic trials, to be held June 29–30 at the Los Angeles Memorial Coliseum. The presence of foreign-born collegians such as Boston University hurdler Dave Hemery and USC sprinter Lennox Miller added to the pre-Olympic flavor in Berkeley.

Hemery, a twenty-three-year-old Englishman and recent convert from the high hurdles, gave notice that he'd be an Olympic medal contender by winning the 400-meter intermediate hurdles in 49.8 seconds. Miller, a Jamaican, won the 100 meters, placed a close second in the 200, and anchored USC to victory in the 4 x 100 relay. Running the third leg for USC was O. J. Simpson, the football star who would win the Heisman Trophy that fall. In his first NCAA appearance for San Jose State, Evans circled the ash-and-clay surface in 45.0, four-tenths of a second in front of James. Dick Fosbury won the high jump with a personal-best jump of 7 feet, 2¼ inches, making "conservatives swallow hard by using his colorful 'Fosbury Flop,'" according to the *San Francisco Chronicle*'s report. With world-record holder Jim Ryun sidelined by mononucleosis, Dave Patrick of Villanova won the 1,500 meters in a meet-record 3:39.0.

The star of the show was Gerry Lindgren, the onetime distance prodigy from Washington State. The Spokane native had burst on the scene
four years earlier, shattering a succession of high school records by ridiculous margins. That summer, in the US-USSR dual meet then viewed
as a proxy Cold War showdown, Lindgren scored an epic upset in the
10,000 meters. Robert Kennedy was among the 50,519 spectators at the
Los Angeles Memorial Coliseum who thrilled at the sight of a scrawny,
beak-nosed teenager outrunning the vaunted Soviets. Talking to reporters afterward, Lindgren said he felt the weight of the American system
on his shoulders and couldn't fail his countrymen.

An ankle injury limited Lindgren to a ninth-place showing at the 1964
Olympics in Tokyo. In 1965, Lindgren and other collegians were caught
in the drawn-out war between the NCAA and the AAU. As the national
governing body of amateur athletics, the AAU was fiercely protective of
its authority over US participation in international competitions such
as the Olympics and Pan American Games. The NCAA reasoned that
since it was largely responsible for developing the Olympians through

Gerry Lindgren en route to another win during his incomparable collegiate
career at Washington State. *Washington State athletics*

its collegiate system, it deserved a larger say in how things were run. The NCAA formed an umbrella organization in 1961, the United States Track and Field Federation, in a direct assault on the AAU's authority. The situation got so bad that President John F. Kennedy appointed his attorney general brother, Robert, to try to negotiate a truce. RFK failed, and it took General Douglas MacArthur to arbitrate an agreement in 1963 that assured full US participation in the Tokyo Olympics.

The cease-fire was temporary. NCAA leadership threatened any collegiate athletes who competed in the 1965 AAU Championships that they'd lose their scholarships. Lindgren defied the order and ran anyway, finishing the 6-mile run in a near-dead heat with Billy Mills. Mills and Lindgren were both clocked in 27:11.6, a six-second improvement on Clarke's world record. Lindgren was called to testify a few weeks later at a congressional hearing on the NCAA-AAU feud. "I just remembered why I was a runner," Lindgren said. "That was to be the best representative I could be. So it was wrong to be forced to choose between my country and my school."

No school was going to pull the scholarship of a runner with that kind of moxie, and Lindgren won national collegiate titles at both the 5,000 and 10,000 meters in 1966 and 1967. After spending part of his summer training on Mount Baldy in Southern California to get a feel for altitude running, Lindgren won the 1967 NCAA cross-country title in the 7,200-foot altitude of Laramie, Wyoming. He started his second Olympic campaign strong, claiming his first-ever win over Clarke at the Modesto Relays in the US record time of 13:33.8 for 5,000 meters. On the opening day of the NCAA meet in Berkeley, Lindgren finished 15 seconds clear of the field in the 10,000 meters. Rather than talk about his race afterward, he informed the press that he would boycott the following week's AAU Championships in Sacramento. Lindgren's latest beef centered on the AAU's refusal to recognize Jim Ryun's world half-mile record because it came in a meet sanctioned by the United States Track and Field Federation. "They cheated Ryun from his deserved record," Lindgren said, "and I'm not for any organization that hurts athletes."

With Lindgren adding the 5,000-meter title two days later, Washington State improbably came within one point of tying USC for the team championship. James anchored Villanova to victory in the meet's final event, the 4 x 400 relay. In its meet coverage, the *San Francisco Chronicle* ran an accompanying story from the Associated Press under the headline "Echo Summit Set to Host Olympians." The brief story made no mention of a final Olympic selection meet at Echo Summit, only of a high-altitude training camp. Uncertainty over exactly how the USOC planned to select its Olympic men's track team would only deepen in the coming weeks.

Having already clinched a spot in the Los Angeles trials, Gerry Lindgren's boycott of the AAU meet was mostly symbolic. He didn't need to compete in Sacramento. But his spirit was felt in Sacramento when the AAU agreed just before the meet to finally submit Jim Ryun's two-year-old world record in the half-mile to international officials for approval.

Ryun was still back in Kansas, slowly working his way back from mononucleosis. He had been assured that he would receive a medical waiver to Echo Summit if he needed it. Despite the absence of Ryun, Lindgren, Fosbury, and assorted other collegians, the AAU meet in Sacramento turned out to be one for the ages. Or, more accurately, June 20 turned out be a night for the ages, immediately dubbed "the Night of Speed." In three rounds of the 100 meters—heats, semifinals, and final—the world record of 10 seconds flat was broken by three men and tied by seven others, all within the span of two and a half furious hours. The Night of Speed, indeed.

"There will never be another night like it," Jim Hines said nearly thirty years later, and his words still ring true today.

The two-day meet was held at Hughes Stadium, a horseshoe-shaped facility with a fast clay track. The AAU allowed select foreign athletes to compete in those days, which meant the 100-meter field included Miller, the Jamaican attending USC, and Roger Bambuck, a Guadeloupe-born Frenchman who had won the 200 meters at the 1966 European Championships. But the men to beat in Sacramento were Hines and Charlie Greene, the US rivals expected to battle for the gold medal in Mexico City. In 1966, Greene was ranked first in the world, a spot he relinquished to Hines in 1967. Greene wore sunglasses when he raced, day or night, calling them his "re-entry shades." While great sprinters are often cocky, Greene was in a class by himself. He took great pride in psyching out his opponents, but Hines, an Oakland native who ran for Stan Wright at Texas Southern University, was a tough nut to crack.

"I knew a lot of people were going to run fast in Sacramento," Greene said. "They were in the race with 'The Dudes.' Me and Jimmy were the dudes. You get in a race and hook on with us, you'll run fast. No one even dreamed of beating us."

The fireworks started in the first heat when Hines clocked a wind-aided 9.8. Mel Pender, the Vietnam veteran who received word earlier in the day that he'd been promoted to captain in the US Army, clocked a wind-aided 10.0 in the second heat. The Jamaican Miller won the third heat in 9.9, also aided by illegal breeze. With the wind dipping just inside the legal limit of 2.0 meters per second for the fourth and final heat, Greene, Bambuck, and Jim Green all tied the world record of 10.0.

Pender shot out to an early lead in the first semifinal, just as he had in the 1964 Olympic final before fading to sixth. Hines overhauled Pender at the 80-meter mark and clocked the first wind-legal 9.9 in history. Ronnie Ray Smith, a member of Winter's Speed City group in San Jose, finished four feet behind Hines but was also awarded a 9.9 clocking. Pender and Larry Questad were third and fourth in 10.0. When the announcer informed the crowd of ten thousand that the wind reading was within the legal limit, Hines celebrated with gusto. Greene, warming up for the second semifinal, seethed. "Jimmy took a victory lap, and the son of a bitch hadn't won yet. I didn't appreciate that," Greene said.

Greene matched Hines's new world record in the second semifinal with another legal 9.9. The 10-second barrier in the 100 meters, having outlasted the 4-minute mile and the 7-foot high jump, was shattered three times in ten minutes. At 9:45 PM, with a late-night chill settling in over the sun-baked track, veteran starter Tom Moore called the finalists to their marks.

The eight finalists were old acquaintances who raced each other often and for free. Yes, there were the occasional under-the-table payments from promoters in those days, but the sprinters usually played for more money the night before in poker games than they ever found in hidden

Jim Hines (right) overhauls fast-starting Mel Pender on his way to setting a world record of 9.9 seconds in the 100-meter dash at the 1968 AAU
Championships in Sacramento. *Courtesy of Stan Wright*

envelopes. "Sometimes the race was won the night before at the hotel,"
Hines said. "These guys today lock themselves in their rooms, but we'd
have a couple of cold beers, play cards, go to a movie. We were the best
of friends off the track."

The final proved to be somewhat anticlimactic, in part because it was the third hard 100 of the night. Green overcame Pender's quick start and the powerful finishes of Hines and Miller to win in a wind-aided 10.0. Greene cramped up after the final and had to be assisted to his feet. No victory lap for him.

"The night in Sacramento was magical—a fast clay track, hot as hell, a lot of intensity," Greene said. "That was a great race for me because I beat the people you have to beat to be great."

The International Amateur Athletic Federation (IAAF) accepted only hand times for world records until 1978, but there was a Bulova electronic phototimer in use that night to determine the places. Fully automatic times are slower than hand times because the clock starts ticking the moment the gun fires, removing the human reaction time of hand timing. The automatic time for Hines in his semifinal was a remarkable 10.03, faster than the 10.06 run by Bob Hayes to win the 1964 Olympic title. Greene's time in the second semifinal was 10.10, the third-fastest automatic time in history. Hines would run an automatic 9.95 in Mexico City, but the altitude at the Olympics was probably worth a tenth of a second, and the Tartan track at Estadio Olímpico was even faster than Hughes Stadium's clay surface. "If you look at the surface and the long spikes we had to wear, that race in Sacramento was the fastest ever run," Pender said.

The times were so astounding that the meet director, Al Baeta, called for a steel tape following the semifinals. The race was indeed 100 meters—and a bit more. "We measured it then and there," Baeta said. "It was four inches long. That's what I remember most about that night—sweating out that measurement."

Bob Beamon nearly joined the sub-10 sprinters in the record book when he won the long jump the following evening with a leap of 27-4, three-quarters of an inch off the world record shared by Ralph Boston and Igor Ter-Ovanesyan. Boston qualified for the L.A. trials by jumping an encouraging 26-7¼ in second place. In the men's 200 meters, Tommie Smith needed all of his finishing speed to overhaul John Carlos, the new sprinter on the Speed City block, and Evans claimed his third straight AAU title in the 400. But the meet's most surprising performance—which tickled the delighted crowd—came in the pole vault. Casey Carrigan, a seventeen-year-old from Orting, Washington, finished third at 16-8¼, the highest vault ever recorded by a high school student.

A prodigy who began vaulting in a backyard pit built by his logger father, Carrigan cleared 14-6 as a high school freshman and improved to an eye-opening 15-8 as a sophomore. But his 1968 best of 16 feet fell short of the AAU entry standard, and it took some fatherly lobbying on the part of Paul Carrigan to get his son the last spot in the Sacramento field. "My father wrote this sob letter about how his son was training every day in the rain and cold up in Washington and just needed a chance," Carrigan said. "It worked. That was the beginning of my big year."

The high point of Carreigan's remarkable year would come on a California mountaintop.

———

The NCAA and AAU meets were largely devoid of controversy. Gerry Lindgren had sounded off about the NCAA-AAU imbroglio in Berkeley, and Lee Evans had griped in Sacramento about white entrants receiving more favorable lane draws in the 400-meter qualifying, but the focus at both championships was largely on the outstanding performances of the athletes. The Olympic trials in Los Angeles on June 29–30—or non-trials, as they became derisively known—would prove to be the exact opposite.

The USOC did its best to dress up the proceedings with a veneer of importance. Pigeons flew overhead, just as they did when the 1932 Olympics put Los Angeles on the world map. Bands played, choirs sang, parachutists dropped from the sky, speeches were made extolling the brotherhood engendered by the Olympic movement. In the end, though, the L.A. trials did little more than stoke cynicism in the athletes and generate a nice chunk of revenue for the USOC. Ultimately, the biggest beneficiary wound up being Echo Summit, which became host of the be-all and end-all trials.

The one carrot offered in Los Angeles—that individual event winners would be guaranteed spots on the US Olympic team provided they "maintain the same degree of excellence" through the Echo Summit trials—turned out to be a turnip. Some of the L.A. winners recognized this, such as steeplechaser George Young and 800-meter runner Wade Bell. Others didn't realize their Olympic spots were unprotected until they got to Lake Tahoe.

"L.A. turned out to be a fundraising deal for the USOC," Young recalled. "It really served no purpose."

The non-trials did serve one purpose, though the news wouldn't get out for another month. A decision had been made at the AAU meet that the only way the black athletes would boycott en masse was if two-thirds of them voted in favor. For many, the Sacramento meeting was the first time they had met Harry Edwards face-to-face, and several commented that he was more reasonable than they thought he'd be. During the L.A. trials, a vote was taken at the training headquarters on the Cal Poly Pomona campus. The group voted to go to Mexico City—overwhelmingly, Evans said; by a slim majority, Edwards insisted. Either way, tensions were higher than ever at the Coliseum. The Los Angeles Police Department assigned a plainclothes officer to shadow Stan Wright, the embattled Olympic assistant coach, on and off the track. Wright wasn't the only non-boycotting black person to have his life threatened.

"I was at the L.A. trials but wasn't competing," said Boston, who was nursing a strained knee and received a pass to Echo Summit. "I was on the infield and an undercover guy came up really close to me and said, 'Ralph, we have information that there might be an attempt on your life.' That was one of the most unnerving moments of my life."

Edwards was a conspicuous presence in the general admission section, accompanied by basketball great Bill Russell and a coterie of vocal supporters. The animus peaked when lane assignments were announced for the 200-meter final. Smith was on the far outside in lane eight, Carlos smack up against the curve in lane one. Smith and Carlos berated Wright and Hilmer Lodge, the chairman of the USOC track and field committee, at the officials' table on the Coliseum infield. Denise Smith argued on her husband's behalf. Wright tried to explain that the lane assignments were made by blindly picking .38-caliber shells designated for each athlete out of a hat. (While they weren't live bullets, merely shells from the starter's gun, drawing straws or numbers might have been a more sensitive choice.)

Smith won anyway, clocking 20.2 to finish a march ahead of Hines, the 100-meter winner. Carlos, hindered by the tight inside lane, was fourth. Each of them was headed to Echo Summit.

In Los Angeles, much of the pre-meet publicity centered on USC standout Earl McCullouch, the NCAA and AAU champion in the 110-meter high hurdles. The Detroit Lions had made McCullouch a first-round pick in the 1968 pro football draft, and team officials were pressuring the wide receiver to sign a contract. McCullouch was headed for what looked like a certain victory when he clipped the eighth hurdle, stumbled, and staggered across the finish in seventh place. It was his final track race.

Fosbury won the high jump at 7-1 and headed home to Oregon for some much-needed rest. Dave Patrick, winner of the 1,500 in the convalescing Ryun's absence, went back to Maryland, figuring he had plenty of time to sharpen up for Mexico City. The two were in for a surprise when they reported to Echo Summit. Sixteen athletes were given passes to Echo Summit because of illness or injury, including Ryun, Boston, Mills, Richmond Flowers, and Willie Davenport. Fully 62 percent of the athletes who competed in Los Angeles advanced to the final trials at Tahoe. Given the ambiguous nature of the selection process, it's not surprising that some saw sinister motives on the part of the USOC.

"I think the two trials were held to weed the blacks out," Tommie Smith said.

"You have to go down to nine or ten [places] to get the white cats," Edwards said. "That's why they're doing it. Maybe that's going to be a boys' camp up there."

It wouldn't be a coed camp. Not until 1976 did track officials include men and women in the same Olympic trials. In the pre–Title IX days of 1968, the US Olympic women's team was selected in late August at a two-day meet in Walnut, California. The women's high-altitude camp was in desolate Los Alamos, New Mexico, known to history as the birthplace of the atomic bomb.

"I guess you couldn't have boys and girls together in a trailer park," Fosbury said.

10

MAGIC MOUNTAIN

WHEN HE HEARD about plans to hold a pre-Olympic training camp at Echo Summit, Bill Toomey hopped in his station wagon and drove 500 miles from his Santa Barbara home to Lake Tahoe. Toomey, a gold-medal contender in the decathlon, couldn't wait to get the lay of the land—even if some of it was under snow at the time.

"I really started looking forward to it at that point," Toomey said. "I would have competed under a bridge somewhere, but this just so happened to be one of the most tranquil, beautiful places in California . . . and it was the gateway to the Olympics."

The scheduled dedication ceremony for the Echo Summit track was postponed a week because of Robert Kennedy's assassination. For South Lake Tahoe officials and business leaders, it was a well-deserved chance to pat one another on the back. A Mexican contingent was brought in to emphasize the Olympic connection. The Mexicans and other foreign dignitaries were presented with pine saplings to plant in their home soil.

South Lake Tahoe mayor Don Clarke read a vaguely worded letter from Hubert Humphrey in which the vice president wrote, "I am hopeful the example set by South Lake Tahoe is only the beginning." The ribbon cutting included a ceremonial lap around the track by three runners, the most noteworthy being Van Nelson, a double gold medalist in the 5,000 and 10,000 meters at the 1967 Pan American Games.

Nelson had driven to Tahoe in his 1960 Karmann Ghia convertible immediately after finishing up his classes at St. Cloud State in Minnesota. He was enlisted for the ceremonial lap largely because he was one of the few athletes in town on June 15, but he proved to be a fitting choice for two reasons.

First, Nelson's coach at St. Cloud, Bob Tracy, was instrumental in steering the camp and final trials to Echo Summit. Second, Nelson wound up qualifying for the Olympic team in the 10,000 with one of the best races of his life. Understandably, Nelson doesn't have any memory of the ceremonial lap on June 15, though he has total recall of the 10,000-meter final on September 9—and of one sensory memory he's never shaken.

"The one thing that really stands out is the smell of the ponderosa pine," Nelson said. "It's like a drug. You'd smell that ponderosa pine and rear up on your hind legs, you felt so good."

———————

In early July the first wave of approximately two hundred athletes began arriving for what Harry Edwards called the "boys' camp." Charlie Mays, an Olympic contender in the long jump, was one of a small group that visited the site prior to the Los Angeles trials. "Charlie called and told me about this place that was like paradise," Ralph Boston said. "In fact, they actually lived at a place called the Paradise Inn."

When he did finally arrive, Boston felt as if he'd left the police protection in Los Angeles and the post-King turmoil in Nashville far behind. "Once you walked through that gate at Echo Summit, all that other stuff was someplace else," he said. "It was the most beautiful setting imaginable."

The California Department of Transportation's maintenance yard on the west side of Highway 50 became a mini–Olympic Village. Prefabricated trailers covered with taut, gleaming fabric housed some of the athletes; others would stay in nearby cabins or down at the lake in hotels and rented homes. (A handful slept the occasional night on Walt Little's floor.) Larger trailers were attached to create a dining hall and a weight room. An existing two-story building was used as a medical facility and a place for the athletes to hang out.

A marked crossing was set up across Highway 50 so the athletes could walk back and forth between the trailers and the track. The utilitarian living and eating accommodations were functional, but the track was ethereal. The 400-meter oval was laid out near the base of a granite-studded

Athletes were housed and fed at the Caltrans maintenance yard across Highway 50 from the Echo Summit track. *Courtesy of the Walt Little family*

slope, and the track's pinkish-red surface contrasted spectacularly with the greenery of the trees and the blue of the alpine sky. Only the shot put would be contested outside the circumference of the track. Funnels of lodgepole pine and red fir enveloped the discus and hammer rings and the javelin runways. Several granite boulders were left undisturbed, the most prominent situated next to the high jump pit. Flocks of trees provided natural shade on the backstretch of the track.

"The first thing I wanted to see was the track," said decathlete Rick Sloan. "I crossed the road, went through the trees, and popped right up at the starting line of the 200 meters. I ran one lap and was already out of breath."

There might not have been as much air as the athletes would have liked, but the little they had to breathe was sublime. James, the rising 400-meter star, had gone home to New Jersey after finishing a tired fourth in Los Angeles. It had been a long season for the Villanova sophomore, and he welcomed the chance to take a breather before reporting to Tahoe. Judging from his sensational form in September and October, James found his second wind on the mountaintop.

"I didn't know places like that existed in the United States," James said years later. "I can still taste the air. In the morning it was like a fresh glass of spring water. So crisp. It was delicious."

The training camp officially opened on July 15. Some of the invitees reported earlier; many came later. A handful of stars—Smith, Carlos, Evans, pole vaulter Bob Seagren, and sprinter Ronnie Ray Smith—squeezed in some European meets between the Los Angeles and Echo Summit trials. European promoters were known for providing generous under-the-table payments to lure big-name athletes to their meets. The $2.50 per diem at Echo Summit paled in comparison. Plus, sprinters and pole vaulters figured they needed less time to acclimate to the altitude than their distance counterparts. That wasn't necessarily the case, as Ed Caruthers, the defending trials champion in the high jump, discovered immediately.

"I couldn't jog a mile the first time I practiced there," Caruthers said. "I had to get medical attention."

Russ Rogers, a world-ranked intermediate hurdler with a luminous smile and cocksure attitude, arrived at the summit loaded for bear. Rather than take it easy and get acclimated to the altitude, Rogers put in a full-blown training session on his first day. He told whoever was listening that the altitude didn't feel so bad. Then he fainted, resulting in a split lip and several cracked teeth. A scarier incident occurred when Jim Kemp collapsed and was hospitalized after running the 400 meters in a pretrials meet. Blood samples showed that Kemp had sickle cell anemia, a disorder exacerbated by high altitude. "Jim Kemp was laying on the infield, a black guy, ashen white," Toomey said. "We thought he was near death."

Rogers and Kemp got back on their feet soon enough and were able to compete in the trials. The distance runners had a clearer idea of what they were up against. George Young, a fifth-place finisher in the 3,000-meter steeplechase at the Tokyo Olympics, was having his best season ever in 1968. But he understood from the start that his quest for Olympic gold against the Africans in Mexico City would be an uphill battle.

"There was nothing mysterious about it," Young said. "I knew it was going to have an adverse effect. I just tried to shut it out and work as hard as I could at altitude."

In researching and writing his master's thesis on altitude training, Young determined that the 7,300-foot elevation of Mexico City would have its greatest impact on competitors in the distances from 1,500 to 5,000 meters. The thin air would have less of an effect on the 10,000 meters because the pace was slower. The 3,000-meter steeplechase fell smack in the middle of Young's danger zone, and leaping over four three-foot hurdles and one water jump on each of the race's seven and a half laps would only add to the oxygen debt.

Jack Daniels (center) testing the oxygen intake of Dave Wilborn at Echo Summit. Tom Von Ruden is checking his watch on the left side of the hood.
Courtesy of Jack Daniels

Barometric pressure and the oxygen content of the air decreases incrementally the higher the elevation. The amount of blood pumped by the heart—most of which goes to the muscles during exercise—decreases accordingly. The effects of altitude on the distance events don't really kick in until about 3,000 feet, and the difference between running at 5,000 and 7,000 feet is about the same as going from sea level to 5,000 feet.

Another race in the "danger zone"—the 1,500 meters—happened to be the province of America's most celebrated track and field athlete. Since qualifying for the Olympic team in 1964 as a seventeen-year-old out of Wichita, Kansas, Jim Ryun had set world records at 880 yards, 1,500 meters, and 1 mile. In 1966, he was the youngest person to be named Sportsman of the Year by *Sports Illustrated*. Ryun was even better in 1967, lowering his world mile record to 3:51.1 at the AAU meet.

Two weeks later, in a dual meet between the United States and the British Commonwealth countries in the heat and smog of the Los Angeles Coliseum, Ryun ran his greatest race. He took two and a half seconds off Herb Elliott's venerable record in the 1,500 meters by clocking 3:33.1, the equivalent of a 3:50.1 mile. His Kenyan rival, Kipchoge Keino, finished four seconds back. An Olympic gold medal was all that stood between Ryun and universal acclaim as the greatest middle-distance runner in history.

But the 1968 Olympics weren't being held in Bakersfield or Los Angeles. At the 1967 NCAA indoor meet, Conrad Nightingale of Kansas State introduced Ryun to Jack Daniels, an Olympic medalist in the modern pentathlon who was working on his doctorate in exercise physiology at the University of Wisconsin. Daniels cut to the chase, asking Ryun if he'd given much thought to how much trouble Mexico City's altitude would present to sea-level runners. Not really, Ryun replied. He assured Daniels that he'd put in the necessary work and arrive at the Olympics in great shape.

"Being in shape won't matter," Daniels said. "You have to acclimate yourself to the effects of altitude. Actually, that's a misnomer. You can't acclimatize yourself. All you can do is reduce the impact of the problem."

Daniels convinced Ryun to join him that spring for a test run in Alamosa, Colorado, one of four sites then under consideration to host the 1968 US Olympic training camp. After clocking a 3:53.2 mile at the Compton Invitational in early June, Ryun stopped in Alamosa on his way home to Kansas. In a one-mile time trial at 7,400 feet, Ryun clocked a humbling 4:20. Daniels had made his point, and Ryun rearranged his schedule so he could spend a couple more weeks training at elevations ranging from 7,000 to 11,000 feet.

When Ryun followed up his high-altitude sojourn with world records in the mile and 1,500 meters, many credited his fitness to the time he spent with Daniels in Colorado. But Ryun believed Daniels when he said two weeks or two months or even two years of altitude training couldn't overcome the hereditary advantages of Africans who'd breathed thin air for generations.

Looking ahead to the Olympic year and the prospect of facing Keino on his home turf, so to speak, Ryun went overboard. "I began pushing even harder in training because I knew what altitude could do," Ryun said. "Unfortunately, it broke me down. I'd run a 3:57 on the boards at Madison Square Garden, and outdoors I won the mile and the half-mile at the Big Eight meet, but I felt awful. I went in for some blood tests and found out I had mono. I went six weeks without being able to train. All I could do was take iron, sleep, and pray."

While Jim Ryun convalesced, Jack Daniels treated Echo Summit as a training lab. Daniels had been brought in by the USOC as a consultant to oversee medical testing of the distance runners. He was a curious sight, circling the track in his white Volvo or sitting spread-eagled on the hood as he measured the oxygen intake of runners striding alongside, plastic gas masks covering their mouths and noses.

His six years of studying the effects of altitude on endurance athletes led Daniels to make a recommendation that the USOC implemented at Echo Summit.

"The IOC wouldn't allow any sea-level country to have a country-supported altitude camp that lasted more than six weeks leading up to the Mexico City Olympics," Daniels said. "The idea was that richer countries could have a preparation advantage over not-so-wealthy countries. As a consultant to the US track and field association, I talked them into a trip or two to sea level for a week or so, which spread the total time together longer than six weeks."

Accordingly, prospective US Olympians broke up their time at Echo Summit with brief trips to sea-level meets in Houston; Toronto; Eugene, Oregon; and Walnut, California.

Thinking even further outside the box, the USOC enlisted the services of Carl Stough, or "Dr. Breath," as the athletes called him. While studying choral conducting at Westminster Choir College in New Jersey in the 1940s, Stough became fixated on the breathing techniques needed to strike the right notes. His first job out of college was choir conductor of the First Presbyterian Church in Rocky Mountain, North Carolina. He later worked with the Metropolitan Opera before branching out to assist emphysema patients. He opened the Carl Stough Institute of Breathing Coordination in New York and accepted the USOC's offer to work with the healthiest patients he'd ever encountered.

In a trailer across the highway from the Echo Summit track, Stough put the Olympic hopefuls through a series of breathing exercises that, in his words, "established voluntary control of involuntary muscles affecting the lungs through breathing coordination." Stough worked with dozens of athletes at Echo Summit, including Lee Evans, the 400-meter favorite.

"Dr. Breath taught us how to postpone fatigue by the way we were breathing," Evans said. "When you finish a 400-meter race, your body is screaming for air. If you don't exhale properly, you're putting bad air on top of bad air."

Lou Scott, a distance runner from Detroit, was another Dr. Breath disciple. Nearly fifty years later, Scott could still recite the mantra: Breathe in through your nose, fill up your stomach first, then the lungs. When you exhale, let all of it out until you almost pass out. "Dr. Breath really helped me," Scott said. "I think everyone he saw made the team."

Not all were convinced of Stough's magic. "I thought it was a load of crap," said Jack Bacheler, a dark-horse entrant in the 5,000 meters.

Runners splash through the steeplechase pit in a tune-up meet at Echo Summit prior to the final trials. *Courtesy of the Walt Little family*

For longer runs, the distance men gravitated to Echo Lake, located about two miles northwest of the summit. Echo Lake is actually two lakes: a narrow channel connects the upper and lower portions. The glacial lakes provided a stunning tableau—shimmering blue water ringed by forest and granite mountainside.

"A beautiful place for distance runners to train," steeplechaser George Young said. Another Olympic contender, Van Nelson, remembers taking a four-hour run beyond Echo Lake into the adjoining Desolation Wilderness, one of the most popular backpacking regions in the western United States.

Altitude training was the new frontier in 1968. Two of the top US distance men, Tracy Smith and Tom Laris, followed their own maps. Smith arrived at Tahoe in terrific condition, having won the 10,000 meters in Sacramento and the 5,000 in Los Angeles. When Daniels tested the maximal oxygen consumption, or VO2 max, as it was known in track circles, Smith had one of the highest results of the Olympic contenders, just a notch below the freakish Jim Ryun. Smith did most of his training "down below" in the Tahoe basin, with its 6,200-foot elevation, but he returned to the summit each night to sleep in a trailer. "Live high, train low," he said.

Tracy Smith wasn't as concerned about his ability to acclimate as some of the others. His family owned a fishing lodge outside Bishop on the eastern slope of the Sierra, where he became used to the 8,300-foot elevation. "I think I had an edge on everyone, or the Americans at least, because of that," Smith said.

Laris, a twenty-eight-year-old Dartmouth graduate, steered clear of Echo Summit until the last possible moment. After placing third in the 10,000 at the Los Angeles trials, Laris accepted a transfer from his employer, GE, to work in Mexico City. He didn't do much work for GE while he was there, but he did join a Mexican training group led by Joe Villareal, a standout miler at Texas in the 1950s.

"I didn't have confidence in the US coaches," Laris said. "They didn't know much about altitude. Before leaving Mexico City, I ran a 10,000-meter time trial with Juan Martinez." Martinez, a Mexican runner, was fourth in the 5,000 and 10,000 at the 1968 Olympics, the top non-African finisher in both races.

"Joe told me, 'Stay with Juan all the way. It's going to hurt, but you can do it.' I ran 30:04, and I knew that would be good enough to make the team," Laris said. "None of the other US guys had raced a 10,000 at altitude. I was the only one who knew what it was like."

11

MELTING POT

WHILE HE HAD no high-altitude credentials when he arrived at Echo Summit, distance runner Jack Bacheler acclimated easily to the thin air. Perhaps he was too busy keeping his eyes glued to the ground, tree trunks, and rocks to notice that his lungs needed more oxygen. The 6-foot-6½ Bacheler was a graduate student in entomology at the University of Florida. "If you've been collecting insects since you were five years old, it was nirvana," he said. "I did a lot of high-altitude insect collecting at Echo Summit."

From the bug-collecting distance runner to the madcap army doctor, the group fighting for places on the US Olympic track team included characters of all stripes. The melting pot on the mountain had an abundance of spice.

Growing up—and up—in Birmingham, Michigan, Bacheler was all but forced onto the basketball court. That's what happens when you stand 6-5 in the eighth grade. But when he joined the cross-country team on a lark, Bacheler discovered that he enjoyed running more than rebounding, and he received a partial scholarship to Miami of Ohio.

The world's tallest distance runner (and possibly the tallest entomologist, though records are inconclusive) qualified for the Echo Summit trials by finishing fourth in the 5,000 meters in Los Angeles. Rather than stay in one of the trailers, Bacheler and his wife rented a nearby cabin. "The cabin was about 300 feet higher than the trailers," he said. "We thought that would give us edge."

Considering himself a long shot with nothing to lose, Bacheler trained exceptionally hard at Echo Summit. He got a kick out of running the mountain trails with Gerry Lindgren, "an odd, fun-loving guy," in Bacheler's words. "Lindgren was experimenting with this technique of holding his arms out wide and behind him while he ran. His idea was that he'd bring it out at the trials and surprise everyone."

For Bacheler, whose master's thesis was titled "The Biography of a Flower Bug," Echo Summit offered unexplored territory for the collection of butterflies, moths, grasshoppers, beetles, and dragonflies. "The Echo Summit area was interesting to me in that most of the insects I collected and mounted were ones that don't appear in the Midwest and eastern regions I was familiar with," Bacheler said. "It was a pleasant diversion from the stress of the trials."

Ralph Boston and John Carlos ran sprints up the rocky ski slope next to the track at six in the morning. Some of the athletes worked out furtively, not wanting to show their cards early. Some liked to work out alone; others chose a training partner and stuck together. In the hypercompetitive 400-meter group, Lee Evans trained with Ron Freeman. Larry James did his workouts with fellow East Coaster Vince Matthews. "Lee and I trained together once and he refused to do it again," James said. "He said I made it look too easy." With his high knee lift, Tommie Smith needed time to adjust to the Tartan track. "I spent a lot of time in the air because of the resiliency of the surface," Smith said. "We ran on clay at San Jose State, and the Tartan took some getting used to."

The sound of throwers grunting could be heard on both sides of the highway, from the trees inside the track and the weight room in the maintenance yard. "You had to take more time between sets because of the altitude," said Jim Pryde, a junior-college instructor from Sacramento who was trying to make the US team in the hammer throw.

Randy Matson, the world-record holder in the shot put, lodged in the same South Shore hotel as one of his main rivals, Dave Maggard. Each morning, Maggard sent his two young sons upstairs to wake Matson up. "I loved those little guys," said Matson, whose wife was pregnant with their first child at the time.

Once, while driving back to their hotel following a workout on Echo Summit, Maggard and Matson stopped at one of the roadside vista points on Highway 50 to take in the spectacular view of Lake Tahoe.

"You'd push me off this mountain just so you could win the Olympics, wouldn't you?" Matson said to Maggard.

Randy Matson won three NCAA outdoor titles and set two world records in the shot put while competing for Texas A&M from 1965 to 1967. *Texas A&M athletics*

Matson, a 6-foot-7, 270-pound colossus from the town of Pampa in the Texas Panhandle, was the surest US gold-medal hope in 1968. Four years earlier, as a nineteen-year-old freshman at Texas A&M, Matson won a silver medal at the Tokyo Olympics, nearly beating the world-record holder, Dallas Long. The following year, Matson added nearly three feet to Long's record with a throw of 70 feet, 7¼ inches. He improved to 71-5½ in 1967 and came within 2 inches of breaking the world discus record. Matson led the Southwest Conference in rebounding in his one season on Texas A&M's basketball team and was drafted by both the Seattle SuperSonics of the National Basketball Association and the Atlanta Falcons of the National Football League.

While he didn't engage in the mind games employed by Olympic shot champions Parry O'Brien and Bill Nieder in the late 1950s and early 1960s, Matson didn't fraternize with the opposition, either. He lorded over the ring like a Texas lawman. "I didn't want to be unfriendly, but I came up with Nieder, Long, and O'Brien," Matson said. "They weren't buddy-buddy. I thought they were serious. But I let my guard down with Maggard. We hit it off from the beginning."

The trajectory of Maggard's career was the opposite of Matson's. He grew up in California's Central Valley, the same region that produced Rafer Johnson, Bob Mathias, Tommie Smith, and Lee Evans. Maggard went to UC Berkeley expecting to play linebacker for the Golden Bears, but his football career was cut short by a knee injury. He became a good college shot-putter, finishing fourth at the 1962 NCAA meet. But Maggard never reached 60 feet in his college career—a distance Matson exceeded as a high school senior.

Maggard was a favorite of Cal coach Brutus Hamilton, a beloved figure in the sport who had served as head coach of the 1952 US Olympic team. As much as Hamilton loved the sport—he'd won an Olympic silver medal in the decathlon at the 1920 Olympics—he discouraged Maggard's Olympic dreams. "Dave, it's time for you to get your career going," Hamilton said. "San Francisco State wants you to be their track coach. You've got a family you need to support."

"It might have been the only time I said no to Brutus," Maggard said. "I figured I could do both."

Maggard earned his first world ranking in 1965, when his longest mark was more than 8 feet short of Matson's best. He roomed with Matson on a European tour that summer, the beginning of a lifelong friendship.

In the spring of 1968, Maggard was teaching, coaching, and serving as director of student activities at Los Altos High School on the San Francisco peninsula.

"After the track team was done working out, I'd go home, sleep for 30 minutes, then go back and work out," Maggard said. "I also taught a driver's education class for adults that didn't end until ten at night, and I'd lift for two hours after that. When you work out by yourself, you're always wondering how hard the other guys are working. That drove me to do more."

He asked for two concessions from the Los Altos principal. "I told him I'd coach and teach and make the Olympic team," Maggard said. "But I can't be in the parking lot at seven in the morning, and I can't go to school dances."

Word of his multifaceted work at Los Altos High School had traveled across the Iron Curtain to East Germany. At Echo Summit, Hilmer Lodge of the USOC showed Maggard a telegram he'd received from East German officials. "They're questioning your eligibility," Lodge said. "They saw an article in *Track & Field News* about how you're coaching. They say that's against the Olympic rules." An irritated Maggard informed Lodge that he didn't receive a dime for his coaching duties.

Matson marveled at Maggard's ability to juggle so many obligations.

"Dave had a full-time job and two small kids," Matson said. "I found out in 1969 how hard that is. My throwing never got up to near the level it was before."

Maggard wasn't alone in needing to support his Olympic habit with a paying job. Jay Silvester, the discus record holder, sold insurance to support his family. Silvester's rival, Al Oerter, was a computer programmer on Long Island. Russ Rogers and Norm Tate worked for the Job Corps in New Jersey. About two dozen of the athletes at Echo

Summit were serving in the armed forces. A number of others were teachers, including Ed Burke, the US record holder in the hammer throw. Burke taught political science at Orange Coast College in Costa Mesa, California.

"That was the first and only time in my life when I didn't have to work or go to school," Burke said. "The crisp air, the warm sun . . . you'd walk over to the pole vault pit and take a nap, or go to the dining facility and eat until you couldn't eat anymore. That's what it must have been like to be one of the Eastern European teams, where the athletes were subsidized by the state. All I did was eat, lift, throw, and run. I got in terrific shape."

South Lake Tahoe organizers provided athletes with part-time jobs if they wanted them. Norm Tate drove blood samples from Echo Summit to a testing lab in Sacramento. Lindgren drove high rollers from their hotels to the casinos. Silvester and half-miler Wade Bell were security guards at the track. "Jay and I made sure no one stole a pit," Bell said. "We basically just sat there. It wasn't hard work."

Evans worked as a mechanic in an auto shop. "I'd always been the non-mechanical guy in the family," Evans said. "The guy running the shop had me taking cars apart. The problem was, I didn't know how to put them back together."

It wasn't all work (and work out) and no play, by any means. Local businessmen organized a steamboat cruise on the lake. The casinos were generous with complimentary tickets to the shows. Comedian Bill Cosby, a onetime high jumper at Temple University, showed up at the track. Visits from Cosby and Danny Kaye made the athletes feel like celebrities in their own right.

"Walt Little made life pretty good for us," Rick Sloan said. "We got these cards that let us play any of the golf courses for free. The Olympic staff would say at one of the meetings that they had four tickets to see Bobbie Gentry, who wants to go? We'd raise our hands. We went to the beach and water-skied. It was a fun time."

For some, Echo Summit felt like an all-expenses-paid vacation. For others, it felt like a 1968 version of *Survivor*, sans the production crews and cameras.

"In the midst of this tranquility was psychological warfare," Bill Toomey said. "In most trials, you never see the guys, but at Echo Summit, you had the highly unusual circumstance of putting all these highly motivated guys in trailers on a mountainside . . . eight to ten guys vying for three spots in each event. There were a lot of mind games going on."

"It got tense at times," Dave Maggard said. "At the same time, there was some bonding that took place. People got to know one another, whether they wanted to or not."

"Echo Summit fostered a team spirit in that you became close to a lot of people because you were around them every day," Rick Sloan said. "You got to know people. You wanted them to do well. The setting was a huge part of it—the casinos, the lake, the golf. But the track was the biggest thing. Being around all those guys was almost like being on vacation, though the closer to the trials you got, the more serious everyone got."

Sloan competed in and officiated Frisbee competitions from the discus circle, where arguments broke out over what constituted a foul. Evans remembers the mountain streams. "I wasn't used to fishing for trout," he said. "I grew up fishing for bass and perch." Tate remembers drinking champagne backstage after one of Earl Grant's Stateline shows. "We were treated like celebrities for eight weeks, and we played it to the hilt," Tate said. "We lived like millionaires, even though we didn't have a dime when we got there."

Boston remembers being amazed at how far he could drive a golf ball in the thin mountain air. "I thought I could be a professional golfer, I was hitting it so far," Boston said. "I found out differently when I went back to sea level."

As they did for the tourists whizzing past on Highway 50, the casinos exerted a magnetic pull on the prospective Olympians. Carlos developed a scheme to beat the house in blackjack, convincing Mays, Tate, and Pender to pony up almost $2,000. "We ended up broke and had to hitchhike up the hill that night," Tate said. Rogers scoffed at anyone's willingness to follow the Harlem huckster's lead. "I must have won four or five grand playing blackjack," Rogers said. "I knew what I was doing. Carlos, he was a born loser. He'd grab my chips and leave."

George Frenn, a rambunctious hammer thrower with a penchant for stirring the pot, formed a "syndicate" that he guaranteed would produce big payoffs at the craps table. If you win, you just put down one chip, Frenn explained to his partners on the summit. If you make your point or the pass line wins, you pick up the dollar chip and leave another one down. If you lose, you double your bet and add a dollar. You continue to "double and add one" until you either make a killing or run out of money.

One evening, Frenn was more than $1,000 in the black. He brashly started throwing down hundred-dollar chips. When the dice roll came up fourteen straight "don't passes" in a row, a furious Frenn reached for the dice to see if they were loaded. Several security guards were needed to escort the dead-broke hammer thrower from the casino.

"A couple of people thought they knew what they were doing at the casinos," high hurdler Erv Hall said. "Fortunately for me, there were dime and quarter slots."

Dispensable income was more plentiful than usual among the amateur athletes thanks to the illicit shoe payments made by Adidas and Puma. The real wheeling and dealing would take place at the Olympics, but the rival shoe companies offered payments at Echo Summit to those they thought would be on the medal stand in Mexico City. Dick Bank was the Adidas representative, and he found the practice of clandestine payoffs distasteful. Art Simburg, the San Jose State classmate of Smith, Evans, and Carlos, had no such reservations. As journalist Barbara Smit wrote, "The true losers at Lake Tahoe weren't the athletes who failed to qualify for the Olympic team, but those who walked away with empty wallets."

At one point, the US coaching staff called a meeting to excoriate the athletes for accepting free shoes and possibly more. Sam Bell, the head track coach at California who assisted at the high-altitude camp, was particularly incensed, Silvester remembered.

"I suggested at the meeting that the shoe reps were being very good to the athletes," Silvester said. "Sam Bell became almost apoplectic. He loudly suggested that I leave the camp, set myself up as a professional and get all the free stuff I could. Not much changed after the meeting. The shoe reps simply became more discreet in distributing their wares."

For pole vaulter Casey Carrigan, the youngest camper at seventeen, the shoe shenanigans offered an eye-opening education. "It was real cloak-and-dagger stuff with Adidas and Puma," Carrigan said. "There was definitely money being passed around, but I was too afraid to take any of it. I was afraid I'd lose my amateur status."

———————

Marty Liquori also grew up quickly that summer. A New Jersey native with movie-star looks, Liquori had entered Villanova the previous fall with considerable fanfare. At the 1967 AAU championship meet in Bakersfield—the same race in which Ryun set a world record—Liquori became the third high school runner to break four minutes in the mile. But college freshmen were ineligible for varsity competition, so Liquori came west to Tahoe with no undue expectations. He didn't turn nineteen until September 11. He was a babe in the woods.

"I didn't even watch the Tokyo Olympics on TV," Liquori said. "I had no idea what I was getting into. I was the young guy at Tahoe. Carlos, Pender, and Greene took me under their wing, played cards with me. It was a pretty interesting time. There were so many undercurrents."

The bicoastal rivalry between Oregon and Villanova for middle-distance supremacy was one of those undercurrents. The coaches of the two premier programs, Bill Bowerman and Jumbo Elliott, weren't friendly, and the animosity trickled down. One night on the mountain, Dave Patrick enlisted Liquori's assistance in stealing a large Oregon banner that adorned the enemy's living quarters. An incensed Bowerman threatened to kick the perpetrators off the Olympic team.

Years later, when Oregon runners threw a retirement party for Bowerman, word was relayed to the crusty coach that Liquori would be happy to return the stolen flag. "I don't want Liquori at my dinner," Bowerman growled.

The trailer village was the scene of other boyish mischief. The sprinters passed the time by playing "Dirty Hearts," a card game where the loser of each round has to drink a large glass of water. That meant middle-of-the-night trips to the bathrooms located outside the trailers. "There were steps in front of each of the trailers, and guys would turn them around as a prank," James said. "You'd heard a loud boom in the middle of night and then hear laughter from the other trailers."

———————

The atmosphere would have been different had the Echo Summit trials included women. But the USOC was a conservative organization run by men, much to the consternation of the strong-minded women trying out for 1968 Olympic team. Their team was selected August 24–25 in Walnut. The qualifiers were then granted two weeks of altitude training in Los Alamos, New Mexico, where they were housed at a military installation.

"We were very, very disenchanted," said long jumper Willye White, who qualified for the fourth of her five Olympic teams in 1968. "We were so isolated in Los Alamos. All we could do was go to practice. The guys got to go to Tahoe and had the luxury of high-altitude training as long as they wanted it. They got all the research. We got nothing. But we were used to that kind of treatment. In 1964, [US Olympic men's coach] Bob Giegengack didn't want the girls flying on the same airplane with the boys."

Most of the men didn't give it a thought at the time. That's the way things were done. But Harold Connolly gave it considerable thought, and when it came to speaking out—whether against sexism, racism, or jingoism—the grand old man of the hammer throw threw his 250 pounds around with impunity.

At thirty-seven, Connolly was nearing the tail end of a storied career. A difficult birth and a series of childhood accidents had left his left arm four and a half inches shorter than his right, and his left hand two-thirds the size of his right. Despite the physical handicap, Connolly broke the world hammer record six times between 1956 and 1965. At the 1956 Olympics in Melbourne, Australia, Connolly, the gold medalist in the men's hammer, fell in love with Olga Fikotová, the women's discus champion from Czechoslovakia.

The Cold War romance received international coverage, and their wedding the following year in Prague attracted thirty thousand supporters. On returning to the United States, the couple appeared on *The Ed Sullivan Show* and *To Tell the Truth*. (Amateur rules meant they had to return their $1,000 winnings from *To Tell the Truth*.)

After Czech authorities informed her that she was no longer welcome to compete for her native country, Olga became a US citizen in time to join her husband on the 1960 US Olympic team. They were Olympic teammates again in 1964 and were trying to do it a third time in 1968.

"We had four children and were both working," Hal Connolly said. "We wished we could have gone up to that training camp together, but neither of us could afford to take the time to join the team and take

The 1957 marriage of Olympic gold medalists Harold Connolly (United States) and Olga Fikotová (Czechoslovakia) warmed Cold War hearts. *AP Images*

advantage of the special training. I learned that they were feeding and housing the athletes at a cost of about $8.50 a day. I asked whether they could compensate us since we weren't there, and we got no help whatsoever."

Connolly had lobbied the USOC and US track officials to combine their championship meets. "It wasn't a hot issue to them," he said. "All the advanced teams in Eastern Europe were combined at the time. In meetings they referred to us as boys and girls. That's how they thought about us. It was just ridiculous."

While the US Education Amendments of 1972—known to history as Title IX—made no specific mention of sports, the federal legislation had a tectonic impact on women's athletics, particularly at the high school and college levels. But it came too late to allow Hal and Olga Connolly to compete for Olympic berths on the same playing field.

"That the Olympic Trials and pregame training was separate, and the training comforts unequal for men and women, simply illustrates the era before the wisdom of Title IX," Olga Connolly said nearly fifty years later. "For me, the training situation in 1968 was saved by my parents' immigration to the United States. In that era of amateurism, only their selfless care for our kids and our own personal well-being enabled Harold and me to manage the time and expenditures needed to train for the Olympics."

Olga's husband was equally opinionated on racial matters. Hal Connolly supported the goals of the Olympic Project for Human Rights and would be the most vocal white defender of Tommie Smith and John Carlos when they were expelled from the Olympic Village in Mexico City.

"There were quite a few white athletes who wanted nothing to do with it," Connolly said. "Some had religious objections or philosophical objections. Some of the black athletes in the military were afraid of their positions if they showed support for Carlos, Smith, and Evans. The management of the team began to get apprehensive, very uptight. They didn't quite know how to cope with it. They certainly didn't want to talk about it. They wanted it to just go away."

In late July, while attending a track clinic in Spokane, Washington, Evans told the Associated Press that there would be no black boycott of the Mexico City Games. Evans said he thought Harry Edwards was going to announce the results of the Los Angeles vote earlier but that he apparently preferred to keep people guessing.

"We voted on the boycott at the Olympic Trials in Los Angeles and it was almost unanimous that we go," Evans said. "But it was also 100 percent that we make some kind of protest at the games. What that will be, I don't know."

Harry Edwards was conspicuous in his absence at Echo Summit, both during the training camp and the final trials. US Olympic coach Payton Jordan thought he remembered seeing Edwards once at Echo Summit, but Edwards denied it, despite the camp's proximity to San Jose.

"No, I was never there," Edwards said. "The reason was, word was out that if I went up there, I'd be arrested for trespassing. We didn't want it to become a law-enforcement issue."

But too much ink and videotape had been expended to let the issue die a natural death.

"The newspaper people really enjoyed the controversy," Young said. "They'd ask, 'What do you think of this decision, that decision? Where do you stand on this or that?' It wasn't something I cared to get involved with. I had to get out of there."

Tension arose between Silvester, the white discus thrower from Utah, and some of the black athletes. In fact, his name is the first to come up when black athletes are asked which of the white athletes were most antagonistic in 1968. Decades later, a mellower Silvester tried to explain his stubborn resistance to the racial and political winds buffeting 1968.

"I now understand a bit more about using a venue to espouse your cause to the fullest, but I didn't feel that way then," he said. "I was incensed by it. I worshipped competition. I thought it was a glorious, marvelous experience, and I didn't want anyone interfering with it. To have these people espousing their grievances, I didn't want to hear it."

Burke, Connolly's fiercest rival in the hammer throw, remembers hearing rumors about Black Panthers showing up at Echo Summit, brandishing guns, threatening the athletes. Whether true or not, the existence of such rumors underscores the underlying tensions.

"Those were troubling times," Burke said. "I taught black studies at a school that didn't have any blacks within one hundred miles, so I had an awareness. At the same time, I don't think the white athletes knew the kind of pressure the black athletes were feeling."

———————

Though he steered clear of Echo Summit, Harry Edwards did show up in late July at an unlikely place—the Newell Boathouse on the Charles River, surrounded by members of the all-white Harvard eight-man crew. The Harvard rowers had followed the Olympic Project for Human Rights from afar, and after they won the Olympic trials regatta in Long Beach by a whisker over the University of Pennsylvania, oarsman Cleve Livingston and coxswain Paul Hoffman drove up to San Jose to meet with the California radical. Livingston and Hoffman wore coats and ties; Edwards greeted them in his standard dashiki, beads, and black beret.

"We wanted to find out what it was all about," Hoffman said. "There was no way we'd be boycotting, but we said we'd make a statement on behalf of the Olympic Project for Human Rights and encourage everyone on the Olympic team to have a dialogue with the black athletes. He immediately saw that having the Harvard crew support his cause would make headlines."

At the press conference the following week in Cambridge, six members of the Harvard crew, including Livingston and Hoffman, released a statement that read, in part, "We—as individuals—have been concerned with the place of the black man in American society and his struggle for human rights. As members of the United States Olympic team, each of us has come to feel a moral commitment to support our black teammates in their efforts to dramatize the injustices and inequities which permeate our society."

Edwards accepted their support, telling the assembled media, "It's beautiful to see some white cats willing to admit they've got a problem and looking to take some action to educate their own."

———————

Back on the mountaintop, the most heavily scrutinized black athlete felt obligated to do some educating of his own. Tommie Smith felt it was important to show he wasn't a reverse racist, simply a young man with deeply held convictions.

"I played dominos and cards with the guys, even though I didn't know how to play," Smith said. "I'm not a hater. You can't be a hater and a Christian. The Olympic Project for Human Rights wasn't against whites. It was for freedom and human rights. I respected everyone's opinion. If they listened to what I had to say, I guess it's because I didn't talk much, so when I did, they paid attention."

The card games, Frisbee competitions, casino-busting ventures, and heart-to-heart conversations created a bond among a disparate group of individuals. Track and field is essentially an individual sport, and the ruthless finality of the US trials—top three make the team, everyone else goes home—would normally foster an "every man for himself" attitude. But the celestial setting and time spent together created something different. Rather than weaken the bond, the off-track tensions seemed to strengthen it. John Carlos is a funny guy, the white athletes said. Ed Burke is a righteous dude, the black athletes said. A team was coming together.

———————

Many of them also took steroids together, according to Tom Waddell, an army doctor, conscientious objector, and then-closeted homosexual competing for an Olympic berth in the decathlon. Waddell said he administered steroids to one-third of the members of the 1968 US Olympic men's track and field team. "They came to me with their needles," he said years later.

At Echo Summit, "Tom gave out steroids every day at three o'clock," according to one of his best friends, long jumper Phil Shinnick. "The leadership in US track had no idea this was happening."

Waddell never cared much about what leadership thought. He supported Connolly's efforts to form an athletes' union and angered the army brass by writing speeches for Smith and Carlos in Mexico City. While others resented the intrusion of politics into sport in 1968, Waddell reveled in the discord. "It was a state of ecstasy for me," Waddell said shortly before he succumbed to AIDS in 1987. "I was in heaven."

A New Jersey native, Waddell attended Springfield College in Massachusetts on a gymnastics scholarship. When he was twenty, working as a camp counselor, he met a group of Jewish socialists from New York City. "I fell in love with that group," he said. "They really became my family. I became an extreme activist, particularly in civil rights."

While attending medical school, Waddell worked for a group called the Central Committee for Conscientious Objectors. He ran a medical clinic for the Black Panthers. His classmates referred to him as "Tommie the Commie." In the fall of 1965, spurred by the murder of civil rights volunteers in Mississippi, Waddell took a break from his internship to provide medical care in Selma, Alabama. He spent a night in jail on a false charge of driving recklessly.

A year later, the antiwar doctor was drafted. After breezing through basic training, he was assigned to the Eighty-Second Airborne Division at Fort Benning, Georgia, as a preventative medicine officer. He volunteered for extra training as a paratrooper. But when he was informed in 1967 that he'd be shipped to Vietnam, Waddell filed for conscientious objector status.

"I was always in trouble in the army," Waddell said. "When I refused to go to Vietnam and applied to join the army track team, they said, 'Hurry up, go.'"

Assigned to Fort MacArthur, where fellow soldiers Tracy Smith and Mel Pender trained, Waddell embarked on a crash course in decathlon training. At the 1968 AAU decathlon championships in Santa Barbara, where he no-heighted in the pole vault, Waddell asked Dick Bank, the Adidas rep, for a free pair of shoes. Bank blew him off.

A couple of weeks later, when Waddell scored a 7587 in a pretrials decathlon in Walnut, Bank did an about-face.

"Dick came running up to me after the meet, saying, 'Tom, you want some shoes?'" Waddell recalled. "I said, 'Yes, Dick, I want sixty pair, and I want you to put them all in boxes, and stick them up your ass.' I switched to Puma."

The IOC tried for years to turn a blind eye to the use of performance-enhancing drugs such as anabolic steroids. Avery Brundage turned purple at the thought of his Olympics being tainted by politics or commercial interests, but he expressed little interest in regulating the drug use.

Waddell wrote in his autobiography that he recognized the potential hazards of long-term steroid use and personally took just five milligrams of an oral steroid, compared to the twenty-five milligrams some athletes were injecting. Waddell and Connolly were up-front about their steroid use, but others, including Randy Matson and Al Oerter, were less eager to say whether they did or didn't take steroids. In today's climate, when rampant drug use has torn track and field and other Olympic sports asunder, it's worth remembering that there were no rules against steroids in 1968. In fact, one of the physicians assigned to Echo Summit more or less endorsed their use.

"I don't think it is possible for a weight man to compete internationally without using anabolic steroids," said Dr. H. Kay Dooley. "I did not inquire what the boys were doing on their own. I did not want to be forced into a position of having to report them for use of a banned drug. I can't see any ethical difference between giving a drug to improve performance and wrapping an ankle or handing out a salt pill for the same purpose."

Shinnick, an air force captain whose political views brought him problems similar to those of Waddell's, broke ranks with his friend on the use of performance-enhancing drugs.

"At the time, most of the world-class athletes from other countries were taking steroids," Shinnick said. "I don't like the idea of winning an Olympic gold medal because I took steroids. Steroids are a perversion of the natural process."

With the calendar edging toward September, a couple of tune-up meets offered a preview of the fireworks to come. Evans matched his personal best in the 400 with a 44.9-second clocking on August 17 at Echo Summit. In another meet two weeks later, Evans entered the seldom-run 600 meters, leaving the 400 to Matthews.

In the 600—a lap and a half around the track—Evans clocked 1:14.3, a world's best for the distance. Minutes later, Matthews won the 400 in 44.4, trimming one-tenth of a second off Tommie Smith's world record. Evans had run a world's best at an arcane distance; Matthews had set a world record in one of the classic Olympic events. Though he gamely congratulated Matthews, Evans was steaming inside.

"You bet I was pissed," Evans said. "But it just gave me that much more motivation."

Austin Angell, a Tahoe track enthusiast who spent a lot of time hanging around the track in July and August, detected a chill in the air when September came, a shift that went beyond the onset of autumn. "They screwed around and partied, but when it got to be about three weeks out, they were all business," Angell said. "It's like they flipped a switch."

Before they could get down to business, the question of whether the Los Angeles winners had spots on the Olympic team had to be answered. Evans had gone off to Europe thinking he was already on the team. Fosbury drove north to Oregon to get his belongings together before participating in what he thought would be a "training competition." Dave Patrick, the 1,500 winner in Los Angeles, visited his family in Maryland before arriving at Tahoe. He planned to time his peak for October, when he'd be shooting for a medal in Mexico City.

Bowerman called a meeting in early September to tell the athletes that the coaching staff and USOC brass wanted their input. Should the Los Angeles results be erased in favor of taking the top three finishers in each event from Echo Summit? Since the Mexico City Olympics were being held at altitude, didn't it make sense to send a team that was battle-tested under the same conditions?

Since the vast majority had everything to gain and nothing to lose, the athletes overwhelmingly voted to make Echo Summit the final word in who'd go to Mexico City and who wouldn't. Bowerman was grateful that Patrick went along with the change in plan.

"I'm a patriotic guy," Patrick told the group. "I want to make sure we send our best guys to Mexico City."

Patrick's Villanova teammate, Erv Hall, found himself in the same position. Hall had won the 110-meter high hurdles in Los Angeles, yet he, too, voted against his own interests.

"I thought it was a little strange, putting it to a vote," Hall said. "Obviously, the guys who finished first were outnumbered. But I was kind of macho. Plus, it was sort of a fait accompli. Did I think it was fair? No. But I won the first trials, and I figured I could do it again. It was a case of moving on."

Liquori thinks Bowerman orchestrated the change to give Oregon runners Roscoe Divine and Dave Wilborn a better chance to make the team in the 1,500 meters.

"Dave Patrick was put on the spot," Liquori said. "On the one hand, he wanted to be confident. On the other hand, he agreed to the conditions knowing he wasn't in the best of shape. Dave didn't take a lot of training to get in shape, and [Villanova coach] Jumbo [Elliott] didn't have him training much after the first trials. I didn't learn until later that Bowerman wasn't even the head Olympic coach. Payton Jordan was. I look at it now as the first case of Nike interference in the sport."

Liquori's loyalty to his teammate is commendable, but it's important to note that Nike didn't exist until 1971. At the time of the Echo Summit trials, Phil Knight and his former Oregon coach were partners in Blue Ribbon Sports, a small company that distributed Japanese-made shoes. Distance runners liked training in them, but when it came time to decide what shoes to race in, money talked. Adidas and Puma were kings of the mountain in that respect. Nike's turn would come, but not until later.

As for the decision to nullify the Los Angeles results, Patrick simply wishes he'd had Elliott with him at the fateful meeting.

"I was immature, twenty-two years old," Patrick said. "We should have had coaches with us, someone to speak up for us. Jumbo wouldn't have let that happen in a New York minute."

For better or for worse, the issue was settled. With the exception of the two race walks and the marathon, which were holding their trials in Alamosa, Colorado, the Olympic team would be determined once and for all on the summit overlooking Lake Tahoe.

One hundred seventy-six men vying for fifty-seven Olympic spots in nineteen events. The stakes were even higher than the elevation.

12

TAKE YOUR MARKS

When the starter's pistol finally echoed through the trees in earnest, the final trials didn't exactly roar out of the blocks. The first two days—September 6 and 7—consisted of just one final, the decathlon, followed by an off day. These US track and field trials would be unlike previous versions in profound ways, from the elongated competition schedule to the forested site and spartan spectator accommodations.

It would be "a casual atmosphere, a family-type setup, noncommercial," as South Lake Tahoe publicist Harry Matte put it.

Spectators took shuttle buses up Meyers Grade to the track. Seating in the wooden bleachers was limited to about twenty-five hundred, though organizers said the site could handle up to fifteen thousand if the overflow took advantage of the hillside. An elevated platform built to hold the Longines timing system towered above the finish line. A rudimentary press box accommodated about one hundred members of the Fourth Estate. The reddish Tartan track was six lanes on the curves, eight lanes on the straights. Daily tickets were priced at two dollars for general admission, four dollars for reserved seating.

To duplicate the Olympic format, Bowerman and the USOC track committee stretched the schedule to ten days of competition over an eleven-day span. (Previous US trials were over and done with in two days.) Each of the nineteen events at Echo Summit followed the same qualifying guidelines as Mexico City, even though the number of entrants was much smaller—seven to twelve competitors per event. This proved to be overkill: in the first of four rounds in the 400 meters, for instance, nobody was eliminated.

Postcard courtesy of Austin Angell

"It was bizarre, but it was a first-rate meet," said Bob Jarvis, a Sacramento attorney who has attended thirteen US Olympic trials, including each day at Echo Summit. "You're never going to see anything like it again."

There was no real need for crowd control, and many of the athletes mingled and bantered freely with the spectators. Fans sitting in the front row of the grandstands could practically reach out and touch the sprinters and hurdlers racing by in lane eight. Organizers would estimate the total attendance at one hundred thousand, but that figure is grossly, if not exponentially, inflated. Not that it really mattered.

"You didn't have one hundred thousand people cheering each day, but the athletes performed as if there were," said Payton Jordan, the US Olympic men's coach. "It was an amazing environment. I sat there and drank it in like a big dog."

The decathlon consists of ten events over two days. The first day consists of the 100 meters, long jump, shot put, high jump, and 400 meters. The second day consists of the 110-meter high hurdles, discus, pole vault, javelin, and 1,500 meters. Points are awarded in each event based on the quality of the mark. The competitor with the highest score after ten events is the winner.

Decathletes toil in obscurity until an Olympic year, when the gold medalist receives the unofficial title of "world's greatest all-around athlete." Americans had always expected one of their own to claim the mantle each Olympic year, and they were seldom disappointed. Past Olympic decathlon champions included such hallowed names as Jim Thorpe, Bob Mathias, and Rafer Johnson. But a West German usurper, Willi Holdorf, won the Olympic title in 1964, and another West German, Kurt Bendlin, broke the world record in 1967 previously held by Russ Hodge.

Hodge was his usual formidable presence at Echo Summit, but Bill Toomey was the clear-cut favorite. Toomey coupled great speed and jumping ability with an analytic genius at culling every last point from each discipline. He trained in West Germany in 1965 under noted *Zehnkampf* (decathlon) coach Friedel Schirmer, finishing the season ranked third in the world, one spot below Bendlin and one slot above Hodge.

Russ Hodge throws the discus while tuning up for the decathlon at Echo Summit. *Photo by Harlin Smith, Center for Sacramento History*

In 1966, Toomey and Hodge had waged a pair of epic battles. The first meeting, at the AAU Championships in Salina, Kansas, saw Toomey eclipse the world record with a score of 8234. Three weeks later, in the Los Angeles Coliseum, Hodge edged Toomey by 11 points with a score of 8230. Technical irregularities at the AAU meant Hodge's Los Angeles score became the accepted world record.

Even among the chiseled physiques at Echo Summit, Hodge stood out, a redwood among pines. He carried 235 pounds on a 6-foot-3 frame, massive shoulders narrowing down to a 33-inch waist. He had the tapered legs of a sprinter. In setting his world record, Hodge clocked 10.5 in the 100 meters into a strong headwind. At the same meet, Charlie Greene and Jim Hines, the fastest men in the world, ran no faster than 10.4 and 10.5 in the open 100. Hodge could also put the shot 58 feet, long jump 25 feet, and run the 1,500 meters in 4:12.7, an amazing time for a man his size.

Some of his talent was genetic: Hodge's mother, Alice Arden, had competed in the high jump at the 1936 Olympics in Berlin. But he trained ferociously, if not always wisely. He could bench-press 500 pounds and squat 700 pounds.

Had he been able to stay healthy, Hodge might have gone down as one of history's greatest decathletes. But that magnificent body broke down too many times to count. Between his world record in 1966 and the final trials at Echo Summit, Hodge entered four decathlons and had to withdraw from each with injuries. At the 1968 AAU Championships in early July, which Toomey won with a score of 8037, Hodge strained a quadriceps muscle in the 100 meters and withdrew.

"I liked to train with sprinters, which was a dumb thing to do for a guy weighing two thirty-five," Hodge said. "I wanted to run the 100 meters in 10 flat. I thought I'd be OK at Echo Summit. I calculated what I could do and still get to the Olympics."

Toomey, an iron man who finished thirty-six of the thirty-eight decathlons he entered over the course of his career, led from start to finish at Echo Summit. Toomey's first-day marks included 10.5 in the 100 meters, 25-6¾ in the long jump, and 46.4 in the 400. Though clearly not as sharp as Toomey, Hodge stayed in contention for one of the other two Olympic berths on the first day by putting the shot a prodigious 58-1, the best mark in the twelve-man field by almost a dozen feet.

The decathletes returned to the track the following morning for an 11 AM start in the 110-meter high hurdles. A crowd of fifteen hundred showed up in beautiful weather. Toomey clocked a workmanlike 14.7 in the hurdles, but Hodge pulled a thigh muscle and limped home in 15.5. To his credit, he soldiered on, but Rick Sloan and Tom Waddell were making healthy runs at the second and third Olympic berths. Sloan set a world decathlon record of 6-11¼ in the high jump and cleared 16-1 in the pole vault. Waddell cleared 6-8 in the high jump and had strong marks in the throws, offsetting his weakness in the running events. While he was still in third place through seven events, Hodge could barely walk. He somehow lifted his massive body over 12 feet in the pole vault, but his Olympic hopes were finished.

Sloan, who would later coach Dan O'Brien to the Olympic decathlon title in 1996, received a medical exemption to the final trials after undergoing ankle surgery in May. Echo Summit was just the fourth decathlon of his career. Toomey approached Sloan after the next to last event, the javelin, and said, "Let's work together in the 1,500. You help me break the world record, and I'll help you make the team."

Toomey needed to run the 1,500 meters in 4:31.6 to break Bendlin's world record, a tall task at 7,382 feet. Less than two laps into the race, a laboring Toomey told Sloan, "You're on your own. I'm out."

"I was scared to death," said Sloan, who finished the 1,500 in 4:39.5. "The last two laps felt like I was doing one-legged squats. I don't know if I could have run a tenth of a second faster. Dr. Breath walked me around the track after I finished. I was shot. It wasn't until then that I heard I'd made the team. My parents, my fiancée, they were all there. It was a thrill."

Toomey finished the 1,500 in 4:47.2, giving him a point total of 8222, the third-highest score in history. "I don't usually lie down after the 1,500," Toomey said, "but I remember not wanting to get up at Echo Summit. I was wiped out."

Sloan (7800) and Waddell (7706) were second and third. The US Olympic track trials invariably produces one or two scenes of almost unbearable agony, and the sight of Hodge hobbling his way around the track on one leg in the 1,500 meters at Echo Summit was one such moment. Determined to complete a decathlon after such a long dry spell, Hodge succeeded, finishing tenth with a score of 7186. His 1,500 time of 7:08.2—a pace barely faster than an eight-minute mile—earned Hodge zero points in the tenth and final event.

"It was more emotionally painful than anything else," Hodge said. "I was devastated."

Without disrespecting the valiant decathletes, the crux of the trials began on Monday, September 9. Charlie Greene, Jim Hines, and Ronnie Ray Smith each clocked 10.0 in the 100-meter quarterfinals, an early indication that the thin air would yield fast times in the sprints. Heats of the 400 hurdles were also much faster than ordinary. The altitude would have an opposite effect in Monday's lone final, the 10,000 meters. The longest Olympic track race figured to be greatly affected by the altitude.

Billy Mills was in Echo Summit field, though he didn't want to be. The defending Olympic 10,000-meter champion had come out of semi-retirement with the goal of making the 1968 team in the 5,000 meters. The plan went haywire, to put it mildly.

Mills authored one of the most improbable stories in Olympic history when he won the 10,000 meters in Tokyo. His was the classic rags-to-riches story. Mills was orphaned at the age of twelve. He is seven-sixteenths Oglala Sioux, and he grew up on the Pine Ridge Reservation in South Dakota. As a "half-breed," he felt ostracized by two cultures and struggled to find his way. His ability to run long distances, he'd later say, saved his life.

"In sport I found a third culture that accepted me," Mills said. "I could walk in both worlds."

After a solid but unspectacular college career at Kansas, Mills joined the marines. He had yet to break 30 minutes in the 10,000 when the Olympic year of 1964 rolled around. Several months of uninterrupted training at Camp Pendleton paid dividends when Mills qualified for the

US Olympic team in the marathon. He then qualified in the 10,000, finishing second to Gerry Lindgren at the 1964 Olympic track trials in Los Angeles.

Mills arrived in Tokyo with a 10,000-meter best of 29:10.4, nearly a minute slower than Ron Clarke's world record. Mills figured that if he could shave one second off each of the twenty-five laps, he'd have a fighter's chance.

"I believed in him," said Pat Mills, Billy's wife. "But I was only twenty-two."

Forty-two runners started the Tokyo 10,000, an absurd number that made the second half of the race resemble a rugby match. Lindgren had a sprained ankle and fell out of contention early. "We lapped some of the runners four times," Clarke said. "It was ridiculous. As a matter of fact, the last guy we lapped was the guy who won the 10,000 meters in 1968, [Naftali] Temu."

Clarke led at the halfway point as Mills considered dropping out. "My thought was, I can't finish this, I'm going to have to quit," Mills said. "I truly was going to drop out, but then I saw Pat in the stands. Instead of dropping out, I took the lead."

No American had ever come within 17 seconds of winning an Olympic 10,000, but Mills led Clarke and Mohamed Gammoudi of Tunisia as a clanging bell sounded one lap to go. As the three leaders headed into the first turn of the last lap, they encountered a scrum of several lapped runners. Clarke shoved Mills to the outside. Gammoudi gave Mills a sharp elbow as he burst through the opening into the lead. Mills nearly lost his balance. On the final curve, Clarke passed Gammoudi for a brief moment before the Tunisian reclaimed the lead as Tokyo's Olympic Stadium erupted. Suddenly, on the outside, Mills shot past them both, racing into history with arms upraised. The three runners who followed Mills across the finish line—Gammoudi, Clarke, and Mamo Wolde—would win a combined eight Olympic medals in their careers.

"For one fleeting moment, I was the best in the world," said Mills, whose gold-medal time was an American-record 28:24.4, an improvement of not one but almost two seconds per lap. Clarke magnanimously refused to label the unheralded Native American's stunning win a fluke.

"Billy certainly deserved to win," Clarke said. "He was a very, very good runner, and he got wings on his feet on the last lap."

———————

The wings on Billy Mills were weighted down by age and responsibility in 1968. Mills was thirty years old with a young family and a job selling insurance in San Diego. At the AAU Championships in Sacramento, stomach cramps had forced him to drop out of the 10,000. He gained entrance to the final trials by clocking an encouraging 28:43.6 in August, but he still wanted to run the 5,000, not the 10,000.

"When I got to South Lake Tahoe, I was told I had to run the 10,000 to prove my fitness," Mills said. "But I didn't want to go to Mexico City in the event I'm the defending champion and not have a chance."

Lindgren was also entered in the Echo Summit 10,000, but he wasn't firing on all cylinders, either. He injured a tendon shortly after his double win at the NCAA meet and tried his best to train through it, but he was a shadow of his normal self. But even if Mills and Lindgren had been at their best, the prerace favorite still might have been Tracy Smith, the towheaded winner of the AAU 10,000 and the Los Angeles 5,000.

Smith had shown in the previous two years that he could match strides with the world's best. He finished third at the 1966 International Cross Country Championships in Morocco and was ranked sixth in the world at 5,000 meters. In a 1,500-meter time trial at Echo Summit, Smith had clocked 3:46 to Jim Ryun's 3:44. "I don't remember feeling very stressed," Smith said. "I was pretty confident going in."

The 10,000 final began at 3:30 PM, in conditions that would have been ideal for distance running had the track not been a mile and a half above sea level. Tom Laris, the Dartmouth grad who had prepared in the mountains *above* Mexico City, led a tightly bunched pack through 2,000 meters. One by one, the lead group shrank. Lindgren was the first contender to drop back. Mills, who had looked strong in the first half of the race, experienced the same stomach cramps he had at the AAU meet in Sacramento. The Olympic champion lost contact with the lead group.

At 9,000 meters, Laris, Van Nelson, and Smith received word that Mills and Lindgren were out of it. Smith sprinted into the lead on the backstretch of the twenty-fifth lap and won comfortably in 30:00.4. Nelson was second, and Laris finished third, one spot in front of Mills. Lindgren was even farther back, in fifth. Laris's prediction of the time needed to make the team, based on his time trial in Mexico City, was spot on.

"With four laps to go, all of us knew that all we had to do was keep going to make the team," Smith recalled. "On the last lap, I couldn't resist going for the win. I was in great shape at Echo Summit. I wish I had felt as good in Mexico City as I felt there."

Nelson, the small-college runner coached by Bob Tracy (the man who played a major role in sending the final trials to Echo Summit), was an ecstatic runner-up.

"When I got to St. Cloud in 1964, Bob asked me, 'What are your ambitions?' I said, 'I want to go to the Olympic Games.' He said, 'I'll see to it that you get into the big meets and get the opportunity.' I'm so glad he was there at Echo Summit to see me do it."

The painkillers Mills took before the race wore off at the three-mile mark. He consoled himself by thinking he'd get another shot—the one he wanted—in the 5,000-meter final four days later.

The schedule split each day into morning and afternoon sessions. It didn't make sense for spectators to go back down to the lake during the break, so there was a lot of milling about. At most US track meets, the 100-meter final attracts the greatest interest, but most meets aren't held on a mountaintop with no spectator parking. The Tuesday crowd for the 100-meter semifinals and final was no more than two thousand.

The 1:00 PM semifinals eliminated just three sprinters. The eight finalists returned two hours later to determine who'd be going to Mexico City. The temperature for the final was sixty-three degrees, considerably cooler than sprinters prefer. Mel Pender, the 5-foot-5 Vietnam veteran, led out of the blocks, just as he had at the Tokyo Olympics before fading to sixth. Hines wound up winning in 10 seconds flat, followed across the line by Greene and Pender. Ronnie Ray Smith of Bud Winter's Speed City contingent placed fourth, earning a spot on the Olympic 400-meter relay team.

Less than a year after taking enemy fire in the Mekong Delta, the thirty-year-old Pender was an Olympian for the second time by virtue of his third-place finish at Echo Summit. "I got out of the blocks fast and God helped me the rest of the way," Pender said. "I thought my track days were over in 1964, but I beat those young boys to make my second Olympic team. No sprinter my age had ever done what I did. I was built like a brick shithouse with no drugs in my body."

As was the case for the Night of Speed in Sacramento, hand timing was used for the official results at Echo Summit. Again, however, officials had access to a fully automatic unit to determine final places. The automatic times for the 100-meter final at Echo Summit were 10.11 for Hines, 10.15 for Greene, 10.20 for Pender, and 10.22 for Ronnie Ray Smith. Fast, but not as fast as the times in Sacramento. Not that any of them much cared—there would be ample opportunity to break records in Mexico City.

The shot put ring and sector were located just outside the first turn of the track, giving spectators a close-up view of the proceedings. Matson had suffered a rare loss in late August to George Woods, but the world-record holder expected a massive throw in the trials final. "I warmed up with a standing throw of sixty-seven feet, and normally I pick up about five feet from that," Matson said. "I thought I was going to break the world record."

Matson not only did not challenge his world record of 71-5½ but also finished third for the first time in four years. Woods and Maggard threw big personal bests in the opening round—68-0¼ for Woods, 67-4¼ for Maggard. Matson reached 67-1¼ in the second round, and that was it.

"It's a lot like hitting a golf ball," Matson said. "You get off a little bit and you try to correct it. I just pressed."

Echo Summit was the only time Maggard beat Matson in his life. "The only way I could beat him was to break his leg or for him to have a bad day," Maggard said.

Extremely quick and light of foot for a man carrying 295 pounds on a 6-foot frame, Woods trained at night after working full days in a Los Angeles insurance office. "There was a street light at the end of the football field," he said. "I couldn't find my shot half the time, so I ended up painting it white. Ah, the good old days."

The first world record ever set in the parking lot of a beginner's ski hill came the following day, September 11. The 400-meter intermediate hurdlers had shown the previous two days that it would take a very fast time to win the final.

Ron Whitney, the world's top-ranked intermediate hurdler in 1967, arrived at Tahoe the man to beat. But Whitney's position heading into the final was more precarious than he'd anticipated. In unseasonably hot conditions—the mercury reached ninety-two degrees on September 10— the semifinals were staggeringly fast. Geoff Vanderstock of USC finished a stride ahead of Whitney in the first semifinal. Vanderstock's 49.2 clocking was just one-tenth of a second off Rex Cawley's world record.

In the second semifinal, Tom Wyatt clocked 49.3 to edge Boyd Gittins. The quality of the semifinals was such that Nick Lee and Andy Bell missed qualifying for the final even though they each ran 49.7, a time fast enough to have won a medal in each of the previous thirteen Olympic Games. Ordinarily, eight runners advance to championship finals, but the unorthodox six-lane track made the Echo Summit final a superexclusive affair.

Fast semifinals sometimes result in tired finalists and slower times. That wasn't the case at Echo Summit on September 11. The crowd cheered lustily for Paddy McCrary, the local favorite from UC Berkeley in lane four. Vanderstock drew lane six, to the immediate right of Gittins. Whitney would be able to monitor most of the field from lane three.

Wyatt and Gittins went out fastest, streaking over the first 36-inch hurdle in unison. Whitney got out slowly, losing the stagger to Wyatt in lane one. When the hurdlers emerged from the trees on the far turn, Gittins was in front. Vanderstock was coming on fast, however, and he glided into the lead over the eighth hurdle. Whitney was sixth and last with just two hurdles remaining.

Running the race of his life from the outside lane, Vanderstock crossed the finish line two meters ahead of Gittins. Whitney corralled the tiring Wyatt in the hurdleless final 35 meters to claim the third Olympic spot.

"It seemed like I was running downhill, it felt so good," Vanderstock said. "The hurdles were coming at me so quickly."

Occidental coach Dixon Farmer ran up to the panting Vanderstock and showed him his stopwatch. "It was a touch under 49 flat," Vanderstock remembered. Indeed, the official time was 48.8, three-tenths faster than Cawley's 1964 record. The electronic time was only a tad slower: 48.93.

Geoff Vanderstock set a world record of 48.8 seconds in winning the 400-meter intermediate hurdles. © *Don Chadez*

Gittins was second in a collegiate-record 49.1. Whitney's 49.2 was his fastest ever.

The world record thus passed from one USC graduate to another.

"Rex [Cawley] was one of the reasons I came to USC," Vanderstock said. "Before I went to Echo Summit, he gave me some workouts to do. Meet these times and you'll break my record, he said. One of the times he told me to do was 60 seconds for 500 meters. Two weeks before the final, Bill Toomey, Ron Whitney, and I ran a 500-meter time trial, and we all broke 60. I knew I was ready, but I tried to tamp everything down, not to get too excited too early. Fifteen steps between hurdles . . . it's all about timing."

Cawley and other experts had foreseen greatness from Vanderstock from the moment he arrived at USC two years earlier. Gittins, however, was the closest thing Echo Summit saw to a UFO.

At the Los Angeles trials in late June, Gittins finished a nonqualifying fifth in his preliminary race because of an identified flying object. "Some pigeon droppings hit me in my eye," Gittins said. "I was lucky to finish. It's hard enough to have depth perception in the hurdles with both eyes. I had to close one eye."

Gittins was granted a spot in a runoff the next day, which he won. He arrived at Echo Summit with a best time of 50.5. With nary a pigeon in the sky, he improved to 50.1 in the heats, 49.5 in the semifinals, and 49.1 in the final to become one of the most unlikely 1968 US Olympians.

"The first day I tied the school record, the second day I tied the collegiate record, and the third day I tied the world record," Gittins said. "And I finished second all three times. It was frustrating, but it was fun. I had a ball."

With shadows lengthening and the crowd still buzzing over the fastest 400 hurdles race in history, the eight finalists in the 800 meters lined up for the day's concluding event. Most eyes were on the tall runner in the pink shorts and blue singlet of the Kansas Jayhawks. Jim Ryun had seemingly put his Olympic year troubles behind him when he ran a

3:55.8 mile at sea level in mid-August, but he wasn't as experienced or confident racing two laps as he was four, and he still wasn't satisfied with his altitude preparations. Complicating any prerace predictions was the uncertainty over how much the high altitude would affect a race lasting more than 100 seconds.

"The 800 was on the border as to whether it helped or not," said Tom Farrell, a 1964 Olympian who was rounding into shape nicely at Echo Summit. "I was in a tough place in 1968. How do you beat Jim Ryun? And here you've got Wade Bell. There's potentially only one spot on the team left."

Farrell had finished fourth in the Los Angeles trials race won by Bell, the world's second-ranked 800-meter man in 1967. Farrell was more of a 400–800 runner; Bell and Ryun were more the 800–1,500 types, meaning they relied as much on strength as speed.

Mark Winzenried, an eighteen-year-old seen by all as a future star, led the finalists through the first lap in 52.8 seconds, a solid pace. Winzenried maintained his lead down the backstretch and into the final curve, when the runners vanished behind the trees. When the leaders came back into view, a gasp went through the crowd. Where was Ryun?

Behind the trees, Ryun suddenly stopped running. Bell had to swerve to the outside to avoid tripping over him. Farrell patiently stayed on the curve throughout, winning in 1:46.5. Bell recovered from his near fall to place second in 1:47.1, becoming the second Bowerman-coached athlete to make the 1968 Olympic team. Kenny Moore had earlier qualified in the marathon trial race in Alamosa, Colorado.

The battle for third was fierce, with Ron Kutschinski edging Winzenried by two feet at the wire. Kutschinski needed supplemental oxygen after the race. Winzenried broke down in tears after coming so close.

Ryun, meanwhile, thought better of simply quitting behind the trees. After what seemed like an eternity, he reappeared, jogging across the line in 2:02.6. He grabbed his sweats and left the track without talking to the pack of reporters.

"I had exercise-induced asthma and had to stop," Ryun later explained. "It just so happened it was behind the trees. I remember wondering, oh my Lord, what's going to happen in the 1,500? I wasn't in the best place, confidence-wise, after the 800."

The place Farrell had fallen in love with the year before, when he joined Tracy for the test run in South Lake Tahoe, provided one of the most satisfying experiences of his running career. "I had a ball up there," Farrell said. "Of course, if I had finished fourth, I probably would have hated the freaking place."

Thirty years later, when members of the 1968 Olympic men's team gathered in New Orleans for a reunion, Farrell and his wife, Chris, were surprised to receive an apology from triple jumper Norm Tate. The way Tate remembered it, Chris Farrell had tried to find a seat in the stands on one of the afternoons her husband was running. The black women who at the time were married to John Carlos and Tommie Smith refused to move over and make room for Chris and a friend. "John's and Tommie's wives were very vocal about the [Black Power] protest," Tate said. "They said something to Tom Farrell's wife that bothered me. I was taught that the most important thing is how you treat people, and those were nice people. I was caught up in being black and having white friends, but not everything is black and white."

In New Orleans, Tate apologized to the Farrells for the long-ago incident—for not saying anything when Chris was treated rudely. Chris Farrell said she didn't remember it but thanked Tate for his concern.

"Norm Tate is nine feet tall in my opinion," Tom Farrell said. "He must have carried it with him for thirty years. That team really did have a bond and a friendship. It was a special group."

Sandwiched between the 400 hurdle and 800 finals—and between the trees on the infield—was the discus final. The ring wasn't visible to most of the spectators, and what took place out of view wasn't particularly dramatic. Jay Silvester clinched victory with his second-round toss of 207 feet, 6 inches. Gary Carlsen was second at 205-2, 6 inches in front of Al Oerter's 204-8. Fourth place was another dozen feet back.

Like a bear coming out of hibernation, Oerter needed time to get oriented in an Olympic year. While Silvester stretched the world record to 218-4 at Modesto in late May, Oerter was stuck throwing 195-footers. Oerter wasn't concerned at first. He had just one number circled on his calendar: October 15, the date of the Mexico City final. But as the spring turned to summer, Oerter penciled in September 11, just to be safe.

In 1956, Oerter finished second at his first trials behind Fortune Gordien. In 1960, he was second to Rink Babka. In 1964, Silvester shunted Oerter to second again. Each time, Oerter won Olympic gold. His Olympic victory in Tokyo came despite torn cartilage in his ribs that nearly forced him to withdraw midway through the competition.

"All my life I've trained through the trials, except in 1968," Oerter explained. "I was pretty far down the list. Up in Tahoe, I had to put out a little bit, to make sure I made the team."

Under Payton Jordan's discerning eye, Oerter worked diligently at Echo Summit on his technique, never his strong suit. "I'm a thrower,

Al Oerter kept his hopes for a fourth Olympic gold medal in the discus alive by placing third at Echo Summit. *AP Images*

not a technician," Oerter said. "I needed to get with Payton and have him yell at me, tell me what I was doing wrong."

Years after he retired—and the consummate Olympian didn't really retire until his early fifties—Oerter remembered Echo Summit fondly.

"I'm sure some environmentalists today would complain, but it was a wonderful place to train," Oerter said. "The Olympic Games were at hand. You didn't concern yourself with the trailers or the food, because at that time, all of the athletes were one hundred percent focused.

"The only thing that scared the hell out of me was when the jets went overhead. It sounded like thunder rolling through those mountains."

The Echo Summit trials were halfway done. More thunder was on the way.

13

OUT OF THIS WORLD

Bob Seagren arrived at Echo Summit fashionably late, a sixteen-foot pole strapped to the side of his Corvette. He looked and felt like a million bucks. He'd just gotten back from vaulting his way across Europe, competing in six meets in twenty-nine days. He'd already qualified for the Olympics, right?

Wrong. And if the news that his Los Angeles win counted for nothing didn't wipe the smile off Seagren's handsome face, being carted off the mountain on his back most certainly did.

A week before he had to prove himself all over again, Seagren's back seized up to the point where he couldn't move. An ambulance transported the Olympic favorite to Barton Memorial Hospital in South Lake Tahoe.

"I pinched a nerve in one of my vertebrae, and they couldn't tell me whether it would be a day or a month before it got better," Seagren said. "It was excruciating. I was getting Demerol shots every two hours."

After spending four days in the hospital, Seagren returned to his trailer on the summit and did nothing for twenty-four hours. The next day he ran a couple of wind sprints and tried planting his pole in the box. While not completely out of the woods—he had a congenital back condition—he knew he'd at least be able to give it a shot.

The pole vault was the first of four finals to be held September 12, followed by the javelin, 200-meter dash, and 3,000-meter steeplechase. Fans who had never seen a world record would see two within a matter of minutes.

Seagren was just eighteen when he burst on the national scene in 1965. Pole vaulters tend to be the gregarious types, and Seagren struck up an instant friendship with his older and more experienced rival, John Pennel. In 1963 Pennel became the first man to set a world record using a fiberglass pole, clearing 17 feet. Although he was favored to win a gold medal at the Tokyo Olympics, Pennel injured his back beforehand and wound up eleventh.

Pennell and Seagren became roommates in late 1965, sharing an apartment in the Southern California community of Glendale. "I was fortunate in that I didn't have to have a job, but that wasn't the case with a lot of athletes," Seagren said. "John had to go to work in the morning."

While the carefree Seagren bounced between junior colleges and Pennel worked to pay his share of the rent, the roommates took turns breaking each other's world records. In 1967, with Pennel sidelined by wrist and shoulder injuries, Seagren upped Pennel's record by an inch with a 17-7 vault in San Diego. Two weeks later, at the AAU Championships in Bakersfield, Seagren lost not just his national title but his world record. USC sophomore Paul Wilson cleared 17-7¾ to Seagren's 17-4. Wilson never made it to Echo Summit—a serious back injury ended his career prematurely.

Seagren's back loosened up as the trials final progressed, and he clinched the win by making 17-4 on his second attempt. Seagren then had the crossbar raised to 17-9, or 5.41 meters, a new world record. "The pine trees lining the runway made the bar look like it was set at seven feet," he said later. He sprinted down the red runway, planted his black pole in the box, flew skyward, and corkscrewed his body cleanly over the bar. He finished the day by taking three shots at 18-0½, narrowly missing on his second try. Friends back home were shocked at the news. The last they'd heard, Seagren was flat on his back in the hospital.

"I found out it was a congenital defect and I just hyperextended it," Seagren said. "I learned how to warm up and exercise to prevent that from ever happening again."

Joining Seagren on the Olympic team were Pennel, the twenty-eight-year-old veteran, and Carrigan, the seventeen-year-old wunderkind. Each cleared 17 feet. "I'd been praying outside my trailer every night, asking God to please help me make the Olympic team," Carrigan said. "When

Bob Seagren wound up breaking the world record in the pole vault, looking, in Tommie Smith's words, as if he were falling out of the trees. *Courtesy of the Walt Little family*

I jumped seventeen feet to move into third place, I remember thinking, 'There really is a God.'"

As the excitement from the pole vault began to die down, the best starter in the business, Tom Moore, called the six finalists in the 200 meters to their marks. John Carlos was in lane four. Tommie Smith drew the dreaded inside lane. Smith won his semifinal earlier that afternoon in 20.2. Carlos won his in 20.3. The day before, Carlos clocked 20.1 in the heats, equaling his fastest ever.

Carlos had been telling anyone who'd listen that he was going to "come out of the trees and break the world record." The bravado was old hat, but his competitors had noticed a newer, more serious Carlos at Echo Summit. He ran early-morning sprints up the ski hill. He'd cut his weight from 197 to 186 pounds.

Rest assured, the weight loss didn't mean he'd shed the Harlem swagger. A boom box announced his arrival at the starting line. Along with sunglasses and the all-red uniform of the Santa Clara Valley Youth Village, the Speed City summer affiliate, Carlos wore a red pair of Puma 68s, or as they'd soon be known, "brush spikes."

While conventional track shoes had six spikes on the sole and two on the heel, the new Puma model had sixty-eight tiny brushlike spikes on the sole. Smith, also representing the Santa Clara Valley Youth Village but dressed in green shorts and a blue top, opted for a pair of conventional Pumas.

The six sprinters were set and coiled when Larry Questad let out a yelp. An insect had crawled across his hand. Moore called for a reset. The gun sounded and the crowd waited anxiously. Out from behind the trees streaked Carlos, leading Larry Questad and Jerry Bright off the curve by at least two meters. Smith was even farther back. "When I saw a plethora of people in front of me, I thought God didn't want me to make that team," Smith said.

Carlos maintained his lead down the stretch, crossing the finish line in a hand-timed 19.7, three-tenths of a second below Smith's world record. "You got nothing on me, Bob!" a joyous Carlos shouted at Seagren after the race. The electronic timing system caught Carlos in 19.92, making it the first indisputably sub-20-second clocking in history.

Smith rallied in the homestretch, stretching out his long legs to finish second in 20.0 (20.18 electronically). The battle for third was the closest of the trials as Questad, Bright, and Tom Randolph each crossed the line in 20.2 seconds. The automatic timer was able to separate them, though just barely: Questad 20.28, Bright 20.29, and Randolph 20.29.

John Carlos setting a world record of 19.7 seconds in winning the 200 meters over Tommie Smith (168) and Larry Questad (42). © *Rich Clarkson*

As Carlos cooled down after the race of his life, an official had the gall to tell him the 19.7 wouldn't be accepted as a world record because of his shoes. Carlos brushed the wet blanket off by telling reporters, "You saw it, and you'll write it, and everybody will know there was somebody in those shoes. I felt like I could have run it barefoot."

Questad called his parents in Idaho to share the exciting news.

"Hello?"

"Hi, Mom. Guess what? You'd better pack your suitcase for Mexico City," Questad said.

"I've got a surprise for you," she replied.

"What?"

"You've been drafted."

"Mom, couldn't you have waited to tell me that tomorrow?"

John Carlos displaying the controversial Puma "brush spikes" he wore in setting an unrecognized world record in the 200 meters. © *Don Chadez*

Prior to competing in the Olympics, Questad returned to Billings to take his physical. He failed. "Chronic urticaria," he said. "I got the hives from wool. What a blessing."

Frank Covelli won a wind-hampered javelin final, and the two-record afternoon ended with George Young winning the steeplechase. That same evening—or early the next morning, perhaps—local police took their first Olympian into custody.

Someone had given Carrigan a fake ID so he could celebrate at the Stateline clubs that night. That's when things "got out of control," in Carrigan's words.

"I was running away from this guy and I knocked over a lady," Carrigan said. "I'd had a little bit to drink. I got arrested. I was so wound up with making the team that I told this security guy, 'Do you know

His second-place finish at Echo Summit was one of the few losses of Tommie
Smith's career. © *Rich Clarkson*

who I am? Do you know what I just did?' He didn't seem too interested.
They took me to jail, and my mom had to bail me out."

Charges were dropped. On a more poignant (and sober) note,
Carrigan's father received news of his son's accomplishment—not the

arrest—on the radio while driving a logging truck on the back roads of Washington.

"He pulled over and started crying," Casey said.

With the high jump final not scheduled until September 16, the tenth and final day of competition, Dick Fosbury had plenty of time to get a feel for what awaited him. Too much time, maybe.

"We spent all week watching guys make the team and not make the team," Fosbury said. "The atmosphere was very, very intense. We all looked out for each other, which made it hard to see people you'd become friendly with not make the team."

An airline ticket agent set up a table next to the track—Echo Summit's version of the Grim Reaper. "As soon as someone didn't make the team, they shipped 'em out, just like that," Tate said. "Guys had been there six to eight weeks, and then they were told to leave immediately. It was so cold-blooded."

That's long been the nature of the US Olympic track trials, starting in the 1920s and continuing through the present. Few countries dare choose their teams solely on the results of one competition, figuring Olympic medal contenders shouldn't be ruled out for having an off day in one selection meet. In the United States, as the 1968 Olympic men's coach Payton Jordan put it, "The man steps up to the line and selects himself."

Nothing was quite that simple in 1968, as the Los Angeles imbroglio illustrated. But once the final trials began in early September, the bottom line was as clear as the crystalline waters of Lake Tahoe: top three or bust.

Norm Tate knew the feeling of being a bust. He had entered the 1964 Olympic trials in Los Angeles as one of the favorites in the triple jump. Whether it was the pressure or bad luck, he messed up his steps and finished a distant seventh. The day before, his good friend Charlie Mays missed making the Olympic team in the long jump by three-quarters of an inch.

"We sneaked a bottle of whiskey onto the plane and got drunk, we were so depressed with not making the team," Tate said. "On the flight home, we made a promise to one another. We were going to make the Olympic team in 1968."

Exactly four years later, but this time on Friday the thirteenth, Tate made good on his drunken vow. After squeaking into the Echo Summit final as the sixth of seven qualifiers, Tate opened with a jump of 52 feet, 6¼ inches. That mark held up for third place behind Art Walker and Dave Smith.

"It was an obsession of mine, to make the Olympic team," Tate said. "I was the happiest man at Tahoe."

The sight of a sprinter appearing suddenly from behind the trees was exhilarating. A sixteen-pound hammer flying out of the forest like a stray cannonball was something else entirely. "You'd hear a yell and then another yell: 'Heads up!' More than once a hammer tore branches off the trees," decathlete Rick Sloan said. "You'd run for the track when you heard 'Heads up!' It wasn't the safest environment."

For that very reason, hammer throwers are accustomed to being relegated to fields far off the beaten track. Harold Connolly set one of his world records in what looked like a rock-filled quarry. Hammer throwers ranked low on the Tahoe totem pole. "We usually practiced at South Tahoe Intermediate School," Jim Pryde said. "If we wanted to throw at Echo Summit, we had to organize it with the javelin and discus throwers."

Bowerman tried to keep the hammer off the schedule at a pre-trials meet in Eugene, Oregon. "The hammer throw is a foolish event," Bowerman said in a meeting at Echo Summit. "If I had my choice, it wouldn't even be on the Olympic schedule."

Those were fighting words to George Frenn, the combustible hammer thrower. "If the hammer is good enough to be in the Olympic Games, it's good enough to be in your stinking meet. I say that no one should go to Oregon unless they put the hammer in." When the other athletes burst into applause, Bowerman had no choice but to grudgingly relent.

Despite the fear and loathing they engendered, hammer throwers came from royal lineage. The event originated in the British Isles, where Henry VIII was an early practitioner. In those days, an actual sledgehammer was thrown for sport. The event then evolved into its current form, where the thrower spins three or four times in a circle, propelling a sixteen-pound orb attached to a four-foot wire with a handle on the end. In the early part of the twentieth century, the "Irish Whales"—New York City policemen who migrated to America in the Irish diaspora—lorded over Olympic hammer circles.

Connolly proved to be a worthy successor to the leviathans, but the best US thrower in 1968 was Ed Burke, the junior-college teacher from Southern California. Burke supplanted Connolly as the American record holder in 1967 with a throw of 235 feet, 11 inches. As Burke began winding up for his opening throw in the Echo Summit final, Frenn tried to unsettle him with a derogatory comment about Burke's skills.

"Frenn had never been within ten or twenty feet of me," Burke said, his disgust apparent decades later. "I answered him by saying, 'Oh yeah? Watch this.' I won the event on my first throw."

Burke's opener flew 224-1. Touché. Al Hall placed second to qualify for his fourth Olympic team, as did Connolly in third. Frenn finished in the dreaded fourth spot. "I wouldn't have made the team if one of the athletes' father hadn't died," Connolly said, referring to Tom Gage, the second-place finisher at the Los Angeles trials who left Tahoe to be with his family.

His days as an Olympic medal contender were over, but Connolly would be heard from in Mexico City. He made sure of that.

———

The 110-meter high hurdles had been one of the strongest US events for decades, and few expected to see anyone other than an American standing atop the medal stand in Mexico City. Willie Davenport and Earl McCullouch were ranked first and second in the world in 1967, a year in which US hurdlers claimed seven of the top eight slots. But the forecast at Echo Summit was hazier. McCullouch, the 1968 NCAA and AAU champion, signed a professional football contract days after his crack-up at the Los Angeles trials. Davenport pulled up with a groin injury in his qualifying heat at the AAU meet and needed a medical exemption to be added to the Echo Summit field.

Davenport had one of the most illustrious careers in US Olympic history, qualifying for four Olympic teams in the high hurdles and one as a bobsledder, making him one of the first two African Americans to compete in the Winter Olympics. But in September 1968, Davenport's sole Olympic experience consisted of getting hurt in Tokyo and not making the final.

His second Olympic go-round got off to a rocky start. He quit the track team at Southern University before the 1968 season following a dispute with the Jaguars' coach, Dick Hill, over Davenport's irregular practice habits. At the Pelican Relays on April 19 in Baton Rouge, Louisiana—the first time the meet had been integrated—Davenport lost decisively to Tennessee's white hurdler, Richmond Flowers. Davenport was so shaken by the experience that he apologized on a local television station. He told his fans he wouldn't lose again.

Although he was just twenty-five in 1968, Davenport gave off an older vibe. When he didn't receive any major scholarship offers coming out of Howland High School in Warren, Ohio, he enlisted in the army as a paratrooper. He kept his hurdling skills sharp competing for a local sports club while stationed in Germany from 1961 to 1963. At the 1964 Olympic trials, Davenport registered one of the biggest upsets of the meet, finishing first in a field that included Hayes Jones, the eventual Olympic champion. After receiving his army discharge in 1965, Davenport enrolled at Southern, and he rebounded from the injury in Tokyo to rank first in the world in 1965, 1966, and 1967. Even Hill, the esteemed coach who felt Davenport needed to take practice more seriously, called his hurdling form the best he'd ever seen.

Echo Summit offered Davenport the perfect environment to turn a disappointing season around.

"It was the one time the United States did something to assist the athletes," Davenport said. "They weren't concerned about the facility's future use or the cost. It was done to accommodate the athletes. We hadn't seen that before. My mission was to make the Olympic team and win a medal. The mission was to compete, and that's what we did. You live in trailers? No big deal. You do what you have to do."

Running into a strong headwind, Davenport won the Echo Summit final in 13.4 seconds. Leon Coleman and Erv Hall were second and third in 13.5. Flowers, who hadn't fully recovered from an early-June hamstring injury, finished fifth.

"I was [a] shell of myself at Tahoe and couldn't get it done," Flowers said.

Minutes after the final, Flowers received a call from Tennessee football coach Doug Dickey. Dickey told Flowers to hurry back to school, that he had a starting spot in the backfield waiting for him.

"I jumped on that," Flowers said. "That allowed me to quit thinking about it. Not making the Olympic team probably bothers me more now than it did then."

Thirty years later, one of the greatest Olympians of all time marveled at the collection of talent gathered on the summit overlooking Lake Tahoe.

"I think it was the greatest track team ever put together," Davenport said. "Take the hurdles, the 100, 200, and 400—we left people at home who could have won an Olympic gold medal. We could have taken fifth- or sixth-placers who would have kicked butt. It says a lot about America that we had so many great athletes."

The fourth and last final on September 13 was the 5,000-meter run. Billy Mills had planned his entire season around competing in the 5,000 rather than the 10,000, the event in which he won a gold medal in Tokyo. But when the gun sounded at 4:30 PM for the 5,000 final, Mills wasn't one of the seven starters.

Mills said he was told he couldn't run because he hadn't petitioned for entry in the 5,000 when he sought an exemption into the 10,000 final. "I was told I didn't fill out the form properly," Mills said. "I didn't sign any form." The confusion only escalated. More than seventy athletes signed a petition requesting that Mills receive a spot in the qualifying heat. When yet another meeting was called to discuss the matter, Gerry Lindgren made an impassioned case that Mills deserved a shot in the 5,000. Then things got really bizarre.

The US team staff asked Mills to run a 5,000-meter time trial the same day as the qualifying heat. Ron Clarke, the world-record holder from Australia, happened to be at Tahoe doing some high-altitude work. Clarke agreed to pace Mills through a trial run. Mills clocked 14:32.8, a good time at 7,377 feet, but it wasn't good enough to change the minds that mattered.

"I was caught up between the white leadership and the civil rights movement," Mills said. "The leadership was afraid of a conflict with the black athletes, because if I ran the 5,000, I might keep a black athlete off the team. It was an angry year, and I understand prejudice. I'd been called a prairie nigger. But I should have had the opportunity to run."

The only black entrant in the 5,000 meters was Lou Scott, a silver medalist at the 1967 Pan American Games. Scott says he didn't feel the need to fight the pro-Mills petition because he knew who was the better runner in 1968. "I was going to make the team," Scott said. "One of those three spots was going to be mine."

In winds gusting up to thirty miles per hour, Bob Day opened a big lead on the field through the first eight laps. The bug collector Jack Bacheler left the trailing pack and set out after Day. The trees inside the track made it more difficult for the pursuer to always know how much ground needed to be made up, but it also posed a challenge to the front-runner. "It lent a different flavor to the distance races," Bacheler said. "When I was going after Day, I'd get around the trees and pick it up, or at least I thought I was picking it up."

Day backed off the pace in the final four laps and was content to cross the line in tandem with Bacheler in 14:37.4. The race for third turned out to be one of the fiercest battles of the trials. Scott had a

30-meter gap on Lindgren with two and a half laps remaining, but it began shrinking precipitously.

Lindgren had been told he needed to run the 10,000 at the Los Angeles trials to be admitted to the Tahoe field. By that point his ulcers were acting up, on top of the Achilles he'd injured at the NCAA meet. He dropped out of the Los Angeles 10,000 after four miles but was given a medical exemption anyway. "I was in really bad, bad shape," Lindgren said.

Lindgren said he was pelted with pine cones and needles by several black athletes as he tried to chase down Scott on the closing laps of the Echo Summit 5,000. "They really wanted a black guy to make the team," Lindgren said.

Entering the final homestretch, Lindgren pulled even with Scott. But Lindgren had expended too much effort chasing Scott down to have anything left for a finishing kick. Scott crossed the line six-tenths in front. Lindgren lay spread-eagled on the infield afterward, oblivious to the rock poking into his back. Scott didn't feel much better. "I couldn't sit down, lay down, stand up," Scott said. "When I finally came to, everyone was gone."

———————

Getting kicked off the UTEP team in April for refusing to compete against Brigham Young University didn't hinder Bob Beamon's performances in the slightest. In fact, he kept getting better and better. He beat Ralph Boston by a foot in Modesto. Beamon then came within three-quarters of an inch of matching the world record at the AAU meet in Sacramento and won the Los Angeles trials easily. Beamon's 1968 performances called to mind a prescient comment Boston had made a couple of years earlier to Gayle Hopkins, another top jumper. "If this guy ever learns what he's doing, look out," Boston told Hopkins.

The company Beamon kept at Echo Summit helped lay the groundwork for his historic jump in Mexico City. He satisfied his hankering for basketball by playing pick-up games at the intermediate school in South Lake Tahoe, and he wasn't averse to visiting the casinos. But the

Bob Beamon soaring through the thin air to win the long jump. © *Don Chadez*

biggest takeaway from his month on the mountain was that he began seeing the long jump as a craft.

"It was an incredible place to train, to seriously train and be around the greatest track and field athletes of all time," Beamon said. "It gave me a lot more insight into technical training, into clearing up the rough edges.

"What I found out is that the long jump is more than just jumping. It's running, gaining a psychological edge. I actually didn't work with coaches. One day I'd work out with Tommie Smith, another day with John Carlos. What's the saying? If you're with the best, you can expect the best."

Beamon wanted to lay down a big jump in the first round of the September 14 final. Boston had the same intention, and the 1960 Olympic champion opened the final with a wind-aided jump of 27-1¼. Beamon was up next. He sprinted down the runway, launched his body high into the air, and touched down at 27-6½, the longest jump of his life. Since the wind reading of 3.2 meters per second exceeded the legal limit of 2.0 meters per second, it didn't count as a new world record. "The wind reading didn't mean much to me," Beamon said. "I wasn't there to break any records. I wanted to jump as far as I could and make the team."

Beamon jumped a wind-legal 27-1 on his second jump and passed his four remaining attempts. Boston also shut it down early. But the battle for the third spot went the full distance.

The principles were Phil Shinnick and Charlie Mays, and they had a history. At the 1964 Olympic trials, Shinnick edged Mays for third by three-quarters of an inch. Mays drank whiskey with Tate on the flight home, vowing to make amends in 1968. After failing to qualify for the final in Tokyo, Shinnick set his own goal—to set an Olympic record four years hence in Mexico City. Those ambitions collided head-on beneath the trees at Echo Summit.

Mays graduated from the University of Maryland Eastern Shore, a historically black college, and later served a couple of terms in the New Jersey state legislature. His fingerprints were all over a variety of schemes at Lake Tahoe. In return for making speeches to the local chamber of commerce, he and Tate received the free use of an automobile from a local car dealer. "Charlie was a hustler," Tate said.

While Mays steered clear of the racial issues dividing the black athletes in 1968, Shinnick was an unapologetic radical. His first paper at the University of Washington addressed segregation in Seattle. "We're only five generations removed from slavery," Shinnick said. "We still have the ghosts. Whites inherited a certain racism." When he spoke out in support of Harry Edwards and the Olympic Project for Human Rights in 1968, Shinnick, a lieutenant in the air force, was threatened with a court martial. He also had a chip on his shoulder from a five-year-old snafu that had cost him a world record.

At the 1963 Modesto Relays, Shinnick stunned Boston and the rest of the track world by jumping the incredible distance of 27-4. Shinnick's mark never received recognition as a world record, however, since there wasn't a wind gauge positioned along the long-jump runway. Boston and other eyewitnesses vouched for the jump's legality—a hurdles race run at the same time and in the same direction had a legal wind reading—but the experience left Shinnick embittered.

Midway through the Echo Summit final, Shinnick had a solid grip on third place at 26-6½. "You're on the team," Boston told him. But Mays responded in the fourth and fifth rounds with wind-aided jumps of 26-8 and 26-9¼. Shinnick fouled narrowly on a jump well beyond 27 feet and finished with a pair of 26-5¾ jumps—good, but not good enough.

Shinnick insists he was the victim of a conspiracy engineered by Payton Jordan and implemented by Mays. Neither Jordan nor Mays are alive to offer their sides of the story, but Shinnick said the US coach put his arm around Mays in the middle of the competition and offered some advice. As Shinnick ran down the runway for his next jump, Mays sprinted alongside him, just a couple of meters away.

"When I came out of the woods, he was right there, trying to spook me," Shinnick said. "I think the powers that be saw me as a white guy who was willing to speak out. I'm still stunned by the whole thing. It's very personal. I have this dream where a spider is racing down at me. Payton Jordan is the spider."

Shinnick says Jordan apologized to him many years later.

"That's what you get as an athlete—great highs and great lows," Shinnick said. "I'd never trade that tsunami for anything. Tahoe was a tidal wave coming from all directions. It created a bond. It's something you can't buy."

The long jump and the 400 meters were the only finals scheduled for September 14. Had the Nevada sports books established a betting line before the trials began on the event most likely to yield a world record, the favorite would have been the 400. Vince Matthews lowered the world record to 44.4 on August 31 in a tune-up meet. The hurdles record set by Geoff Vanderstock over the same distance only heightened expectations.

Larry James looked like his April self after having a Tahoe dentist correct some problems he had with his teeth. Ron Freeman beat Lee Evans in a pair of pretrials races, and Matthews was obviously in sensational form. But betting against Evans still looked like a fool's errand, given his knack for winning close races by the sheer force of his will.

Evans drew lane six for the final. Matthews was lined up directly to Evans's left in lane five. James drew the third lane. Rounding out the six-man field were Freeman in lane two, Jim Kemp in lane one, and Hal Francis in lane four. The temperature at the 3:50 PM start was a mild sixty-three degrees.

As Evans prepared to take his mark, he saw his coach, Bud Winter, gyrating his shoulders and arms just beyond the first curve. Winter was doing what his Speed City disciples called the "snake dance," a shimmy designed to keep them relaxed. Evans waved his arm to acknowledge receipt of the message.

Matthews tore through the first 200 meters in 20.7 seconds, making up the stagger on Evans. "When Matthews passed me, I told myself I'd better [get] going," said Evans, who passed the midway point in 21.1, the same split as James. The order changed dramatically as they vanished

Lee Evans (50) edging Larry James in their epic 400-meter showdown at Echo Summit. © *Don Chadez*

from view by the trees: James was in front entering the homestretch, trailed by Evans and the fading Matthews.

James, in the white jersey and navy shorts of Villanova, appeared to have the race won halfway up the final straight. But Evans, wearing the number 50 on his black jersey, dipped into his seemingly bottomless well of desire and overhauled James in the last few strides. The sound of cars on Highway 50 was inaudible through the cheering.

The fully automatic timing system clocked Evans in 44.06, rounded down to 44.0 in the official results. James was second in 44.19 (44.1), also far below the previous world record. Freeman finished fastest of all, claiming the third Olympic berth in 44.62 (44.6). Matthews was fourth in 44.86 (44.8).

The five finalists other than Matthews improved their personal bests by an average of six-tenths of a second. According to IAAF scoring tables that compare the relative value of marks across all of the Olympic events, Evans's 44.06 was superior to every other world record at the time.

"I haven't been this tired since I came up here," Evans said in a postrace interview. James admitted to "sort of giving up" in the last few strides. "I tightened up in the last 10 yards," he said. "I couldn't move."

Evans wore the same model of red Puma 68 shoes that Carlos wore in the 200-meter final two days earlier. The IAAF refused to ratify either mark as a world record. As a result, James received official credit for setting a world record in the 400 even though he lost the race. The fuss over brush spikes was largely forgotten when Evans and Tommie Smith took the records even lower at the Olympics in Mexico City, but the entire affair had more to do with the rivalry between Adidas and Puma than with any concerns about a level playing field. Horst Dassler, the son of Adidas founder Adi Dassler, refused to cede an inch of ground to his loathed brother Rudolf, the Puma chieftain.

"It was all politics," Evans said. "Horst Dassler had the shoes banned because he knew if he didn't, everyone would have worn them. Those brush spikes were nice. When you put your foot down, the track felt so easy."

The 400-meter men took the initiative in resolving another potential controversy at Echo Summit. Evans, James, Freeman, and Matthews knew that in 1964, the US Olympic staff had inserted Henry Carr, the 200-meter champion, into the 4 x 400 relay team in place of Theron Lewis, the fourth-place finisher in the 400 at the Olympic trials. Lewis left Tokyo without getting a chance to compete. The fear was that US sprint coach Stan Wright might make a similar move in 1968, substituting Tommie Smith for Matthews or Freeman. Smith had clocked what was then the fastest 400-meter split in history (43.6) on the US team that broke the three-minute barrier by clocking a world-record 2:59.6 in 1966. Evans, James, Freeman, and Matthews set up a meeting with Wright to gain assurance that there wouldn't be a repeat of 1964.

"It's nothing against Tommie personally," James told Wright. "It's just that the guys don't want any politics in this thing."

Wright told them not to worry, and the four rivals practiced their baton passes enthusiastically at Echo Summit following the trials. They even adopted their own chant: "We don't jive—2:55,"—the time they planned to run in Mexico City.

14

HIGHS AND LOWS

WITH ONE DAY to go, all but six of the Olympic berths available at Echo Summit had been filled. Nine other spots had been awarded in three separate races in Alamosa, Colorado: the marathon on August 18, and the 20- and 50-kilometer walks on September 7 and 10. The record-setting frenzy on the summit was over, consigned to history. But the eight men who clawed for the last six open seats on the flight to Mexico City gave Echo Summit the final-day send-off it deserved.

Fall was in the crisp air as fans disembarked from the shuttle buses in the early afternoon of September 16. The schedule consisted of just two finals—the high jump and the 1,500 meters—but both events had star power. The high jump featured Dick Fosbury, inventor of the newfangled Fosbury Flop. The 1,500 had Jim Ryun, the world-record holder. Neither Fosbury nor Ryun could be considered a lock, however.

After winning the Los Angeles trials and thinking he'd already booked passage to Mexico City, Fosbury competed in four meets, winning just one and never jumping higher than 6-10. He'd need to be much better than that to succeed at Echo Summit against a deep field of experienced straddle jumpers. Ed Caruthers and John Rambo were 1964 Olympians. Otis Burrell and John Hartfield finished the 1967 season ranked fourth and seventh in the world. And no one quite knew what to make of Reynaldo Brown, a seventeen-year-old neophyte with a string of 7-foot clearances.

Among the 1,500-meter finalists, Ryun possessed the best finishing kick, a lethal weapon in a slow-paced race. But he still felt out of sorts at altitude, and his debacle in the 800-meter final five days earlier did not engender confidence. In early June, when Ryun was sidelined by mononucleosis, *Sports Illustrated* put Dave Patrick on its cover with the headline "On the Heels of Jim Ryun." The national exposure hardly jinxed the Villanova senior: Patrick won the NCAA title in meet-record time and finished first in the Los Angeles trials. Tom Von Ruden and Marty Liquori had looked strong throughout the training camp. In fact, when the USOC offered to pay for the airfare of athletes who wanted to go home for a few days before the final trials began, Von Ruden instead went to Leadville, Colorado, where he trained at 10,000 feet above sea level.

They may have stood shoulder to shoulder on the starting line at 3:30 PM, but mentally speaking, Ryun's three main challengers were in much different places. Their states of mind influenced the final result—in two cases, favorably; in the other, ignominiously.

While Ryun, Patrick, and Liquori were all highly acclaimed high school runners, Von Ruden came from humbler roots. He attended high school in Notus, Idaho, population 324, where he played football and basketball and ran track, even though his school didn't have one. The nearest track was in Caldwell, eight miles away.

"I could have gone unnoticed in Idaho," Von Ruden said. "I played whatever sport was in the season. I was a skinny kid with braces. In football, I played halfback and safety, punted, kicked off. I won the mile at the state meet twice with a best of 4:35.9. I wouldn't have made any lists in Southern California."

The track coach at Caldwell, Ralph Tate, didn't care what the stopwatch said about the tall, wiry guy gliding smoothly and quickly across his track. Tate called Ralph Higgins, the track coach at Oklahoma State, and insisted that he offer Von Ruden a scholarship, sight unseen. Three years later, Von Ruden ran a leg on the Oklahoma State two-mile relay team that broke the world record. He finished second to Patrick in the 1966 NCAA outdoor mile and graduated with bests of 1:47.9 in the half-mile and 4:01.1 in the mile.

After college, Von Ruden enlisted in the army to further his running career. The arrangement worked out nicely in 1967, when he won the 1,500 meters at the Pan American Games and ranked fifth in the world.

But the plan went awry in 1968, leaving him a nervous wreck at Echo Summit.

"I had written orders to go to Vietnam," said Von Ruden, whose two-year commitment was set to expire in October 1968. "I'd wander off into the forest and ponder the possibilities. I knew going into the final that nobody wanted to finish in the top three more than me. I had to make the Olympic team. It was a life-and-death situation for me. It was either Mexico City or Vietnam. How's that for pressure?"

Dave Patrick was the latest in a long line of great Villanova milers. The greatest of them all was Ron Delany, an Irish import who won the 1,500 meters at the 1956 Olympics in Melbourne, Australia. Patrick was a promising underclassman when he sought out Delany for advice.

"Mr. Delany, how do you get ready for the big races?" Patrick asked.

"Dave, there's a fine line between being worried and being concerned," Delany replied. "If you're worried, you're not going to be ready. If you're concerned, you respect the competition and you'll do your best."

Patrick earned a place in the Villanova pantheon by winning practically every big race he entered. Despite being hampered early in the 1968 season by a fractured bone in his foot, Patrick got stronger as the Olympic season progressed. At the IC4A Championships in early June, he ran a personal-best 3:56.8 in the mile with a 54-second last lap. His wins in Berkeley and Los Angeles stamped him as Ryun's most serious challenger. The question in most minds wasn't how Patrick would perform at Echo Summit; it was whether he could win a medal in Mexico City.

But Patrick's mind wasn't where it needed to be following the vote to negate the Los Angeles results. Von Ruden sensed as much when he rode one of the shuttle buses with Patrick shortly after the vote was taken.

"Dave said he wished he hadn't given up his spot," Von Ruden said. "For him to say something like that . . . I felt it opened the door a little for me."

Marty Liquori turned nineteen five days before the 1,500-meter final. It would be easy to say he had the least to lose of all the finalists, but that wasn't how he thought, even at his tender age. Instead, he thought about all he had to gain. It didn't hurt that he was having the time of his life.

"I had a great time, up there, training hard in a beautiful environment," Liquori said. "Just seeing Jim Ryun on a day-to-day basis and finding out that he wasn't a very good ping-pong player. Getting to meet Danny Kaye, gambling in the casinos, almost getting thrown in jail for being underage.

"I remember that early in the camp, I couldn't sleep. I'd never had a beer in my life, but someone told me that if you can't sleep, drink a six-pack of beer before you go to bed. I guess that's when I started drinking."

Liquori's boyish insouciance masked the intensity he brought to his training. No one breaks four minutes in the mile at age seventeen without putting in the work, and with Villanova coach Jumbo Elliott largely absent from Echo Summit, Liquori followed the speed-oriented workouts provided by surrogate coach Pete Peterson. "Some adjusted to altitude training better than others," Liquori said. "I was able to adjust. I was strong as an ox up there."

At Essex Catholic High School in New Jersey, Liquori ran for Fred Dwyer, himself an outstanding miler at Villanova in the 1950s. That's the way it worked at Villanova: one great miler passing the torch to another. But there wasn't any rule about having to wait for your turn.

––––––––––

The last thing Jim Ryun wanted to see was a fast early pace. He needn't have worried. Ryun and Dave Wilborn led the field of eight finalists through a plodding first lap. The pace remained slow through 800 meters, reached in 2:13, a high-school pace. The real racing didn't start until the backstretch of the third lap, when Wilborn shot into the lead.

With 500 meters remaining, Ryun intentionally dropped to the back of the pack, giving him the space he needed to swing wide and launch his fabled kick. Liquori, running more aggressively than Patrick, pulled even with Wilborn as the bell sounded for the last lap. Patrick was third with 400 meters remaining. Von Ruden was eighth and last.

With one lap remaining in the 1,500-meter final, Villanova teammates Dave Patrick and Marty Liquori (100) are in good position. Dave Wilborn (right) leads, but Jim Ryun (far left) has swung wide to begin his finishing kick. *Don Chadez*

Ryun exploded down the backstretch, taking the lead and expanding it with each long, powerful stride. As the runners came into view off the final turn, renowned broadcaster Jim McKay, calling the race for *ABC's Wide World of Sports*, set the scene for a national television audience:

"Who will get second and third? Tom Von Ruden is moving up through the pack right now. He could do something. Ryun, sneaking a quick look as he leads into the homestretch. Liquori is second, Von Ruden is third now, and Patrick is way back. Patrick isn't going to make it!"

Ryun ran his last lap in a blazing 51.9 seconds, his final 800 in a sizzling 1:51.5. The winning time was 3:49.0. Liquori (3:49.5) and Von Ruden (3:49.8) left Patrick a well-beaten fourth in 3:52.0. Ryun's winning time in the final was slower than the 3:48.8 Patrick and Liquori ran in the previous day's semifinal.

Liquori squealed with joy after crossing the final line, finally acting his age. Patrick pounded his fists in frustration before the finish line.

Liquori wanted to console his teammate but couldn't find him. Patrick headed into the woods, alone.

He didn't realize it at the time, but when Patrick lined up for the 1,500-meter final, he was on the wrong side of Delany's sage advice about the difference between concern and worry.

"I remember being on the starting line and not feeling very confident," Patrick said. "I didn't really have a game plan. Entering the home straightaway, I remember wondering, Where is my kick? Where did it go? I remember a burning sensation in my thighs. What the hell is that?"

Ryun had packed his 1964 Plymouth before the final, eager to return to Kansas to be with his fiancée, Anne Snider. The sun was just beginning to drop below the tree line when Ryun headed east. Sixteen hours later he was in Manhattan, where Anne was a student at Kansas State. He figures he averaged close to one hundred miles per hour.

Dave Patrick and Bill Clark were the only Los Angeles winners who didn't place in the top three at Echo Summit. Clark was injured at Echo Summit and finished eighth in the final, two minutes behind the winner, Tracy Smith. Following the USOC's original statement that the winners at Los Angeles would be awarded Olympic spots provided they "maintain the same degree of excellence" at Echo Summit, Clark's omission from the US team made more sense than Patrick's. Patrick's semifinal time in the 1,500 meters was the fastest of the competition. On the other hand, Ryun, Von Ruden, and Liquori all advanced to the 1,500-meter final in Mexico City, making the United States the only country with three finalists. The top three from Echo Summit all acquitted themselves well in Mexico City. What Patrick might have done had he been able to train for another month with a clear head, no one knows.

"It is what it is," Patrick said. "I can forgive, but I can't forget."

———————

Even more so than the metric mile, the high jump was a four-man show—perhaps the best show of the entire Echo Summit run. At the very least, it was the most intimate. "It felt kind of tight with the trees around," Caruthers said. "You'd never seen anything like it, but it was beautiful."

Because the view from the grandstands was obstructed by trees, spectators were allowed on the infield to watch. "There was a rock that was probably seven or eight feet high, right in the middle of the trees," Fosbury said. "It was obviously natural, so they weren't going to move it. It would have taken a D8 to move that thing. During the competition, spectators sat on the rock to get an elevated view of the high jump."

Burrell, thought to be one of the leading contenders, failed to clear his opening height of 6-11. When Rambo and two others missed three times apiece at 7-0, four jumpers remained in the competition: Hartfield, Caruthers, Fosbury, and Brown. Those four all cleared 7-1 on their first attempts, Brown setting a lifetime best.

Pole-vaulter Casey Carrigan was the only athlete at Echo Summit younger than Brown, who wouldn't turn eighteen until December. Brown's family moved from Los Angeles to Compton when Reynaldo was a child. In a predominantly black community known for producing excellent athletes (and today, rappers), Brown stood out early. He high-jumped 6-5 in the ninth grade and excelled on the basketball court. When he won the California state title in 1966 as a Compton sophomore, Brown surprised the school's track coach, Willie Williams, with an audacious question.

"What would it take to make the Olympic team?" Brown inquired.

"Uh, that's going to be a tough journey," Williams replied.

"I'm ready for it," the fifteen-year-old said. "All I need is for you to show me what it takes to get there."

Seeing that Brown was serious, Williams said, "OK, let's start working."

Brown cleared 7 feet for the first time on April 20, 1968. He was a straight-leg straddler, meaning he didn't bend his lead leg when going over the bar as most straddlers did. Brown cleared 7 feet several more times that spring and summer but still wasn't viewed as a serious contender in such a competitive event.

"A lot of people doubted me because I was so young," Brown said. "I told them I was different."

Echo Summit was a new world to the inner-city kid. "Living in Compton, I'd never been out of the city," Brown said. "Tahoe was the farthest trip I'd ever made in my life. We lived in trailers. It was beautiful. I was an observer. I saw what the other high jumpers did and started to do what they were doing, except more. Whatever it took, I was going to do it."

The bar went up to 7-2. Hartfield maintained his lead by clearing on his first attempt, the highest jump of his life. Caruthers and Brown flew over on their second attempts. Fosbury missed his first two tries and was in serious trouble.

"I was not on top of my game," Fosbury said. "When the bar went to 7-2, I knew I needed to be clean. I wasn't. I didn't make it until my third jump. When we got to 7-3, I was in last place."

Fosbury was in fourth place, actually, but it might as well have been last, given the circumstances. With zero misses up to that point, Hartfield was in a commanding position. Nobody in the field had ever cleared 7-3. It was practically inconceivable that his three challengers would all make a height that only five men in history had cleared. "If you were watching that competition, you'd be thinking there's no way John Hartfield wouldn't be on the team," Caruthers said.

Hartfield was a twenty-three-year-old graduate of Texas Southern University, where his coach was Stan Wright, the 1968 US Olympic assistant. Wright had recruited him out of Denver, where the muscular 6-foot-3, 175-pound Hartfield starred in football and basketball as well as the high jump. His teammate at Texas Southern, record-setting sprinter Jim Hines, remembered a time when they were walking across the football field after track practice. Hartfield asked the ball boy for a football, which he proceeded to punt seventy-five yards on the fly.

Hartfield was married to Wright's daughter, Toni, who was five months pregnant when her husband stood on the brink of realizing their dream.

"We knew we were going to Mexico City," Toni Hartfield said. "My only question was whether my doctor would let me go if John qualified."

At 7-3, Caruthers was up first in the jumping order. He grazed the bar but it stayed upright. Next up was Brown, who stunned everyone but himself by making it. "Here's a guy who should be at home starting his senior year in high school, and he's clearing 7-3 at the Olympic trials," Caruthers said. "Crazy."

Hartfield narrowly missed his first attempt at 7-3. Fosbury, batting cleanup, soared over the bar with room to spare. "I had a fantastic jump," Fosbury said. "I killed it. I'm celebrating, I bounce out of the pit . . . and then Dear Old Coach asked the officials to measure the bar."

Dear Old Coach was Berny Wagner, who intruded on the proceedings by informing the high jump officials that Fosbury's jump was an

Dick Fosbury clearing the bar in the high jump final at Echo Summit. *Courtesy of Track & Field News*

Oregon State school record. As such, it needed a second measurement, at least according to Wagner. The officials brought out a ladder and tape.

Hartfield, meanwhile, was going through his prejump routine, bending over, looking at the ground in deep concentration. As Hartfield raised his head and prepared to take his second attempt, he saw the ladder and a bunch of officials blocking his path.

"He doesn't know what was going on," Fosbury said. "He has to wait. He's rattled."

Wagner's request for a measurement took several minutes to complete. His concentration broken, Hartfield missed his last two attempts.

"His last attempt, I'll never forget it," Fosbury said. "It wasn't a bad attempt, but he brought down the bar, rolled off the back of the pit, and ran off into the woods. I didn't see him again for twenty-plus years."

Fosbury neglected to mention one of the more wrenching parts of the story. Ralph Boston completes the tale. "That's one moment I remember so clearly," Boston said. "Hartfield missing that third attempt, disappearing into the woods, his pregnant wife running after him."

Hartfield died of cancer in 2012 following a distinguished career as a teacher, coach, and record-setting masters athlete in the Houston area. His widow confirmed her inadvertent role in one of the most heart-wrenching moments at Echo Summit.

"I remember being disappointed, of course," Toni Hartfield said. "He was leading, and then they stopped to do the measurement with Fosbury. John was really upset, but he got over it pretty quickly. We had to get back to real life."

Was Wagner's call for a measurement in the middle of a fraught competition legitimate, or was it underhanded gamesmanship?

"I don't think so," Fosbury said. "Berny was a stickler for the rules. Berny honestly wanted to make sure my jump was a school record and an all-time collegiate record. I don't think he was trying to break anyone's rhythm."

Dwight Stones, Fosbury's successor as the king of the floppers, was a high school sophomore in the fall of 1968, which means he was nowhere near Echo Summit. But he jumped against Wagner's athletes in the 1970s and is familiar with the story. Wagner died in 2013.

"That was no accident," Stones said. "Berny was a bastard, God rest his soul."

Since Caruthers, Brown, and Fosbury all cleared 7-3 on their first attempts, the final results were determined on the basis of who had the fewest misses throughout the entire competition. Caruthers was first, Brown second, and Fosbury third. Hartfield was fourth. No man had ever cleared 7-2 and finished worse than second in a high jump competition until September 16, 1968.

"That was my exposure to the intensity of US trials," Fosbury said. "In many ways, it's more intense than the Olympic Games."

There was one more mountain to climb, and it wouldn't be as pretty or peaceful as the first one.

15

INTERLUDE

PEACE AND QUIET didn't suddenly break out while US Olympic hopefuls slept soundly at their alpine retreat. The ancient Greeks suspended their wars for the Olympics, but 1968 afforded no such pause.

In the two months of altitude training and competition at Echo Summit, more than one thousand US soldiers lost their lives in Vietnam. Police and protesters clashed violently on the Chicago streets outside the Democratic National Convention. Soviet tanks crushed Czechoslovakia's quixotic quest to give socialism a human face. Feminists disrupted the Miss America Pageant in early September by tossing bras in the trash and crowning a sheep. Mexican students launched street demonstrations that grew in frequency and intensity as the Olympics drew closer.

The Republican presidential nominee, Richard Nixon, turned the counterculture's peace sign into a symbol for victory in the Vietnam War. In accepting his party's nomination on August 8 in Miami, Nixon presented an apocalyptic vision of the 1968 landscape. "As we look at America, we see cities enveloped in smoke and flame," he said. "We hear sirens in the night. We see Americans dying on distant battlefields abroad. We see Americans hating each other; fighting each other; killing each other at home." Nixon called on the "forgotten Americans, the non-shouters, the non-demonstrators," to rally around the flag.

In those days there were no tablets, laptops, cell phones, or Twitter accounts, not at Echo Summit or anywhere else. (Even today, cell phone coverage at Echo Summit is hit-and-miss.) For two months, Bill Toomey and his colleagues might as well have been residing on a different planet.

"Now everyone remembers the Vietnam War and everything else that was going on in 1968, but we were removed from that when we were up at Tahoe," Toomey said. "There was a real positive feeling up there.

It was the calm before the storm. When we left, that ended the tranquil part of the journey."

———————

Some of the newly minted Olympians left the summit before reassembling in Denver for team processing. Bob Seagren drove home to Southern California along with Geoff Vanderstock. "We were riding pretty high," Seagren said. "We both made the team and broke the world record." Jay Silvester drove an hour east to Reno, where he took advantage of a strong quartering wind to throw the discus 224 feet, 5 inches—6 feet beyond the world record he'd set in the spring. He couldn't have headed into his Olympic meeting with Al Oerter feeling more confident.

Many of the Olympic qualifiers took the opportunity to stay at Echo Summit for another week or two to decompress and continue breathing the thin air. US assistant coach Stan Wright encouraged the sprinters to stick around and practice the baton passes so crucial to relay success. Just as Wright assured the top four finishers in the Echo Summit 400—Lee Evans, Larry James, Ron Freeman, and Vince Matthews—that their spots on the 4 x 400 relay team were secure, he told the top four in the 100 meters the same thing with respect to the sprint relay. The US 4 x 100 relay in Mexico City would consist of Charlie Greene, Mel Pender, Ronnie Ray Smith, and Jim Hines. While the Americans were seen as a lock for the gold medal in the 4 x 400 relay, the margin for error in the 4 x 100 was narrower. Teams from Jamaica, Cuba, and France all had enough speed to give the US foursome a run for its money, especially if the Americans botched any of their handoffs.

Both relay teams took test runs on September 28 at a meet in Victoria, British Columbia. A capacity crowd of five thousand turned out for a four-nation meet involving about one-third of the US Olympic men's team along with athletes from Jamaica, Canada, and Trinidad and Tobago. Evans anchored the 4 x 400 team to a comfortable win, but what happened in the short relay put the US coaching staff in the hot seat—and led to an extraordinary final footrace on the track in the forest.

Stan Wright entered two US sprint relay teams in the Canadian tune-up—the Olympic unit of Greene, Pender, Ronnie Ray Smith, and Hines, and a "B" team consisting of Charlie Mays, Larry Questad, John Carlos, and Tommie Smith. To Wright's dismay, the "B" team won in 39.1 seconds, the same time as the A team, but a stunning result nonetheless. When Wright walked into a postmeet party that evening, Carlos, Questad, and Mays greeted the coach with shouts of "We're going to Mexico City!"

Wright immediately called his boss, Payton Jordan, the US head coach, in South Lake Tahoe. "I feel like an ass," Wright told Jordan. They decided to schedule a runoff for the following Wednesday at Echo Summit. Wright requested ten accredited timers to make everything official, and he beseeched Jordan not to let the media know about any of it.

Eight of the world's fastest men gathered for one final shoot-out at the Echo corral. Hurdler Willie Davenport was one of the few spectators, lending vocal support to the "B" team. Wright's timers took their positions at the finish line. John Carlos broke the quiet with his usual hoarse-voiced jive, most of it directed at an unusually quiet Charlie Greene. Still upset over the "B" team's grandstanding in British Columbia, Mel Pender seethed.

"Even if they had beaten us, I don't think Stan would have replaced us," Pender said. "I really don't. But it didn't matter, because we kicked their ass. Kicked it good."

Indeed, the "A" team led the runoff from the gun to the finish line, winning by about three meters. Their time was a shocking 38.4, six-tenths of a second faster than the official world record. The time wouldn't be submitted for record consideration, but it's fair to say six world records were bettered at Echo Summit—four during the trials, the 400 mark set by Vince Matthews set in a pretrials race, and the relay runoff.

The "B" team, second in 38.8, also faster than the world record, accepted the result with surprising grace. The sprinters exchanged hugs while Wright breathed a mountainous sigh of relief. He and Jordan were almost as happy with the "B" team's response as they were with the "A" team's resounding win. The coaches nodded at the realization they were thinking the same thing.

This really is a team we're taking to Mexico City.

Stan Wright, the same coach who'd been labeled an Uncle Tom by Harry Edwards during the height of the boycott madness, gained further respect from the black athletes by taking a last-minute stand against IOC president Avery Brundage.

Speaking at the National Press Club in Washington, DC, Brundage said, "I don't think any of those boys will be foolish enough to demonstrate at the Olympics. I think if they do they will be properly be sent home. This is permanent Olympic policy."

The "boys" weren't pleased. Twenty-one black athletes signed a petition demanding Brundage's removal as IOC president. Asked to comment on Brundage's remarks, Wright said, "It appears Mr. Brundage is inciting some sort of action with these statements." Behind the scenes, the USOC arranged a conference call with Brundage and the US coaching staff. Wright told the IOC chieftain that the US athletes, black and white, took great exception to his remarks. Brundage denied that they were directed at any particular group and apologized if any offense was taken. Brundage's waffling didn't change how Wright and the black athletes felt about him, but the apology dampened any rekindling of the boycott talk.

The US Olympic men's track and field team gathered in Denver in early October for the last stop on the journey to Mexico City.

"When we went to the airport in Reno, there was a gloominess, a sadness," Toomey said. "We knew we were leaving this hallowed ground." Ed Caruthers felt as though they'd already had their Olympics. "I was sad to leave," he said. "It was a special place."

Members of the US women's track team were in Denver as well. "We were all checking each other out," Norm Tate said. The men and women were issued uniforms and the outfits they'd wear in the opening ceremonies on October 12. Randy Matson had filled out a form earlier in the year requesting a size 52 extra-long coat. In Denver, he was issued a 52 regular. "We were always the poorest-outfitted team at the Olympics," Matson said.

The black athletes held a lengthy meeting in Denver to determine what course of action they'd take in Mexico City. Ralph Boston was asked to chair the proceeding. It quickly became apparent that a boycott was out of the question, and the talk ranged from the serious to the absurd. Someone suggested that they paint their shoes black to show fealty to the cause. The idea went nowhere. "We couldn't dye our shoes black, because then we wouldn't get our money from the shoe companies," Evans said. How about everyone wearing black socks? Triple jumper Art Walker said they made his feet sweat. Black armbands? Mel Pender said that would cut off circulation in his bulging biceps.

"Every time a reasonable type of protest came up, there were always dissenters," Tate said. "It was eventually decided that if you get up on the medal stand, do your own thing." Evans did come up with one suggestion that met with widespread approval: if Avery Brundage awards the medals for your event, show your disapproval by wearing black gloves for the traditional handshake.

Tommie Smith did more listening than talking. "In Denver, each athlete gave his reasons for not wanting to boycott," Smith recalled. "I respected their opinions. We decided to go and do what we felt we should do individually. I never considered the boycott a hoax. To me, it was real. But it needed to have the backing of the rest of the black athletes. You can't do it alone. That's suicide."

S. T. Saffold, Smith's best friend from San Jose State, was in Denver the same time as his college roommate. Saffold was a wide receiver for the Cincinnati Bengals, who were playing the Broncos that weekend at Mile High Stadium. Saffold was drafted by the San Diego Chargers in 1967 but left the team and returned to San Jose State. In the spring of 1968 he received a call from Bengals assistant Bill Walsh, who with legendary coach Paul Brown was developing the "West Coast offense" that Walsh later immortalized while winning three Super Bowl championships with the San Francisco 49ers. Walsh, a San Jose State graduate, was intrigued by Saffold's athleticism. Saffold had played one season of college football after his basketball eligibility expired in 1966.

The Bengals were staying at the same Denver hotel as the Olympians. During a one-hour break between meetings, Saffold got together with Smith, whom he hadn't seen in quite some time.

"It was very interesting to see how politically involved Tommie had become," Saffold said. "The assassinations of Martin Luther King and Bobby Kennedy affected him greatly. He said something to the effect of, 'I don't know what I'm going to do in Mexico City.' The Olympics are a dream for track and field athletes, and the shelf life for the world's fastest man is a year or two at most. He had some misgivings about whether he even wanted to qualify.

"When we talked in Denver, he wasn't sure what he needed to do, but he sounded pretty confident that he'd use that platform to make a statement. I observed a real serious sense of responsibility on Tommie's part. It was almost a burden."

––––––

Mexican president Gustavo Díaz Ordaz would have had to be blind not to see the massive demonstrations spreading across borders and oceans like a virus in 1968. Polish students were clubbed on the streets of Warsaw. Thousands of West Germans marched to protest the release of a Nazi judge who had sentenced hundreds of people to death during World War II. Columbia students occupied university buildings in New York City. The largest demonstrations occurred in France, where students and workers nearly toppled Charles de Gaulle's government. Czech students were active in the Prague Spring that led to Soviet tanks in August.

The student movement was international in scope, and Mexico wasn't immune to its grip. When he wasn't fingering Communists for blame as tensions mounted, Díaz Ordaz suspected an infiltration of dissidents from the United States, France, and West Germany. The Mexican government had invested more than $150 million in the Olympics—roughly $1 billion in today's dollars—and Díaz Ordaz wasn't about to let a horde of dissatisfied students disrupt his nation's big parade.

Five decades on, historians are still trying to piece together exactly what happened on the evening of October 2 in the Plaza de las Tres

Culturas in the Tlatelolco section of Mexico City. A crowd of ten thousand—mostly students, but also encompassing parents, women, children, and the elderly—assembled to hear speakers talk about civil liberties and the need to remain strong against government oppression.

The plaza was surrounded by thousands of troops. The Olimpia Battalion, organized and trained to provide security at the Olympic Games, accessed surrounding rooftops and balconies. Members of this unit were distinguishable by their white gloves. Shortly after 6:00 PM, two helicopters buzzed the protesters, firing off flares. The Olimpia Battalion opened fire from the balconies. With the exits closed off by troops, panicked students trampled one another. The killing went on for an hour, subsided, then resumed. The government-controlled media reported thirty-eight dead, including four soldiers, and put the blame on students who allegedly fired first. Independent studies later estimated the number of dead at three hundred. Thousands more were arrested and detained.

Athletes from around the world were arriving in Mexico City while the bloodstains on the plaza were still fresh. Matson remembered being spooked by the sight of soldiers holding machine guns at the airport when he landed.

"We'd heard there had been student riots and protests," Matson said. "There was even talk that the Olympics would be canceled. We were pretty selfish about it. We were concerned that the Olympics would be canceled. We didn't really understand what was going on."

Brundage arrived in Mexico three days before the Tlatelolco massacre. After meeting with Pedro Ramírez Vázquez of the Mexican organizing committee, Brundage assured Matson and everyone else that the Games would go on.

"The Games of the 19th Olympiad, a friendly gathering of the youth of the world in amicable competition, will proceed as scheduled," Brundage said. "We have conferred with the Mexican authorities and we have been assured that nothing will interfere with the peaceful entrance of the Olympic flame into the stadium . . . nor with the competitions which follow."

Once he got a look at the dilapidated housing surrounding the Olympic Village, Al Oerter understood the Mexican students' frustration.

"I thought the demonstrations were well founded," Oerter said. "No more than two hundred meters outside the stadium were shacks with corrugated roofs. It was like the Mexican government gave them a gallon of paint and told them to fix them up. Here was this wonderful stadium, and there was abject poverty just around the corner."

Ralph Boston heard when he arrived in Mexico City that the government had dumped the slain students' bodies in the ocean. "King, Kennedy, Russian tanks in Prague, now people were getting killed in Mexico City," Boston said. "What a tough, strange time."

16

MEXICO CITY

THE TLATELOLCO MASSACRE immediately became known as *La Noche Triste*, or Night of Sorrow. Ten days later, Janice Romary carried the US flag into Estadio Olímpico during the opening ceremonies of the XIX Olympiad. Romary, a six-time Olympian in fencing, was the first US woman accorded the honor. She was also an eleventh-hour substitute. The honor was originally given to hammer thrower Harold Connolly, who, in keeping with the rebellious spirit of 1968, declined.

Parry O'Brien carried the US flag at the opening of the Tokyo Olympics in 1964 and raved about the experience to Connolly. The two-time Olympic shot put champion noted that his picture appeared on the front page of newspapers nationwide, and that the exposure helped his business interests back home. In initially accepting the USOC's offer, Connolly was swayed by the feelings he experienced at the 1956 Olympics, when he watched the US flag raised and heard "The Star Spangled Banner" ringing across Melbourne Cricket Ground in honor of his gold-medal performance.

But the twelve years since Melbourne had soured Connolly on the way his sport was run. He remembered how track officials had ignored his request for combining the men's and women's trials at one site. Mostly, he resented the expectation that he'd blindly follow a tradition he considered silly—that the US flag bearer refuse to dip the flag when passing the host nation's head of state. When he started the tradition at the 1908 Olympics in London, Ralph Rose allegedly said, "This flag dips for no earthly king." At the 1936 Olympics in Berlin, when German-born gymnast Al Jochim refused to dip the Stars and Stripes as he paraded past Adolf Hitler, the practice was carved in stone. To dip the flag was un-American.

"I knew the history of the thing," Connolly said. "It isn't right that we walk in and we're the only country that refuses to make a gesture of respect. It bothered me. I refused to be a party to it. They told me that if I dipped the flag, I'd be arrested and sent home."

Janice Romary continued the tradition initiated sixty years earlier by a shot-putter twice her size. She did not dip the flag when leading her US teammates past Díaz Ordaz. Neither has any subsequent US flag bearer at the Winter or Summer Olympics.

Sleeping conditions in the Olympic Village made some of the US Olympians long for the trailers of Echo Summit. The concept of an Olympic Village originated with the 1932 games in Los Angeles, where local organizers felt they needed to offer affordable housing to convince other nations to make the long trip to Southern California during the height of a worldwide depression. Los Angeles organizers built a mini-city in neighboring Baldwin Hills that received glowing reviews.

The concrete high-rises of Mexico City's Olympic Village continued the practice of bringing the world's athletes together. Too closely together, in Jay Silvester's view. Already tense about his looming discus showdown with Al Oerter, Silvester complained to US coach Payton Jordan about the noise some of the black athletes were making with their boom boxes and late-night parties. Silvester asked to be moved to quieter quarters. "It was wearing me down," Silvester said. "I pleaded with Payton to give me another place. He said, 'Sorry, Jay, I can't do it. We'd be accused of segregation.'"

Shot put favorite Randy Matson slept in one room with fellow throwers Dave Maggard and Ed Burke, where their beds practically bumped up against one another. Matson had sleeping issues, but his bigger problem was getting going in the morning. "Maggard and I were big coffee drinkers, and we were told that caffeine is illegal, that it was one of the drugs they were testing for," Matson said. "We quit drinking coffee."

The younger Olympians tend to find the hectic atmosphere more agreeable than their older counterparts. Such was the case for Reynaldo

Brown, the seventeen-year-old high jumper. "It was exciting to meet the Soviet athletes because of all the talk about the US versus Russia," Brown said. "I wanted to see what these people were really all about. It was like a happy homecoming. Everyone had a smile on their face."

Bob Seagren also found the atmosphere in Mexico City festive and welcoming. "I think Mexico City was the last of the free and open Olympics," Seagren said. "My parents literally walked into the Olympic Village every day. If you were out on the street in a warm-up suit and put up your thumb to hitchhike, there was almost a traffic jam to see who could pick you up first."

The first final on the Olympic schedule was the men's 10,000 meters. African runners who had lived and trained at altitude their entire lives swept the medals. Kenyan Naftali Temu, looking fresh as a daisy, outsprinted Mamo Wolde of Ethiopia for the gold medal. Ron Clarke, the world-record holder from Australia, was unconscious for ten minutes after wheezing across the finish line in sixth place. The top American, Tracy Smith, was eleventh. The juxtaposed images of Temu heading straight into a spirited victory lap and Clarke flat on his back with an oxygen mask strapped to his face prompted a new wave of denunciations about the fairness of holding the Olympics at high altitude. Chris Brasher, the gold medalist in the steeplechase at the 1956 Olympics, wrote in the London *Observer*, "I feel like throttling the whole of the IOC."

The US gold rush started the day after Temu's victory, when Matson and George Woods finished first and second in the shot put.

Montezuma's revenge likely thwarted an American sweep of the medals: Matson's good friend and fast-closing rival, Dave Maggard, contracted turista on the morning of the qualifying round and lost twelve pounds in the next twenty-four hours. Maggard finished fifth in the final, three and a half feet behind Matson's winning throw of 67 feet, 4¾ inches.

"Dave had really bad luck," Matson said. "If he'd been healthy that day, I'd have had to throw farther than I did to win."

As Matson's experience illustrated, the IOC's first foray into drug testing was inauspicious, to put it generously. Just one athlete in Mexico City was disqualified, and not for steroids or amphetamines but for alcohol. Hans-Gunnar Liljenwall, a Swedish entrant in the modern pentathlon, admitted afterward to drinking a few beers to calm his nerves before the pistol-shooting portion of his event. The Swedish team had to return their bronze medals. Matson waited around after the shot put to be told where to report. No one showed up, so he went back to the Olympic Village.

"Two days later, we got a message—take a drug test," Matson recalled. "I'd been drinking coffee and taking sleeping pills since my event ended. I never took it."

Gender testing also took place in Mexico City for the first time in Olympic history. The International Amateur Athletic Federation (IAAF), the governing body for track and field, had instituted compulsory gender testing two years earlier, likely a factor in the sudden retirements of the Soviet Union's top female athletes, Tamara and Irina Press. Polish sprinter Ewa Klobukowska, a double medalist at the Tokyo Olympics, failed a chromosome test in 1967. In Mexico City, eight hundred female athletes submitted to buccal scrapings, where tissue taken from the inner cheek is examined to determine the athlete's chromosomal pattern. Two of the tests required clarification before officials cleared both athletes as women.

Sprinter Jarvis Scott and her US teammates treated the sex tests as a joke. "They called you in and did what they needed to do," Scott said. "We'd come out of the room and say, 'I'm a man, I can't participate.' It was funny, but not funny."

The orgy of record breaking in the sprints and jumps began an hour after Matson's ho-hum win in the shot. All eight finalists in the men's 100 meters were black, an Olympic first, including three Americans: Jim Hines, Charlie Greene, and Mel Pender. Hines had equaled the Olympic record of 10.0 in the semifinals despite getting a poor start, so he looked like the man to beat. In the final later that evening, Pender's blinding start gave him an early lead. But Hines summoned another great finish and streaked across the finish line in 9.95 seconds, the first sub-10 electronic clocking in history. Jamaica's Lennox Miller edged Greene for the silver medal, 10.04 to 10.07. Pender went from second place to sixth in the final 20 meters.

Hines had said before the Games that he'd wear a glove if he were forced to shake Brundage's hand during the medal presentation. Brundage wisely refrained from presenting any medals in men's track and field. Hines accepted his gold medal without incident from Lord David Burghley, president of the IAAF and the 1928 Olympic champion in the intermediate hurdles. Burghley's character was dramatized in the Oscar-winning movie *Chariots of Fire*. The actor playing a fictionalized version of Burghley in the film places champagne glasses on the hurdles as a device to keep him from touching them in practice. Not true, said Burghley's daughter, Lady Victoria Leatham. "He was never one to waste champagne," she said.

––––––––––

The discus showdown between Silvester and Oerter figured to be one of the highlights of the Games. Silvester led the qualifying with a throw of 207 feet, 9½ inches, smashing Oerter's Olympic record by nearly 8 feet. But the slate was washed clean the following day, both by the rules—qualifying marks don't carry over to final—and by a deluge of cold rain from the leaden Mexican sky.

Even before the rain wreaked havoc on Silvester's psyche, Oerter's peers knew better than to ever bet against him in an Olympic final.

"As we watched Oerter go through the whole training situation, there was never any doubt in our minds who was going to win," Maggard said. "I've never seen a better competitor in my lifetime." Connolly echoed Maggard's comments. "There's a magic about him when he's competing," Connolly said. "He's nervous before the meet. He doesn't eat well and his hands shake. But once the event is about to start, a calmness settles over him. The other athletes see it, and it intimidates them."

The officials asked the discus finalists if they'd like to delay the start an hour to let the rain pass. They voted yes and retreated to a room beneath the stands. Oerter remained on the field, continuing with his practice throws. "I was throwing very well in the rain," Oerter said. He also understood the effect his obliviousness would have on the others. "Even if they're not looking at you, they're watching."

Changing into a dry uniform did nothing for Silvester's nerves. "I just laid in that room and melted into the training table," he said. "I was nervous and exhausted. When we came back out, the discus felt like it weighed ten pounds. I had no snap. I was flat as a pancake. I didn't handle it well."

Oerter exceeded his lifetime best on three of his six throws, reaching 212-6½ in the third round to reclaim his Olympic record and become the first track athlete to win four consecutive gold medals. Silvester fouled half his throws and wound up fifth at 202-8, the lowest moment in his career.

"It was the easiest Olympic competition of my career," Oerter said. "I certainly didn't expect that."

———

Press reports back home noted that Oerter and Wyomia Tyus, in the women's 100 meters, were the only US winners on the third day of the track program, as if that constituted a debacle. That story line ignored what the American men were up against in the 800 meters and the 400-meter hurdles—a pair of British Commonwealth subjects in record-setting form. Dave Hemery of Great Britain cleaved seven-tenths of a second off Geoff Vanderstock's month-old record in the 400 hurdles, and Ralph Doubell of Australia matched the world record in winning the 800.

Hemery had beaten Vanderstock at the NCAA meet in June, so his win wasn't a big surprise. It was the manner in which the British-born, US-trained hurdler annihilated the field on a rain-soaked track that left statisticians slack-jawed. Hemery hit the halfway point in 23 seconds and maintained his overwhelming lead in the homestretch, clocking 48.12. Vanderstock was second coming off the final hurdle but was nipped at the line by a German and an Englishman, missing a medal by 0.04 seconds.

"My best friend literally went from second to fourth in one step at the finish," Seagren said. "My heart died for the guy."

The race for gold in the 800 meters was a two-man battle between Doubell and Wilson Kiprugut of Kenya. Doubell's superior kick brought him home in 1:44.3, two-tenths in front of Kiprugut. Though Tom Farrell claimed the bronze for the United States in a lifetime-best 1:45.4, he wasn't happy with his performance. "I think I did too much training at Tahoe," Farrell said. "Looking back on it, I think I needed a coach. I didn't talk to Bill Bowerman; he was coaching Wade Bell and other guys. I talked to Payton [Jordan], a good friend, but I basically coached myself."

Bell's chances for a medal in the 800 were ruined by a gastrointestinal ailment he picked up on his second day in Mexico City. Bowerman went to his grave believing Bell was ready to run 1:43 and win the gold medal. A severely weakened Bell couldn't make it past the first-round heats. "I lost seven pounds in three days and had no strength at all," Bell said. "I always say I left my heart in Mexico City."

The Olympic program in men's track and field consisted of twenty-four events. In 1968 there were just twelve women's events, and media coverage of the US women's team in Mexico City was a fraction of that accorded to the men. No one got shafted more than Wyomia Tyus. Her victory on the evening of October 15 made her the first sprinter, male or female, to successfully defend an Olympic championship in the 100 meters. Tyus, a product of Ed Temple's Tennessee State dynasty, put an exclamation point on her historic Mexico City win with a world-record clocking of 11.08. When she had returned home to Georgia following her first Olympic win in Tokyo, the city of Atlanta had thrown a parade for her that abruptly stopped when it reached the white neighborhoods. She came to Mexico City harboring no illusions about suddenly receiving equal treatment.

"Coach Temple prepared us for whatever we might run into, especially being black women from the South and not getting recognition," Tyus later said. "I always say pioneers are the last ones to get recognized. And that's OK, because you know you've had a place in history and you've done what you could do."

———————

Harry Edwards didn't go to Mexico City. The founder of the Olympic Project for Human Rights received sharp criticism for not seeing the movement he'd started through to its completion. But a year of death threats and surveillance from the FBI had left Edwards more than a little gun-shy. Instead, his confidant, Louis Lomax, arranged for him to attend a black writers' conference in Montreal, Canada, beyond the clutches of US law-enforcement authorities.

"Louis Lomax pointed out that if I went to Mexico City and any of the athletes suffered the same fate as the Mexican students, it would be on me," Edwards said. "I thought Louis was being overly cautious, but people forget that was a dangerous time, 1968. There'd been lots of deaths in the civil rights movement, oftentimes with the participation of local police forces. People thought we were being paranoid, and maybe we were. But we weren't wrong to be."

As S. T. Saffold had picked up from their conversation a few weeks earlier in Denver, Tommie Smith felt he had no choice but to do something dramatic in Mexico City. First, though, he had to win the 200-meter final on October 16, which meant reversing the order of his Echo Summit loss to Carlos. "I could not lose," Smith said.

Smith tied the Olympic record of 20.3 in winning his first-round heat on the morning of October 15. Peter Norman, an obscure Australian who arrived in Mexico City with a best of 20.5, won his heat in 20.2. Smith matched Norman's hours-old Olympic record that afternoon in the quarterfinals. Carlos cruised into the semifinals with a pair of easy wins. After one of the qualifying races, Smith and Carlos briefly talked about making some sort of protest on the victory stand. The understanding seemed almost telepathic. Smith had already asked his wife, Denise, to buy a pair of black gloves.

Sixteen sprinters advanced to the semifinals scheduled for the next afternoon. Carlos won the first semifinal in 20.1, bringing the Olympic record down another notch. Smith matched Carlos's time in the second semifinal, but in slowing down near the finish, he injured his left adductor muscle. Ice bags were applied to Smith's groin as he lay flat on his back underneath the stadium. Eighty thousand spectators were filling the seats above, excited about an evening schedule that featured finals in the 200 meters, 3,000-meter steeplechase, pole vault, triple jump, and javelin.

With the start of the 6:00 PM final just forty minutes away, Smith tried jogging. Not bad, he thought. He accelerated to 60 percent of his top speed and felt OK. He reminded himself that he didn't feel anything close to 100 percent before the Echo Summit final and still managed to qualify for the Olympic team. Still, he wasn't certain how the leg would hold up under the stress of an Olympic final.

"I really didn't know whether I could run the final until a few minutes before," Smith said. "I didn't know whether I could pull the throttle."

Smith drew lane three for the final. Carlos was immediately to his right in lane four. When the gun went off, Carlos exploded around the curve, opening a lead of about 3 meters. Smith, cutting into the lead with each of his nine-and-a-half-foot strides, blew past Carlos with an unrivaled burst of speed down the homestretch. Despite throwing his arms out wide in celebration and coasting the final 15 meters, Smith crossed the line in an electronically timed 19.83 seconds.

In turning to watch Smith blow past on his left, Carlos ignored Norman two lanes to his right. The white Australian edged Carlos for the silver medal, 20.06 to 20.10. Smith's record stood untouched for a month short of eleven years.

"When I got under the stands to congratulate them, things felt very strange," Stan Wright said. "A gut feeling told me something was going to happen, and I didn't know what the hell it was."

The image of Smith smiling euphorically as he crossed the line—a picture of joy—is superseded by the somber image of two black Americans bowing their heads and raising gloved fists during the playing of their national anthem on the medal stand. Smith's right arm was ramrod straight. Carlos's team jacket was unzipped, his left arm bent. Smith had a black scarf around his neck, Carlos a set of beads his wife gave him. The Americans placed one Puma shoe on the stand next to their stockinged

Tommie Smith (center) and John Carlos (right) on the victory stand in Mexico City. The silver medalist, Peter Norman (left) of Australia, wore an Olympic Project for Human Rights button to signal his support for the American sprinters. *AP Images*

feet. Norman showed his solidarity by wearing an Olympic Project for Human Rights button.

"I'm one of the most patriotic people around," Smith said. "I was telling the truth about an issue. It might have made me unpopular, but it wasn't wrong. I can't sing. I can't dance. The only thing left is silence. One of the most prominent landmarks in the United States is the Statue of Liberty. If you look at my victory stand, you'll see a lot of similarities."

The smattering of boos heard during the playing of the anthem became a cavalcade when Smith and Carlos raised their fists in defiance as they exited the field with their medals. But the real blowback came the following day, when the IOC threatened to send the entire US team home unless the USOC took decisive action against Smith and Carlos and anyone else who intended to follow suit.

Worried about how the black athletes would react when they learned of the imminent decision to expel Smith and Carlos from the Olympic Village and revoke their visas, USOC officials enlisted Jesse Owens to pacify the mutinous troops.

The meeting was a disaster. Owens started by asking Connolly and the handful of other white athletes in attendance to leave the room. Lee Evans and Vince Matthews loudly defended their right to stay. Owens, the sharecropper's son who'd won four gold medals at the Nazi Olympics in Berlin, issued familiar words about how politics have no place in the Olympics. "I was disappointed with Mr. Owens's worldview and tone in his scolding of Tommie Smith's and John Carlos's behavior," said US distance runner Jack Bacheler. The athletes left the meeting incensed. Owens left in tears.

When word got out the morning of October 18 that Smith and Carlos had been sent home, the anger grew. Triple jumper Art Walker called the expulsion ridiculous, asking how the USOC could justify not dipping the flag in the opening ceremonies but then turn around and condemn Smith and Carlos for making their own political statement. Ron Freeman said, "It's freedom of speech. I don't think what they did warranted them being expelled from the Olympic Games. I don't think they did anything wrong."

Overnight news reports didn't make a big deal of the protest, but when the IOC and USOC laid the hammer down the following day, press coverage turned against the sprinters. A young *Chicago American* columnist named Brent Musburger referred to Smith and Carlos as "black-skinned storm troopers." John Hall of the *Los Angeles Times* called their action "a discredit to their race—the human race." Arthur Daley of the *New York Times* was particularly critical of Carlos, who did in fact threaten some aggressive members of the media as he exited the Olympic Village. "When the ultrabelligerent Carlos stomped out of the Olympic Village yesterday, he was asked where he was going," Daley wrote. "'I'm going home,' he snapped, brushing interviewers out of his way. 'Do you mean the United States?' maliciously asked a bystander."

By reacting the way they did, the IOC and USOC leadership made the Smith-Carlos controversy far bigger than it would have been otherwise. But not all of their US teammates agreed with what the sprinters did.

"To me, they were two guys who were totally misled and used by Harry Edwards," said Larry Questad, the white sprinter who finished sixth in the 200 meters. "I considered them sprinters who also happened to be black. It's not like they had to go to the back of the bus."

Vanderstock felt Smith and Carlos should have voiced their feelings at a press conference, not on the awards stand. "Can't we just have a track meet here?" Vanderstock asked. "Look at what happened afterward: Munich, boycott; Montreal, boycott; Moscow, boycott; Los Angeles, boycott. All because of politics."

Oerter said he might have done the same thing had he been subjected to the racism Smith and Carlos faced in their daily lives. At the same time, the discus great felt they sacrificed something special.

"The medal ceremony is something that sticks with you forever," Oerter said. "I thought they missed out, so I felt for Tommie and John."

The man caught between a rock and a hard place was Evans, who was scheduled to run in the final of the 400 meters the evening of his teammates' expulsion. On their way out of town, Carlos and Smith met with their Speed City comrade, urging him to run. "It was heavy on my back," Evans said. "I was in shock. I feared for my life." On his way to the track for the most important race of his life, Evans got in a heated exchange with Douglas Roby, president of the USOC. The two had to be separated.

The start of the men's 400-meter final was delayed by a commotion around the long jump pit. Evans, Freeman, and Larry James were expected to sweep the medals. The big questions were, What effect would the Smith-Carlos affair have on Evans? Would the gold medalist take the world record below 44 seconds? And what sort of demonstration was planned for the awards ceremony?

Evans traded in the brush spikes he wore at Echo Summit for a conventional pair of Pumas. When the gun finally sounded, he tore down the backstretch into an early lead. Evans said afterward that he used the ire he felt toward the USOC as fuel on the far curve. He still had the lead as the field turned toward home. Once again, James was a formidable opponent. Once again, the distance between the two of them at the finish was a meter at the most.

And once again, Evans prevailed, this time in the world-record time of 43.86 seconds. James was second in 43.97, Freeman third in 44.40. Evans credited Freeman for not letting him back off in practice at Echo Summit. "I've had a lot of different coaches over the years, but Freeman made me go through the workouts at the most important time," Evans said.

The thin air obviously contributed to the otherworldly records established in Mexico City, but at the start of the year, who could have imagined a time below 44 seconds not being fast enough to win a gold medal in the 400? Certainly not the silver medalist.

"I made one mistake in 1968," James said. "I told a very good friend of Lee's what I planned to do. My objective was to run 43.9 and win two Olympic gold medals. I learned a lot about Lee that year. His mindset wasn't about time. It was about seeing himself in front at the finish."

Evans, James, and Freeman wore black berets to the medal ceremony. They took them off during the playing of the anthem and waved them overhead once the music stopped. Asked why he looked so happy on the victory stand, Evans replied, "It's harder to shoot a guy who's smiling."

Evans took heat from some black people for not taking a stronger stand. In his 1970 book, *The Revolt of the Black Athlete*, Harry Edwards wrote, "Evans tried to do the impossible—he attempted to stand up and be counted on both sides of the fence at once. And, because this is a struggle for black survival in which there is no middle ground, he failed on both accounts, or so some felt."

Edwards blamed the book's editors for inserting that passage without his knowledge. "It sells books if there's a rift or a tear," Edwards said in 2017. "I apologized to Lee. Tommie and Lee were there from the beginning. Lee was powerfully involved, but after Smith and Carlos, he knew the other guys didn't have their gold medals."

Edwards was referring to James, Freeman, and Matthews, the "we don't jive—2:55" guys. Evans and company still had some unfinished work to do.

Ralph Boston went to Mexico City thinking he was no worse than cofavorite in the long jump with Bob Beamon. "Little did I know," Boston said.

Boston nearly became the sole favorite when Beamon fouled twice in the qualifying round. With Beamon one jump away from elimination, Boston, or "the Master," as Beamon referred to him, took his flustered rival aside and offered the right words of encouragement. "Bob, don't lose your confidence," Boston said. "Just take it easy and you'll definitely make the final."

Taking off well behind the board, Beamon jumped 26-10¼, making the final with room to spare. Beamon felt like an entirely different man the next morning. He'd spent the night with his girlfriend in a Spanish villa rented by Mel Zahn, a Californian who hoped to recruit Beamon and other black Olympians to join his track club. Beamon woke up refreshed after breaking the athletic taboo against having sex the night before a big competition. (The wife he had promised the girlfriend he'd divorce was also in Mexico City, but Beamon wasn't overly concerned.) Zahn secured a limousine to chauffeur Beamon to the stadium. Warming up, Beamon felt unusually light on his feet. Boston overheard Beamon tell himself, "I feel I can jump twenty-eight feet today."

Olympic Stadium was about half-filled when the long jump final began at 3:30 PM. The temperature was seventy-four degrees Fahrenheit, about fifteen degrees cooler than the day before. The Tartan runway was harder and firmer as a result. The first three jumpers had trouble adjusting their approaches to the takeoff board and fouled. The dark sky was signaling rain as Beamon prepared for his first attempt. "Before the rain comes, let's put everything together on this one," he told himself. Curiously, Beamon was wearing a pair of Adidas spikes on his feet. He'd worn Puma shoes in the previous day's qualifying round. Beamon wasn't the first Olympian to accept cash envelopes from both of the German shoe companies, but he'd soon be the most celebrated.

"I was more of a Puma person, but when I put on the Adidas long jump shoe, it felt a lot better," said Beamon, who was rewarded with a lifetime Adidas contract. "I cared more about which shoe fit best."

At 3:46 PM central time, Beamon sprinted down the runway and hit the white board perfectly with his right foot. He seemed to hang suspended in the air before touching ground near the far end of the sand pit, skipping twice like a rock on a glassy lake.

"I didn't think he was ever going to come down," Payton Jordan said.

"That's twenty-eight feet," Boston told Lynn Davies, the defending Olympic champion from Great Britain. Nonsense, Davies said. Boston responded, "That's *more* than twenty-eight feet."

Officials took an unusually long time peering through the special measuring device designed to compute the distance of a jump without the need of a tape. Beamon had jumped beyond the machine's ability to compute. Officials called for a steel tape to measure the perfect jump. Finally, the distance appeared on the scoreboard: 8.90 meters. Beamon, untutored in the metric system, looked confused.

"Bob, you jumped 29 feet," Boston told him. The imperial distance was actually 29-2½, nearly 2 feet beyond the world record of 27-4¾ shared by Boston and Igor Ter-Ovanesyan of the Soviet Union.

Beamon collapsed on the track, trembling and nauseous. Boston and US teammate Charlie Mays tried to help him to his feet. When he regained his equilibrium, Beamon sprinted and hopped joyfully up and down the track. Dozens of spectators leaped over the fence and surrounded him. The measurement and celebration lasted more than fifteen minutes, delaying the competition and the scheduled start of the men's 400-meter final. The rest of the long jump final was held in a downpour.

"I thought I was fine until, lo and behold, Bob Beamon opened up like that," Boston said. "Not only did he open like that, the heavens opened up."

Klaus Beer, an East German Boston had never heard of before, won the silver medal with a jump of 26-10½. Boston was third at 26-9½, giving him a complete set of Olympic medals. Mays fouled three times. Davies quit after taking one half-hearted jump. Beamon accepted his gold medal in black socks and rolled-up sweatpants to demonstrate his support of Smith and Carlos.

Beamon's jump represented the greatest single improvement on a world record in track and field history. The largest previous extension of the long jump record occurred in 1935 when Owens leaped 26-8, 6 inches beyond the old mark. The record had advanced 8¾ inches in the thirty-three years since. Beamon, who added 21¾ inches to the record, had an interesting thought afterward: *Would I have jumped 30 feet if I hadn't had sex last night?*

Beamon's flip-flop between Puma and Adidas was part of a larger drama involving the feuding Dassler brothers. The cloak-and-dagger machinations began in 1965 when Horst Dassler secured an exclusive arrangement with Mexican Olympic officials to sell Adidas shoes in the Olympic Village. The agreement also allowed for the free import of Adidas shoes from Germany; Puma was taxed at ten dollars per pair. When Puma tried to dodge the excise tax by packing its shoes in containers that looked like the ones used by Adidas, Mexican officials impounded the Puma imports. Puma had Art Simburg collect athletes' signatures for a petition demanding that its shoes be allowed into Mexico.

Simburg was performing his duties when he was suddenly whisked away by Mexican security agents. He spent three days in the *cárcel* before the US State Department secured his release. Simburg's arrest and incarceration was an untimely distraction for his fiancée, the gold-medal sprinter Wyomia Tyus.

Puma ultimately arranged for British athletes to retrieve the shipment of shoes out of the compound. The amateur ideal was vanishing right beneath Brundage's nose, but the IOC czar was powerless to stop it. The Dasslers reportedly paid out more than $100,000 to track and field athletes in Mexico City.

Mexicans were used to living in the shadow of the United States, but the sound of "The Star Spangled Banner" echoing across the track must have grown tiresome nonetheless. Seagren won a nine-hour pole vault competition in which the three medalists all cleared 17-8½, a half inch shy of the world record the American favorite set at Echo Summit. (Of the four world records set at Echo Summit, Seagren's was the only one to survive the Mexico City onslaught.)

Seagren's gutsy decision to pass 17-6¾ in the Olympic final made the difference as Claus Schiprowski of West Germany and Wolfgang Nordwig of East Germany took the silver and bronze medals. With his narrow win, Seagren continued the US streak of having won every Olympic pole vault competition since 1896.

Willie Davenport and Erv Hall added to the US cache with gold and silver medals in the 110-meter high hurdles. Davenport's official time was 13.3, matching the Olympic record Hall set in the semifinals. The high hurdles final was held on the tension-racked day after the Smith-Carlos protest. "I didn't come here to talk about black power or anything like that," Davenport said at the postrace press conference. "I came to talk about the race today."

Bill Toomey led the decathlon from start to finish, once again maximizing his strengths and minimizing his weaknesses. His first day was historic. He ran the 100 meters in 10.4, long jumped 25-10, and clocked 45.6 in the 400 meters. Toomey's score at the end of ten events was an Olympic-record 8193, slightly inferior to his Echo Summit total but enough to defeat the West German pair of Hans-Joachim Walde and Kurt Bendlin.

Toomey's star-crossed American rival Russ Hodge was in Mexico City working as a spotter for ABC. "I was praying for Bill," Hodge said. "I had a tear in one eye because I wasn't competing, and a tear in the other eye for Bill, because he did it."

The most surprising US medal of the Mexico City Games came in the 50-kilometer racewalk. Just three years after switching from distance running to racewalking, Larry Young claimed the bronze medal. No American had ever finished higher than seventh in the grueling 31-mile race. "I wasn't even considered a dark horse," Young said.

The music Young heard after accepting his bronze medal was Beethoven's "Ode to Joy." Mexico City marked the first Olympics in which East and West Germany fielded separate teams, but not until Munich four years later would their flags and national anthems be used in the medal presentations. "Ode to Joy" was the compromise hymn selected for the combined German team starting in 1956. The winner of the 50-kilometer walk in Mexico City was Christoph Hohne of East Germany. "Auferstanden aus Ruinen" (German for "Risen from the Ruins") would become a most familiar anthem as East Germany flexed its muscles over the next five Olympiads.

Mexico City wasn't a bed of gold and bronze medals for everyone on the US men's team. Dave Maggard in the shot put and Wade Bell in the 800 meters saw their Olympic dreams fall victim to Montezuma's revenge. Ed Burke saw his medal hopes ruined by human error. Burke came to Mexico City expecting to win a medal. What he didn't expect to encounter was an official who didn't know the rules.

Twice in the final he started turning in the slick circle before aborting the effort and starting over. Twice a Mexican official called him for a foul, even though the rules allowed a thrower to start his motion over, provided the ball of the hammer didn't touch the ground outside the circle. After a heated discussion, the officials finally granted Burke an additional throw, but it wasn't far enough to put him the top eight and receive three more attempts. He finished twelfth and quit the sport.

"It was a nightmare," Burke said. "I thought, I've spent my entire life for this? Forget it. I can start a family and start a regular life."

In pole vault qualifying, Casey Carrigan needed to clear 16-1 to advance to the final. The high school senior sailed over the bar, but an official reaching for Carrigan's pole appeared to knock it through the uprights. The rule would be changed the following year, but in 1968 a vaulter's pole wasn't allowed to pass under the bar. Carrigan's jump was ruled a miss, even though he cleared the bar by a foot and a half. "I cried on and off for three days," Carrigan said. The same ruling cost US teammate John Pennel a medal in the final. Pennel's successful clearance of 17-8½ was ruled a miss when his pole followed him into the pit.

―――――――――

Prior to 1968, just one athlete from Ethiopia or Kenya had won an Olympic medal in track and field: Abebe Bikila, the two-time marathon champion from Ethiopia. In Mexico City, altitude-born runners from those African nations collected nine medals, including gold in the 1,500 meters, 3,000-meter steeplechase, 10,000 meters, and marathon. Mohamed Gammoudi, a Tunisian who won the 5,000 and placed third in the 10,000, grew up at sea level but spent much of the year leading up to the Olympics training in the French Pyrenees.

Aside from Jim Ryun, George Young represented the best US shot to win a gold medal in the distance races. Young hadn't lost a race all year at any distance, from the mile to the marathon, and Mexico City was his third Olympics. He'd done as much altitude training as any US runner, but the best he could do was third place in the 3,000-meter steeplechase final. Young held the lead approaching the final water jump, at which point Benjamin Kogo and then Amos Biwott roared past.

Biwott, a steeplechase novice who was either nineteen or twenty-one years old, depending on the source, sprang over the hurdles as if he'd receive extra credit for height. While the other runners got their feet wet negotiating the water jumps, Biwott's shoes were completely dry when he broke the tape. Young valiantly outsprinted Kerry O'Brien of Australia for the bronze medal. "I missed by a few ticks," Young said. "That's done, said and gone."

Ryun's main rival should have been dead on his feet by the time the 1,500-meter final rolled around on October 23, the final day of Olympic track and field. Kip Keino had run with the leaders in the 10,000 meters before dropping out with a stomach cramp with two laps remaining on the opening night. He finished a close second to Gammoudi in the 5,000 meters four days later. Counting heats and finals, the summit meeting with Ryun in the 1,500 was Keino's sixth race in eight days.

Keino knew he couldn't match Ryun's kick in a slow-paced race. Ryun knew he couldn't hold a fast early pace at 7,350 feet. When Ben Jipcho sacrificed his own chances to assist his more famous teammate with a 56-second opening lap, Ryun went to the back of the pack. "I knew what altitude would do to me if I went too fast," Ryun said.

West German teammates Harald Norpoth and Bodo Tümmler attempted to keep pace with the Kenyans while Ryun continued to hold his fire. Keino took the lead with two laps remaining and, incredibly, increased his killer pace. Ryun moved up from fifth to second on the final lap, but Keino was far in front and still going strong. Keino finished in 3:34.9, an Olympic record and the second-fastest 1,500 meters in history. Ryun was second in 3:37.8, a time he had thought would be good enough to win. Given the altitude and the number of races he'd already run, Keino's performance ranks among the greatest in track history.

"Keino, oh my God," said Tracy Smith, the 10,000-meter US Olympian. "He has to drop out of the 10,000 with gallstones, he gets upset by Gammoudi in the 5,000, and then he does that in the 1,500? It was like he raced himself into shape."

There should have been no shame in placing second to a champion of Keino's caliber, but that's not how Ryun's loss was perceived back home.

"There was an awful lot of criticism, but they didn't understand the effects of altitude," Ryun said. "I'm honored to have won a silver medal. It's one of the most disciplined races I've ever run. When I passed Tümmler and Norpoth, I could see the lights were on but nobody was home. That's because they tried to keep up with Keino's pace."

Several years later, when they were competing on an ill-fated professional track circuit, Jipcho apologized to Ryun for playing the sacrificial lamb in Mexico City. "He said he was asked by the Kenyan federation to run a fast pace to kill me off," Ryun said. "He didn't need to apologize, but I appreciated the sentiment."

The Ryun-Keino showdown took place on Sunday, October 20, the final day of track and field competition. If Ryun's gallant but unsuccessful run for a gold medal was a disappointment to American fans, the closing act still had more than its share of red, white, and blue.

The United States broke the world record in all three relays—the men's 4 x 100, women's 4 x 100, and men's 4 x 400. Sprint coach Stan Wright took a gamble in leaving Charlie Greene in the leadoff spot on the men's 4 x 100. Greene had injured a tendon above his left knee in the 100 meters, and he looked terrible in relay qualifying. With Carlos banished from the Olympics, the only available replacement was Questad. Questad had run for US Olympic head coach Payton Jordan at Stanford, but Wright stayed with Greene. "Charlie should not have run," Questad said. "They wanted to run black or not run at all."

Cuba beat the United States in the heats, and Jamaica lowered the world record to 38.3 in the semifinals. The Americans entered the final as underdogs for the first time in Olympic history. But Greene ran a solid leadoff leg in the final, and Hines overhauled Cuba's Enrique Figuerola on the anchor leg en route to the gold medal and a new world record of 38.2. The Cubans mailed their silver medals to Harry Edwards to demonstrate their support of the Olympic Project for Human Rights.

The US women also set a world record in winning the 4 x 100 relay. They dedicated their gold medals to Smith and Carlos, a generous gesture given the way they'd been ignored by their black compatriots in the run-up to Mexico City.

The 4 x 400 foursome of Matthews, Freeman, James, and Evans didn't quite run the 2:55 they'd planned, but they didn't jive their way around the track, either. The US clocking of 2:56.1 chopped more than three seconds off the world record. The grilling they'd received after the US sweep in the 400 meters prompted James to recommend to his teammates that they skip the postrace press conference. The others agreed. Enough had been said already. "I got assaulted by the Philadelphia media," James said. "They told me I had to talk. I told them I was sorry, but we agreed to have no comment."

World records were nice, but nothing during the entire track schedule captured the Mexican crowd's fancy more than the sight of Dick Fosbury turning convention upside down. The high jump final provided a welcome respite to eight days of often suffocating turmoil and controversy.

Fosbury had eighty thousand people eating out of his hand. No announcement was needed when he was next up in the jumping order. The crowd loved the way he rocked back and forth, clenching his fists, psyching himself up for a good minute or two before each attempt. Mostly, they thrilled at the spectacle of the lanky American flying over the bar backward.

"They got a big kick out of watching something so different," Fosbury said. "It must have seemed strange to the marathon runners, because when they entered the stadium, it was dead silent."

Fosbury cleared his first six heights on his first try, somersaulting out of the pit with a grin and a peace sign. When Soviet jumper Valentin Gavrilov missed three times at 7-3¼, Fosbury and US teammate Ed Caruthers were assured of the top two spots on the victory stand. Caruthers needed to clear 7-4¼ to have any chance at beating Fosbury. He knocked the bar off three times.

Fosbury put some additional shine on his gold medal by flopping over 7-4¼ on his third try, breaking the American record. As the crowd screamed in delight, US marathoner Kenny Moore interrupted the tail end of his 26-mile journey by throwing his arms up in the air and dancing a jig. The scene was one of pure joy. A German journalist watching from the press box exclaimed, "Only a triple somersault off a flying trapeze with no net below could be more thrilling."

As he did at Echo Summit, Caruthers jumped a career best, just as Fosbury had done, clearing 7-3¼ for the silver medal. Caruthers might have left Mexico City empty-handed had he not chosen expediency over principle early in the competition.

"In 1968, with all the stuff going on, MLK being killed, the marches, it seemed like you had to do something," Caruthers said. "We had agreed to compete in black socks. But the only ones I had were dress socks, and I'd never worn them before. On my first jump, my foot slipped when I planted. I said, 'Crap, I can't do this. I don't want to be thinking about socks when I'm in an Olympic final.' I took them off."

Caruthers wore the dress socks to the awards ceremony, a nod of support to his black teammates, but few noticed. Theirs was the last final presentation of the final day, and the stadium was half-empty.

The gringos had one hell of a run. The US men won twenty-four medals in Mexico City—twelve gold, five silver, and seven bronze. Americans broke world records in the 100, 200, 400, long jump, and both relays. Had automatic timing been the standard in 1968, the number of world records set by US men would have climbed to eight: Erv Hall clocked 13.38 in the semifinals of the 110-meter hurdles, and Davenport clocked 13.33 in the final, marks that statisticians have retroactively credited as world records.

Toomey, Seagren, Fosbury, Matson, Davenport, and Oerter set Olympic records. Beamon's world record in the long jump lasted twenty-three years. The 4 x 400 relay record went unsurpassed for twenty-four years.

Payton Jordan's comments earlier in the year about the boycott had irritated Lee Evans and some of the other black team members, but the Stanford coach's steady hand and basic decency proved indispensable in Mexico City. When members of the 1968 team gathered in Sacramento to be honored at the 2000 Olympic trials, Jordan reflected on the experience.

"I've gotten a lot of credit for being the coach of one of the greatest teams ever," Jordan said. "It embarrasses the hell out of me. It wasn't one man. There was a national desire to succeed—people like Walt Little, Carl Stough, Bill Bowerman, and Stan Wright. I know I'm leaving people out. I think the results and the closeness of the group says that what we did was right, even though there were a few exceptions. It was a tough year. You had to be pretty strong to keep your balance. Strong people held together during what could have been a very chaotic thing. I know I'm biased, but I don't think there's ever been a team like it. I love all of them."

Toomey, the decathlon winner, credited the track in the forest for the US showing in Mexico City.

"It is my honest opinion that South Lake Tahoe is written on a part of every performance that went on the victory stand in Mexico City," Toomey said. "I know that without the times there, my medal would have had a German home."

17

LEGACIES

WHEN TOMMIE SMITH returned to the Olympic Village the night of his protest, he said to his roommate, "I'm glad that's over."

Kenny Moore prudently held his tongue. But Moore immediately saw the irony in Smith's words. "I remember thinking, it will never be over," Moore said.

Smith and Carlos left Mexico City in a blaze of controversy and recrimination. When their connecting flight landed in San Jose, there were no supporters on hand to greet the record-setting sprinters, only a gaggle of aggressive journalists. Smith had a twenty-one-year-old wife, a baby son, and no job. North American Pontiac, where he'd worked washing new cars in the back lot, had cut him loose before the Olympics. He was scared, to put it plainly.

At least Carlos and Evans were still eligible to compete collegiately for San Jose State, giving them a post-Olympic purpose. The Spartans brought Bud Winter his first NCAA team championship in 1969, powered largely by Carlos, who won the 100 and the 200 and anchored the San Jose State sprint relay team to victory. Evans was upset in the 440-yard dash at the NCAA meet by newcomer Curtis Mills, who broke Smith's world record with a 44.7 clocking. The loss didn't prevent Evans from ranking first in the world for the fourth straight year.

To finish up his teaching credential, Smith returned home to Lemoore, where he worked for a semester as a student teacher at his old elementary school. When he couldn't find a permanent teaching job, he signed a professional football contract with the Cincinnati Bengals. He spent two and a half years on the team's taxi squad before being cut. Smith's marriage fell apart. His fifty-seven-year-old mother died

Tommie Smith reflects on his 1968 experiences at the Echo Summit reunion. *The USDA Forest Service*

suddenly, her early passing caused, Smith believed, by the ostracism and hate mail she received in the conservative valley town following Mexico City.

"The pressure of Mexico City had taken my mother, had broken up my marriage, and had left me without a way to make a living," Smith wrote later. "It was time for me to leave world records, victory stands, and silent gestures alone for a while."

Though he didn't threaten the record-breaking times he clocked at Echo Summit and in Mexico City, Lee Evans remained one of the top 400-meter runners in the world for another four years. He qualified for the 1972 Olympics as a member of the US 4 x 400 relay team but ended up watching the Olympic final from the Munich stands—the victim, in a cruel twist, of another victory-stand demonstration.

Vince Matthews and Wayne Collett finished one-two in the open 400 meters at the Munich Olympics. The third US entrant, John Smith, pulled up with a hamstring injury and didn't finish. It's hard to call what Matthews and Collett did on the victory stand a protest; rather than raise a fist or bow their heads, they basically looked like two guys standing on a street corner, waiting for the bus after work. Collett stood casually with his hands on hips. Matthews stroked his goatee. Neither looked at the flag.

Incensed that two more black Americans had again defiled the awards ceremony, the IOC expelled Matthews and Collett not just from the remainder of the Games but from all future Olympics. With Smith injured, the United States didn't have enough eligible quarter-milers to field a relay team. Evans, the man who removed his black beret in Mexico City in part because he wanted to give Matthews a chance to win a gold medal in the relay, was the odd man out in 1972.

"What happened in Munich was like getting a divorce," Evans said. "I couldn't talk about it for five years. Two Olympic gold medals is nice, but three would have been better."

Art Simburg, the Puma shoe peddler who spent time in a Mexico City jail, introduced Tommie Smith to Jack Scott shortly after Smith's football career ended. Scott would later make headlines for harboring Patty Hearst when the newspaper heiress turned revolutionary went on the run with the Symbionese Liberation Army. But in 1972, when he was named the athletic director at Oberlin, a liberal arts college in Ohio, Scott's reputation as a critic of the sports establishment was on a par with that of Harry Edwards. It didn't hurt Scott's reputation in left-leaning circles that Vice President Spiro Agnew, in a speech to football boosters in Birmingham, Alabama, labeled him the "guru from Berkeley."

Scott hired three black coaches at Oberlin, including Smith, to head up the basketball and track programs. When Scott left Oberlin after falling out of favor with the school's administration, Smith's days were numbered. He returned to California to accept a job at Santa Monica

Community College, where he coached track and taught sociology classes for twenty-seven years.

John Carlos was the world's best sprinter in 1969 and 1970, tying the world record in the 100-yard dash at his favorite meet, the West Coast Relays in Fresno. He tried his hand at professional football but had even less success than Smith. His ex-wife, Kim, committed suicide in 1977, and Carlos drifted through much of the 1970s and '80s. He regained his footing as a track coach and counselor in Palm Springs. He received an honorary doctorate degree in 2005 from Texas A&M University-Commerce, which was known as East Texas State when Carlos spent a turbulent year there before transferring to San Jose State. (Smith received an honorary doctorate from San Jose State in 2005.)

Carlos now lives in the Atlanta area, as does Smith. Their relationship, which was never close, deteriorated when Carlos wrote in his autobiography that he intentionally let Smith win in Mexico City. Recent years have seen a rapprochement of sorts. The media seeks Smith and Carlos for comment whenever a prominent athlete takes a race-related stand, as San Francisco 49ers quarterback Colin Kaepernick did in 2016 when he kneeled during the playing of the national anthem to protest police brutality.

As Carlos noted at the Echo Summit reunion in 2014, their victory stand is now seen through a much different lens. San Jose State unveiled a statue depicting their Mexico City protest in 2010. The National Museum of African American History and Culture in Washington features a similar statue, along with an exhibit devoted to the racial climate surrounding the Mexico City Games. When the US Olympic and Paralympic teams were invited to the White House in late 2016, the USOC asked Smith and Carlos to join them.

President Obama paid tribute by saying, "Their powerful silent protest in the 1968 Games was controversial, but it woke folks up and created greater opportunity for those that followed."

Harry Edwards never relinquished the pulpit he commandeered in 1968 with the Olympic Project for Human Rights. His three decades as a professor of sociology at UC Berkeley were characterized by overflowing lecture halls, a messy but ultimately successful battle over tenure, and a silver- and fork-tongued ability to continue admonishing the sports establishment on race-related matters. Edwards served as a paid consultant for Major League Baseball and the San Francisco 49ers, where with head coach (and San Jose State graduate) Bill Walsh he worked to increase coaching opportunities for black people in the NFL.

"The establishment has changed to the extent that they decided to invite me in," Edwards said. "But I'm like the Statue of Liberty; I've been in the same position since Day One."

Smith, Carlos, and Lee Evans criticized Edwards for failing to join them in Mexico City, but the three Olympians later came to see their association with him in a broader, more nuanced light.

"Harry had an ulterior motive," Smith said. "I do believe that he used us, in the sense that he used us as a door for change. The Sixties was a time of social change, and here were these two world-champion athletes who could help him make change."

Edwards now says he never expected the OPHR to foment a black boycott of the Mexico City Games.

"No, it was never visualized as a full-blown boycott," Edwards said. "Charlie Greene and Mel Pender were literally running under [military] orders. Jim Hines and Ralph Boston—they were associated with black schools that told them if they were the least bit associated with the Olympic Project for Human Rights, they'd be kicked out of school. We never approached the boxers because they'd turned their backs on Muhammad Ali in 1967. We knew they weren't going to support a boycott.

"There was never any vision that it would be a uniform boycott. But we hoped there was an opportunity to make a statement at the Olympics, which were the second-most political forum in the world, behind only the United Nations. If you can keep the sports establishment focused on your primary goal, you have a chance to do something else.

"At the end of it all, I had a pretty good idea of what strategies were viable. I understood what we were up against. I could not control what the athletes would do once they got to Mexico City, but I had a pretty good idea that Smith, Carlos, and Evans would do something.

"Today a lot of the guys say they were behind the Olympic Project for Human Rights, and that's fine. But in 1968, Tommie and John Carlos said hey, this is a serious thing. . . . Martin Luther King had been shot down, four girls died in the Birmingham church bombing, Medgar Evers was assassinated."

Edwards called the Olympic Project for Human Rights his most lasting achievement. "The image of Tommie Smith and John Carlos on that podium in Mexico City—that statement will be here long after I'm gone," Edwards said. "What people think about that statement is irrelevant. The statement is there and it speaks for itself."

Jim Hines, the sprinter who set world records in the 100 meters and sprint relay in Mexico City, believes Smith and Carlos tarnished the accomplishments of their nonprotesting teammates.

"The Olympic 100-meter dash decides who is the world's fastest human," Hines told Moore in a *Sports Illustrated* article written twenty-three years after Mexico City. "When it's overshadowed by a political move, it's hard not to think about it, especially when people can't even remember you. The '68 Olympic team was the best in history, but it was discredited by what Tom and John did. The glove situation cost us all."

Hines had hoped to follow in the footsteps of Bob Hayes, the 1964 Olympic gold medalist who had a Hall of Fame professional football career with the Dallas Cowboys. Hines was a sixth-round draft pick of the Miami Dolphins who caught two passes in ten games over the 1969 and 1970 seasons, earning one of football's all-time great nicknames: "Oops."

"I'd been drafted by the Miami Dolphins, and I explained that that wasn't me with the glove," Hines said. "But they believed we all had to know about it. I would have tripled my money from the Dolphins if it weren't for that. The gesture cost me a total of $2 million."

Kenny Moore narrowly missed winning a marathon medal at the 1972 Olympics in Munich, finishing fourth. He then embarked on a lengthy writing career with *Sports Illustrated*. In 2006 Moore wrote the definitive biography on his college coach, Bill Bowerman.

Not surprisingly, Moore's articles on distance running are particularly incisive. One of his most memorable pieces chronicled a 1995 journey to Ethiopia, where Moore and a photographer tried to unravel the mystery of why Mamo Wolde, the 1968 Olympic marathon champion who had edged Moore out of a bronze medal in Munich, had been imprisoned by the Ethiopian government. Moore was able to visit Wolde in prison and illuminate his plight, but the Ethiopian runner was held without charges for another seven years. Wolde died in 2002, shortly after being released from prison. Moore also wrote a lengthy feature about Gerry Lindgren's bizarre postrunning career, in which Lindgren abandoned his family and went under an assumed name for a number of years.

In Mexico City, Moore witnessed firsthand the vituperation Smith and Carlos received for what he called an act of deep conscience.

"I had no political leanings other than to get along and do my best in sport," Moore said. "That team had great camaraderie. I knew Tommie and John were right, but it took me years to realize how right they were. I could kick myself that I didn't realize it earlier."

The USOC's board of directors appointed Bill Bowerman to be the head coach of the 1972 US Olympic men's track and field team. Stan Wright was bitterly disappointed not to get the head job, but he swallowed his pride and served as one of Bowerman's assistants. While the Munich Olympics are mostly remembered for the terrorist attack that left eleven Israeli athletes dead, Wright is best known for not getting two of his sprinters, Eddie Hart and Rey Robinson, to the starting line in time for their qualifying races in the 100 meters. Wright had been given an incorrect schedule, which he and the sprinters realized when they stopped by an ABC truck on their way to the stadium and saw their races being run on television. Hart, a gold-medal contender, never got an opportunity to challenge the eventual winner, Valery Borzov of the Soviet Union.

Angered by hostile questioning at a press conference, Bowerman refused to do an interview with Howard Cosell of ABC Sports. Wright did the interview, primarily to let people know the sprinters weren't at fault. Cosell tore Wright apart. The USOC later issued a report that exonerated Wright of blame for the schedule mix-up, but the Munich incident left a scar that never completely healed.

"Sure, it bothers me," Wright said in a 1992 interview. "It will bother me to my grave."

Wright died in 1998, five years after giving a tearful acceptance speech on being inducted into the National Track & Field Hall of Fame. The Olympic ring he received for coaching the 1968 team has been passed down through the family—first to son-in-law John Hartfield, the high jumper who finished a devastated fourth at Echo Summit, then to one of Wright's grandchildren.

Bowerman, who cofounded Nike with Phil Knight in 1971, came up with the "waffle" sole design that set Nike on its way to becoming the largest shoe and apparel company in the world. The address of Nike's headquarters is One Bowerman Drive, Beaverton, Oregon. The man who was instrumental in putting Echo Summit on the track map died a very rich man in 1999 in Fossil, Oregon.

Wade Bell, the former Oregon runner whom Bowerman believed would have won the 800 meters in world-record time in Mexico City had he been at full health, became a certified public accountant. Bell's clients included his wealthy ex-coach. Bell managed Bowerman's numerous donations to the University of Oregon, effectively serving as the Nike cofounder's right-hand man. Knight had offered Bell a job with Blue Ribbon Sports just before the company became Nike. Bell turned the offer down.

"I could have had much more wealth, but that's never been the main factor for me," Bell said.

———

Bud Winter, the innovative coach who turned San Jose into Speed City, died of a heart attack in late 1985, one day after being inducted into the National Track & Field Hall of Fame. Winter's *So You Want to Be a Sprinter* is considered one of the best books on the subject.

Citing budget woes, San Jose State dropped its men's track and field program in 1988. Bud Winter Field was turned into a parking lot. Twenty-eight years later, the university announced that it would reinstate the men's program in 2018, coinciding with the fiftieth anniversary of the Mexico City Olympics. Smith, Carlos, and Edwards were on hand for the announcement.

———————

Avery Brundage was eighty-one in 1968 but clung to his position as president of the IOC for another four years. Brundage wrote his own epitaph at the Munich Olympics when he told a full stadium and a worldwide television audience, one day after a Palestinian terrorist attack left eight Israeli athletes and coaches dead, "The Games must go on." A sentiment that defined his very essence was tarnished, however, by his conflating the murder of the Israelis with a threatened African boycott before the Games that kept the Rhodesian team from competing in Munich. "The Games of the Twentieth Olympiad have been subject to two savage attacks," Brundage said. "We lost the Rhodesian battle against naked political blackmail."

Brundage's successor was Lord Killanin, a personable Irish journalist and author who had presented Smith and Carlos with their medals in Mexico City. Brundage, who had gone to great lengths to conceal the two children he had fathered out of wedlock while presiding over the Olympic movement, married a thirty-seven-year-old German princess in 1973. He died in 1975 at the age of eighty-seven.

———————

Four years after her husband refused to carry the US flag in Mexico City, Olga Connolly, the Czech expatriate who grew up in a country invaded

Ed Burke (right) and Ed Caruthers share a warm greeting at the Echo Summit reunion in 2014. *The USDA Forest Service*

by Nazi Germany, accepted the honor. She had qualified for her fifth Olympic team in 1972. Her husband, Harold, finished fifth in his fifth US Olympic trials, making it the first time in twenty years that he hadn't thrown the hammer at the Olympics.

Ed Burke, Hal Connolly's old rival, dusted off his hammer following a lengthy retirement and threw farther than he did in his twenties. Burke qualified for the US Olympic team in 1984 at age forty-four and was elected to carry the flag into the Los Angeles Coliseum to open the 1984 Olympics.

"That's what I'm known for," said Burke, who continued setting age-group records into his seventies. "It's one of those quirks of fate. People can't remember who won the gold medal, but they remember who carried the flag into the stadium."

Olga and Harold Connolly divorced in 1974. Harold remarried; Olga didn't. Olga was still teaching fitness classes at UC Irvine into her mid-eighties. Harold died in 2010, collapsing in a Maryland gym following a strenuous workout on an exercise bike. His death elicited a glowing tribute from Harry Edwards, who praised Connolly for being one of the few white athletes to publicly support the Olympic Project for Human Rights.

"Harold Connolly was a constant reminder to me, up close and personal, that our struggle was against racism, not against white people," Edwards said. "He remains a model for those who would forge greater intergroup harmony and progress."

—————

As fate would have it, none of the three teenagers who made the Olympic team at Echo Summit made another.

Reynaldo Brown remained one of the world's top high jumpers for the better part of a decade but couldn't duplicate his Echo Summit magic at the 1972 and 1976 Olympic trials. Brown had the unusual distinction of twice finishing second to world-record performances—behind Pat Matzdorf in 1971 (7-6¼) and Dwight Stones in 1973 (7-6½). In both cases, Brown cleared 7-3, the same height he cleared as a seventeen-year-old at Echo Summit.

Casey Carrigan, the prodigiously talented pole vaulter, dropped out of Stanford, moved to Hawaii, and acquired the nickname "Spacey Casey." He resurfaced several years later, climbing to fourth in the world rankings, but an injury prevented him from trying out for the Olympic team in 1976. He had a twenty-eight-year career with the Long Beach Fire Department.

"I feel I wasted my God-given talent to a huge degree," Carrigan said. "But the way my whole life turned out, becoming a Christian . . . if I'd have had a lot of success I might have imploded. I had a great career in the fire service. I feel incredibly blessed."

Marty Liquori had a long, distinguished career, becoming the only American male to rank first in the world in the 1,500 and 5,000 meters. Liquori's win over Jim Ryun in the much-hyped "Dream Mile" at the 1971 Penn Relays put him on the cover of Sports Illustrated. Liquori's problem was one of timing. In 1972, 1976, and 1980, injuries either kept him out of the US trials altogether or left him a shadow of his usual self.

Today, Liquori plays guitar in a jazz band. He's had a lot of time to think about his lone Olympic experience, and he wishes he had the perspective then that he has now.

"We white guys didn't support the black guys as much as we could have," Liquori said. "I was pretty apolitical. If I had it to do over again, things would have been a whole lot different. My reaction at the time was, the Olympics is a sacred thing. Now I look back and say, you've got the world's attention for a second, make your point."

Jim Ryun qualified for his third Olympic team in 1972 but tripped and fell in his Munich qualifying meet, denying him a rematch with Kip Keino. Ryun then joined the International Track Association, a short-lived professional circuit, and had the upper hand in his final races against Keino. While he considers his race against Keino in Mexico City one of his best, given the circumstances, Ryun believes the decision to hold the Olympics at high altitude was a mistake. No Summer Olympics have been held at altitude since.

"If you look at the results, with the exception of me and George Young, who won a brilliant bronze medal in the steeplechase, all of the medals went to runners who lived at altitude," Ryun said. "Put it at sea level and make it a level playing field. The guys from high altitude might have a slight advantage, but the sea-level runners won't be disadvantaged."

Ryun served five terms in the US House of Representatives, where he compiled one of the most conservative voting records of any member of Congress. He was defeated in the Republican primary in 2006. He currently runs a series of running camps.

Months after winning a gold medal and setting a world record as a member of the US Olympic 4 x 100 relay team, Mel Pender was ordered to begin a second tour of duty in Vietnam. Despite being exposed to Agent Orange, the world's fastest late bloomer tied a couple of world indoor

Mel Pender at the 2014 Echo Summit reunion. *The USDA Forest Service*

records in 1972, though he came up short in his quest to make a third Olympic team. Pender went on to become the first black coach at West Point and later worked for the National Football League and National Basketball Association in their community development offices.

While he credits the army for putting his life on a productive path, Pender regrets not being free to express his feelings about racism in Mexico City. "I wish I wasn't in the army at the time, because I'd have been right there with Tommie and John," Pender said. "They're only now getting the accolades they deserve. Those are the two bravest men I've ever met in my life."

As he neared his eightieth birthday, Pender lamented the lack of racial progress made since 1968. He became incensed talking about the early months of Donald Trump's presidency.

"The shit he's doing to this country is ridiculous," Pender said. "This is the United States of America. This isn't the fifties or the sixties. All that stuff is coming back right now. I'd just hope things change before I leave here. I'd love to see people get along."

Jay Silvester bounced back from his Mexico City disappointment to win an Olympic silver medal in 1972. He was leading the Munich discus final until longtime rival Ludvík Danek of Czechoslovakia passed him in the sixth and final round. Conspicuous in his absence from the Munich final was Al Oerter, who retired in 1969 to spend more time with his family. Given the form he showed a decade later when he improved his personal best by 15 feet and finished fourth in the 1980 US trials, Oerter came to regret his decision not to shoot for a fifth gold medal in 1972.

"I left for a very real and valid reason," Oerter said in 1988. "I wanted to be a part of the growth of my daughters. But now that I'm a grandfather and I see that they've turned out fine, maybe they would have grown up fine anyway. There is some regret, yes."

At forty-seven, Oerter qualified for the discus final at the 1984 Olympic trials and continued competing in masters meets into his early sixties. He took up abstract painting and helped found Art of the Olympians, a program that helped Olympians promote their artwork. Though he had heart problems, he refused to have a transplant and died in 2007.

Silvester finished eighth in the discus at the 1976 Olympics and qualified for his sixth US trials in 1980. He lives in Lindon, Utah. When members of the 1968 Olympic team met in New Orleans for a thirty-year reunion, Silvester tried to lay any hard feelings to rest.

"Jay explained to the guys that he had some serious feelings back then," Norm Tate said. "He felt all of the things going on were affecting his training. People change over the years. I think he now understands why the blacks felt the way they did."

Dick Fosbury successfully defended his national collegiate title in 1969, but that was pretty much it for the inventor of the Fosbury Flop. He reapplied to Oregon State's school of engineering. "They took me but said no more track meets—you need to focus on one thing," Fosbury said. "I was the first Fosbury to attend college and really wanted to be an engineer. So I took a sabbatical from high jumping for two and a half years and graduated in March 1972."

Fosbury made a halfhearted and unsuccessful attempt to qualify for the 1972 Olympics before settling in Idaho, where he worked as a civil engineer. His career as a world-class high jumper lasted just eighteen months, but it was a career unlike any other.

"I don't have any regrets," Fosbury said. "Of course, I've thought about the what-ifs—what if I had done those European tours where you make money. Quite honestly, I've never been concerned about running or jumping for dollars. I had an amazing career. It was short lived, but I don't have bad knees or a bad back. I survived cancer. Life is good."

———————

Dr. Tom Waddell and the US Army terminated their tempestuous relationship immediately after the Mexico City Games. He acknowledged his homosexuality in a 1976 *People* cover story. "I hated living a lie," Waddell said in a 1987 interview, weeks before he died from AIDS. "I didn't care if people knew I was gay. I figured the people who liked me were going to continue to like me."

To his very last days, Waddell battled the USOC over the rights to call the event he founded in San Francisco the Gay Olympics. The Supreme Court ruled in the USOC's favor sixteen days before his death. "I don't like the fact that an oligarchy like the USOC can just walk in and trample our rights," Waddell said.

Three weeks before the 1986 Gay Games in San Francisco, Waddell received the AIDS diagnosis. He was released from the hospital in time to compete in the javelin throw, and he won a gold medal for his age group. "They presented me with a special medal, but I wanted one of my own," Waddell said.

Phil Shinnick, the long jumper who narrowly missed qualifying for the Olympic team at Echo Summit, wrote a posthumous tribute to his fellow iconoclast in the *New York Times*. "Of the thousands of athletes I've met, no one developed his potential as much as Tom Waddell, an Olympian, musician, artist, physician, and healer," Shinnick wrote.

Shinnick was imprisoned briefly in the mid-1970s for refusing to cooperate with the FBI in its investigation of Patty Hearst's flight from federal authorities. He led delegations of athletes on tours of the People's Republic of China and the Soviet Union and was named an ambassador of UNESCO in 2000. He practices alternative medicine in New York.

———

Jack Bacheler's affinity for insects got him in hot water with the US Department of Agriculture when he returned to Florida from Mexico City.

"I figured that hiding the cocoons in my used laundry would not create an establishment situation in Florida because their larval host plant doesn't occur in Florida, and I had no intention of allowing the emerged giant silk moths to escape," Bacheler said. "I received a scolding letter from a USDA official pointing out how many of our significant human and agricultural pests are mistaken introductions.

"As a twenty-four-year-old smart ass, I replied that I would never again attempt to bring in live insects from Mexico City after an Olympic Games."

Bacheler made his second Olympic team in 1972, finishing eleventh in the marathon. He earned his doctorate in entomology that same year and did groundbreaking work in boll weevil eradication while serving on the faculty at North Carolina State. He retired in 2013 and took up a new hobby: growing competitive pumpkins. Bacheler's eight-hundred-pound pumpkin took first place at the North Carolina State Fair.

———

Dave Patrick needed therapy to help him come to grips with the overwhelming sense of disappointment he brought home from Echo Summit, when a fourth-place finish lost him the Olympic spot he'd already earned.

"To be honest, it did affect me for years," Patrick said. "I have a lot of baggage. I also have a lot of great memories. We went on a four-mile run once up there and got so caught up in the beauty that we wound up running sixteen miles.

"I have a lot of good memories of Tahoe, and one bad memory."

Payton Jordan, the head US Olympic coach who was not included in the decision to nullify the results of the Los Angeles trials that would have clinched Patrick's berth, did his best to make amends. In 2008, Jordan surprised Patrick at the Penn Relays by informing him that the USOC had made him an official member of the 1968 Olympic team.

"He said a day hadn't gone by that he hadn't thought about my situation at Echo Summit," Patrick said of Jordan. "That was something, for a ninety-one-year-old man to come all the way to Philadelphia to tell me that. I appreciated it."

Jordan died less than a year later at his home in Laguna Hills, California. Seven of his Stanford and Olympic athletes named sons after him.

Once, while Patrick was looking through some of his mother's belongings, he came across a letter he'd sent back in 1968. "Mom and Dad, here's $100 for your trip to Mexico City," the letter read. His mother kept the letter and never spent the money.

"That brought tears to my eyes," Patrick said. "I was working as a waiter at the time. I didn't remember sending the letter."

Randy Matson worked for thirty-five years as a fundraiser for Texas A&M, his alma mater. He stays in touch with his longtime friend and rival Dave Maggard, whose lengthy career in sports administration included stints as the athletic director at UC Berkeley, Miami, and Houston. Maggard also served as director of sport for the 1996 Olympic Games in Atlanta.

"Randy once said, 'Dave, if I trained as hard as you did, I wouldn't be able to move,'" Maggard said with a chuckle. "I said, 'You got your wish, Randy. I can't.'"

Bob Seagren set two more pole-vaulting records in 1972 but settled for a silver medal at the Munich Olympics when international officials banned the pole he'd been using all season. Seagren and Geoff Vanderstock, the USC teammates who set world records at Echo Summit, landed some acting roles after Mexico City. Their credits included *Soap* (Seagren) and *Starsky & Hutch* (Vanderstock). Seagren and Bill Toomey competed in the made-for-television "Superstars" competition, in which athletes from different sports competed for prize money in such events as cycling, weight lifting, tennis, and swimming. Seagren won the first Superstars competition in 1973.

Many of the 1968 US Olympians went into teaching and coaching: Bacheler, Connolly, Carlos, Silvester, Tommie Smith, Van Nelson, Norm Tate, Rick Sloan, Tracy Smith, Lou Scott, and Ed Caruthers, among others. Caruthers, the silver medalist in the Mexico City high jump, tried out for the Detroit Lions before returning to Southern California to teach and coach for more than twenty years.

"I was kind of a borderline kid coming out of high school," Caruthers said. "I didn't know what I wanted to do with my life. I used my experience to let young people know they could get an education and do something they wanted to do for the rest of their lives."

Tom Farrell had the good fortune to retire from his position as global accounts manager for Xerox at the relatively young age of fifty-five. But he leaves his Southern California home for extended spells twice each year to serve as a volunteer assistant coach at St. John's, his alma mater.

"It helps keep me young," Farrell said.

———

Billy Mills, the Olympic hero in 1964 who failed in his bid to make the team again at Echo Summit, cofounded an organization, Running Strong for American Indian Youth, that works to improve the lives of Native Americans. President Barack Obama presented Mills with the Presidential Citizens Medal in 2012, and two years later the Anti-Defamation League made him an honoree in their Concert Against Hate.

Regarding his experiences at Echo Summit, Mills said, "In retrospect, I'm much better off being eliminated than to go down to Mexico City and not make the final. I learned a lesson—don't do anything half-assed."

The brotherhood of the 1968 Olympic team was on full display in 2007 when former Oregon State track coach and Olympic team manager Steve Simmons organized a tribute to Larry James. James, the "Mighty Burner" who received credit for a world record in the 400 meters at Echo Summit, was battling the colon cancer that would claim his life eleven months later on his sixty-first birthday. Among those attending the tribute were Lee Evans, John Carlos, Vince Matthews, Ron Freeman, Norm Tate, Payton Jordan, and three of James's Villanova teammates: Erv Hall, Dave Patrick, and Marty Liquori.

James had a distinguished post-Olympic career. He served in the US Marine Corps Reserve, achieving the rank of major. He earned a bachelor's degree from Villanova and a master's in public policy from Rutgers, and he served nearly thirty years as dean of athletics and recreation at Richard Stockton College in the Pine Barrens of New Jersey. James also served as the manager of several US international teams and was budget chair for USA Track & Field.

Shortly before the 2007 celebration, James spoke of what he considered his three greatest accomplishments.

"First was finishing college," James said. "I came from sparse beginnings. College was a big thing in our house. Second, picking the right woman. I came from a single-parent family. I've been married to my wife, Cynthia, for thirty-seven years. That's very, very important to me, to provide the stability to my family that I didn't have.

"Last, having the opportunity to pass the baton. It's about you when you do it, but when it's over, it's about what you do with it and how you share it. It's about helping others accomplish the things they're capable of."

His son, Larry Jr., spoke at the tribute, saying he was grateful that his father was present to hear how others felt about him. Hall, the 1968 Olympic silver medalist in the high hurdles, presented James with a Villanova shirt emblazoned with "The Mighty Burner—43.9y," referring to his nickname and the fantastic mile-relay split he clocked at the 1968 Penn Relays. The ex-Villanova athletes in attendance then stood and held up their own shirts with the same wording, to the Mighty Burner's delight.

"There is no distance too far, no height too high, to keep us from being here for one of our brothers," Carlos told the gathering.

EPILOGUE

DISTANT ECHOES

THE TRACK IN the forest couldn't be moved until the snow melted the following spring. The Tartan surface was cut up into sections and hauled down the mountain to its new home at South Tahoe Intermediate School. The track was the same, but the elevation was 1,150 feet lower, and there were no trees or boulders on the infield. Still, it served the community's needs for the better part of forty years. In 2007 a new nine-lane track finally replaced the old red relic.

In September 1969, many of the headliners from the previous year's summit meeting returned for the South Lake Tahoe Indian Summer Games. John Carlos won the 100 in a wind-aided 9.9, and Lee Evans clocked 44.5 in the 400. One year to the day after setting his world record at Echo Summit, Bob Seagren won the pole vault at 17-8¾, a quarter-inch shy of his 1968 world-record mark on the summit. A familiar name from Mexico City won the 1,500 meters in 3:37.3—Kip Keino of Kenya, showing once again that he could run fast anywhere, altitude be damned.

Hal and Olga Connolly enjoyed a belated opportunity to compete together at Tahoe, in contrast to the previous summer, when no women were allowed. Payton Jordan delighted the crowd of three thousand by winning the masters 100-meter dash in 13.5 seconds, fleet running for a sixty-two-year-old former Olympic coach.

For a one-day affair in a non-Olympic year, the Indian Summer Games was as successful a sequel as could be expected. But even though he won the triple jump on his return trip to Tahoe, Norm Tate's emotions landed somewhere between wistful and homesick.

"When we came back a year later, it was different," Tate said. "It was the same track, but there was nothing like being on top of the

Runners can barely be seen through the trees at the Echo Summit trials in 1968.
© *Rich Clarkson*

---

mountain." Walt Little Jr., the man most responsible for lighting the South Lake Tahoe flame, continued on as the city's parks and recreation director for two more years before a new mayor and city manager cashiered him. The reason, according to newspaper accounts, was that he didn't have the experience to manage the city's campgrounds. Little and his wife, Vivian, eventually moved to Rio Vista, California, a small town on the Sacramento River, where he bought a stake in the local newspaper and returned to the sidelines of high school football games, getting kids' pictures into the newspaper.

"He was as happy writing about the kids in the delta towns as he was associating with the Olympians at Tahoe," said his son Bill Little.

South Lake Tahoe mayor Norman Woods presented Walt Little (right) with a commendation in 1979 recognizing Little's role in bringing the 1968 Olympic track and field trials to Echo Summit. *Rio Vista News Herald*

Little died in 1999. At the Echo Summit reunion in 2014, his two sons and their families sprinkled some of his ashes at the base of the granite boulder holding the plaque designating the site as a California Historical Landmark.

———

The final major competition on the relocated track occurred in the early summer of 1970, when the AAU decathlon championship was held in South Lake Tahoe. Bill Toomey had retired after reclaiming the world record in 1969, clearing the field for his old rival, Russ Hodge.

Hodge was in great shape, in the midst of his best season in years. His score of 7886 would have been more than enough to put him on the Olympic team two years earlier atop the summit. But the last-place

Friendships developed at Echo Summit stood the test of time. *US Forest Service*

finisher at Echo Summit, John Warkentin, scored a career-best 8026 to deny Hodge his best shot at the national title he'd never win.

———————

Olympic marathoner Kenny Moore visited the Echo Summit site years later. He was disappointed to discover that memories of the track had vanished into thin air. "Neighbors in the area all said essentially, 'You know, we heard something like that happened up here, but we don't know where,'" Moore said.

Harry Marra retired and moved to the Lake Tahoe area after coaching Ashton Eaton to successive Olympic decathlon titles in 2012 and 2016. Marra longs for the echoes of 1968, when he was a college student back east, watching the Olympic trials on television. He was transfixed by the sound of Jim McKay's voice and the sight of larger-than-life athletes competing for the highest stakes in the middle of a California forest.

"To me personally, all the trials held since Echo Summit pale by comparison," Marra said. "I think Echo Summit was the last bastion of

Flags ripple in the breeze at the 2014 Echo Summit reunion. *Photo by Kirby Lee, courtesy of USA Track & Field*

track and field at its height of popularity. Drugs, corrupt leaders, and money have tainted it. I still go to Echo Summit once a year and walk the oval. I get goose bumps every time. Simpler times, I guess."

―――――――――

Ralph Boston keeps in his cell phone a photo of the Echo Summit track taken from high up the ski slope. Lake Tahoe can be seen in the distance. "Lots of trees, lots of nature," Boston said. "Looking back on it, it was so natural, so attuned to nature. Just a really special place."

A friend of Dick Fosbury's had a similar photo enlarged and presented it to the inventor of the flop as a gift.

"When I saw that photo for the first time, I swear I had the same feelings I had when I was standing on the podium in Mexico City," Fosbury said. "The emotion washed over me. It was an incredible place with incredible people. I was a young man then, taking it all in stride, like this happens to everyone who's on the Olympic team. But it only happened to us.

"The setting, the forest in the infield, the giant boulders—for an Oregon kid, it was a mythical place. Mount Olympus is a mythical place, and so is Echo Summit."

The place where the United States found men to match its mountains.

1968 US Olympic Men's Track and Field Team

(Olympic medals in parentheses)

100 meters
Jim Hines (gold)
Charlie Greene (silver)
Mel Pender

200 meters
Tommie Smith (gold)
John Carlos (bronze)
Larry Questad

400 meters
Lee Evans (gold)
Larry James (silver)
Ron Freeman (bronze)

800 meters
Tom Farrell (bronze)
Wade Bell
Ron Kutschinski

1,500 meters
Jim Ryun (silver)
Marty Liquori
Tom Von Ruden

3,000-meter steeplechase
George Young (bronze)
Bill Reilly
Conrad Nightingale

5,000 meters
Jack Bacheler
Bob Day
Lou Scott

10,000 meters
Tracy Smith
Van Nelson
Tom Laris

110-meter high hurdles
Willie Davenport (gold)
Erv Hall (silver)
Leon Coleman

400-meter intermediate hurdles
Geoff Vanderstock
Ron Whitney
Boyd Gittins

Marathon
Kenny Moore
George Young
Ron Daws

20-kilometer walk
Rudy Haluza
Ron Laird
Thomas Dooley

50-kilometer walk
Larry Young (bronze)
Goetz Klopfer
Dave Romansky

High jump
Dick Fosbury (gold)
Ed Caruthers (silver)
Reynaldo Brown

Pole vault
Bob Seagren (gold)
John Pennel
Casey Carrigan

Long jump
Bob Beamon (gold)
Ralph Boston (bronze)
Charles Mays

Triple jump
Art Walker
Dave Smith
Norm Tate

Shot put
Randy Matson (gold)
George Woods (silver)
Dave Maggard

Discus
Al Oerter (gold)
Jay Silvester
Gary Carlsen

Hammer throw
Ed Burke
Al Hall
Harold Connolly

Javelin
Mark Murro
Frank Covelli
Gary Stenlund

Decathlon
Bill Toomey (gold)
Rick Sloan
Tom Waddell

4 x 100 relay
Charlie Greene, Mel Pender, Ronnie
Ray Smith, Jim Hines (gold)

4 x 400 relay
Vince Matthews, Ron Freeman,
Larry James, Lee Evans (gold)

Coaching staff
Payton Jordan (head coach)
Ted Haydon
Johnny Oelkers
Frank Potts
Stan Wright
Mike Portanova (manager)
Bill Bowerman (altitude camp coor-
dinator)

ACKNOWLEDGMENTS

THE SEEDS FOR this story must have been planted in 1968, when my father, John Burns, took the family up to Echo Summit for the Olympic track and field trials. He had wrested a handful of press passes from one of his coworkers at the *Sacramento Bee*. My strongest memory is of walking onto the forested infield and asking Jay Silvester, the hulking discus thrower, for an autograph. Silvester looked at the press pass I handed him, grumbled something about not being a big fan of the media, and signed it for the awestruck eleven-year-old kid. I also remember that my mother and two sisters weren't as excited about being there as I was. My mother, Jeanne, wasn't much of a sports fan, but she taught high school English and supported my journalism career to the hilt. Thanks, Mother and Daddy.

In 2014, when I was working with William Burg of the California Department of Parks and Recreation to have Echo Summit designated a state historical landmark, the US Forest Service office in Placerville threw its full support behind the effort. Laurence Crabtree, Duane Nelson, Cindy Oswald, and Katy Parr—your interest and enthusiasm in Echo Summit fanned the flames, to use a forester's least favorite idiom. Ann and Steve Dunsky in the Forest Service's audiovisual department were also extremely helpful.

I'm grateful that my agent, Barbara Rosenberg, and my editor at Chicago Review Press, Lisa Reardon, took a chance on a story about a long-ago track meet. Their ideas and direction are greatly appreciated. Thanks also to my former boss, Scott Mackey, for helping with the first steps.

A big shout-out goes to Steve Simmons, the former Oregon State track coach and US Olympic team manager who has done so much to keep the memory of the 1968 US Olympic team alive. Besides being one of the most interesting characters I've ever met, Steve has connections that were invaluable in the researching and writing of this book. Tom Lough, a 1968 US Olympian in the modern pentathlon, helped me contact far-flung members of the greatest track and field team in history. Thanks also to Bob and Linda Jarvis, track nuts extraordinaire, for allowing an interloper to hunker down at their kitchen table and study their complete collection of *Track & Field News*, and to Bill Little and Walt Little III, for their recollections of their father's role in bringing the Olympic trials to South Lake Tahoe.

I'm blessed to have a family that not only understands my obsession but generally encourages it. My wife, Dana, supported me for all twenty-five laps of the 10,000 meters. (It helps that she actually likes track.) Thanks so much, Dana. The same holds true for our children, Julian, Ali, Ryan, and Kiki, whose unflagging interest helped immensely, and for my sisters, Cathy Arago and Eileen Noel, neither of whom even remembers going to Echo Summit in 1968.

And thanks to Stalky and Judy Lehman for allowing their son-in-law to write a large portion of this book at their cabin in the eastern Sierra. Whether the 8,000-foot altitude helped or hindered the effort remains up in the air.

NOTES

Starting in 1988 and continuing through 2017, I interviewed more than fifty of the participants at Echo Summit, some of them multiple times, as well as others associated with the event such as coaches and Forest Service personnel. Some of the quotes in this book come directly from articles I wrote for newspapers. Nonprimary source quotes are noted. The results and statistics come almost exclusively from the pages of *Track & Field News*.

Each person I interviewed is listed below, in alphabetical order and with the year of each interview noted:

Austin Angell (2017)

Jack Bacheler (2017)

Bob Beamon (1988, 2017)

Wade Bell (2016)

Ralph Boston (2000, 2017)

Ed Burke (2000, 2010)

John Carlos (2014)

Casey Carrigan (2017)

Ed Caruthers (2016)

Hal Connolly (2000)

Olga Connolly (2017)

Willie Davenport (1988)

Harry Edwards (1988, 2017)

Lee Evans (2000, 2016)

Tom Farrell (2016)

Richmond Flowers (2016)

Dick Fosbury (1988, 2000, 2017)

Charlie Greene (1995)

Erv Hall (2016)

Toni Hartfield (2017)

Bob Healey (2017)

Jim Hines (1995)

Russ Hodge (2017)

Paul Hoffman (2017)

Larry James (2000, 2007)

Bob Jarvis (2017)

Jim Jones (2017)

Payton Jordan (1988, 2000)

Tom Laris (2016)

Doug Leisz (2017)

Harley Lewis (2017)

Gerry Lindgren (2017)

Marty Liquori (2016)

Bill Little (2000, 2014, 2017)

Vivian Little (2000)

Walt Little III (2000, 2014, 2017)

Cleve Livingston (2017)

Dave Maggard (2000, 2016)

Harry Marra (2017)

Randy Matson (2016)

Hardee McAlhaney (2017)

Billy Mills (1994, 2016)

Kenny Moore (1988, 2017)

Van Nelson (2016)

Bill Nieder (2017)

Al Oerter (1988, 2000)

Dave Patrick (2016)

Mel Pender (1995, 2016)

Jim Pryde (2016)

Larry Questad (1995, 2016)

Bob Rice (2017)

Russ Rogers (2016)

Chuck Rohe (2017)

Jim Ryun (2017)

S. T. Saffold (2017)

Lou Scott (2017)

Bob Seagren (2000)

Phil Shinnick (2016)

Jay Silvester (2017)

Rick Sloan (2016)

Tommie Smith (1988, 2017)

Tracy Smith (2016, 2017)

Dwight Stones (2017)

Norm Tate (2000, 2016)

Bill Toomey (2000)

Wyomia Tyus (2004)

Geoff Vanderstock (2016)

Tom Von Ruden (2016)

Willye White (2000)

Stan Wright (1988, 1992)

George Young (2000)

Larry Young (2017)

Prologue: Return to the Summit

"Nineteen sixty-eight was a perverse genius of a year": Lance Morrow, "1968: War Abroad, Riots at Home, Fallen Leaders and Lunar Dreams: The Year That Changed the World," *Time*, 40th anniversary special, 2008, vi.

More than sixteen thousand US soldiers: "Vietnam War Casualties (1955–1975)," Military Factory, 2018, www.the militaryfactory.com/Vietnam /casualties/asp.

Chapter 1: Into the Great Unknown

"It looks more and more": Witherspoon, *Before the Eyes*, 35.

When the vote was taken on October 16, 1963: Witherspoon, 46.

A member of the Mexican delegation, Dr. Eduardo Hay: Witherspoon, 45.

"The Olympics belong to all the world": Guttman, *Games Must Go On*, 123.

"How will the altitude affect": "The Highest Olympics," *Sports Illustrated*, November 4, 1963, 7.

Astrand tested Swedish cross-country skiers: Wrynn, "'Debt Was Paid Off,'" 1157.

"At higher altitudes pathological ECG": Wrynn, 1157.

"Well-conditioned men": "Athletes vs. Altitude," *Sports Illustrated*, March 28, 1955, 33.

"My throat felt on fire": "Athletes without Oxygen," *Life*, March 28, 1955, 27.

The Soviet Union announced in 1965: "Soviet Olympic Body in Study," *New York Times*, March 13, 1965.

In his summary of the conference, Balke: Wrynn, "'Debt Was Paid Off,'" 1159.

The Albuquerque symposium determined: Wrynn, 1162.

"We know that a respiratory thermostat": Bob Ottum, "Getting High in Mexico City," *Sports Illustrated*, October 25, 1965, 31.

"There is this awful sensation": Ottum, "Getting High," 31.

"You begin to acclimate": Ottum, 31.

"The astonishing choice of Mexico City": Roger Bannister, "The Punishment of a Long Distance Runner," *New York Times Magazine*, September 18, 1966, 87.

"It's hard to run against those blokes": Gwilym S. Brown, "Fierce Fight in the Family," *Sports Illustrated*, August 22, 1966, 57.

"Already several countries": Bannister, "Long Distance Runner," 87.

The Soviet Union built training facilities: Witherspoon, *Before the Eyes*, 54.

When collegiate track coaches advocated: Moore, *Men of Oregon*, 140.

"We had to learn how to": Moore, 209.

"I think it was one of those things": Moore, 209.

"Horses are inclined to go" and *"They do not have"*: Witherspoon, *Before the Eyes*, 53.

Chapter 2: Echo Summit

Bill Bowerman assembled a list: Moore, *Men of Oregon*, 209.

In the language of the Washoe: Lekisch, *Tahoe Place Names*, 120.

Oddly, the name change wasn't signed into law until 1945: Lekisch, 128.

"At last the lake burst upon us": Twain, *Roughing It*, 148.

Twain's lone visit to Tahoe occurred: Smith, Branch, Salamo, and Browning, eds., explanatory notes to Twain, *Roughing It*, 614n147.16–17.

Bob Tracy, the track coach at St. Cloud: "Tracy Named Coach of Runners at Tahoe," *Tahoe Daily Tribune*, August 7, 1967.

University of Nevada track coach Dick Dankworth: "Runners Test Heavenly Air," *Tahoe Daily Tribune*, August 11, 1967.

The California and Nevada governors: "Governor Backs Tahoe as Conditioning Site," *Tahoe Daily Tribune*, July 12, 1967.

"Frankly, we are not in first place" and *"This doesn't include"*: "Governor Backs Tahoe."

"It was not a secret that Bill Bowerman": "South Tahoe Praised by Olympic Chairman," *Tahoe Daily Tribune*, September 1, 1967.

Johnson arrived in Placerville: Ellen Osborn, "John Calhoun Johnson: California Pioneer Trailblazer," *Overland Journal*, Summer 2015, 44.

During the peak years of the gold rush: Howard, *Sierra Crossing*, 39.

After serving as adjutant: Osborn, "John Calhoun Johnson," 46.

Johnson's Cutoff was discovered: Osborn, 47.

Previous names included: Lekisch, *Tahoe Place Names*, 34.

Williams, the South Lake Tahoe city manager: "South Tahoe to Make Final Bid as Training Site," *Tahoe Daily Tribune*, September 6, 1967.

The USOC's track and field committee met: "South Tahoe Chosen as Olympic Training Site," *Tahoe Daily Tribune*, September 11, 1967.

Joining Little and Williams in Chicago: "South Tahoe's Hopes High for Success at Chicago," *Tahoe Daily Tribune*, September 7, 1967.

Echo Summit received 85 points: Bob Payne, "Olympic Camp's Press 'Ban' Unpopular," *Spokesman-Review*, August 16, 1968.

As to why the name of the national forest: "How the California National Forests Were Named," US Department of Agriculture Forest Service, 2013, www .fs.usda.gov/detailfull/r5/learning/history-culture/?cid=stelprdb5301043&w idth=full.

The California Department of Transportation, or Caltrans: "U.S. Olympic Athletes to Live at Kingvale While Training," *The Guardian* (newsletter for District 2, Division of Highways), May 1968.

Reagan noted in the release: "Athletes to Live at Kingvale."

Chapter 3: The Mastermind

"He is surely a colorful": Arnold Hang, "The Black Rebel," *New York Times Magazine*, May 12, 1968, 32.

Smith recalls meeting Edwards: Smith with Steele, *Silent Gesture*, 117.

"DEAR TRAITOR": Edwards, *Revolt of the Black Athlete*, 46.

"You don't know me": Edwards, 45.

On October 7, 1967, shortly after returning from Japan: Edwards, 46.

"Looking back on it, the thing that amazes me": Harry Edwards, "Harry Edwards: An Oral History," interviews by Nadine Wilmot, 2005, transcript, University of California Regional Oral History Office, Bancroft Library, Berkeley, 3, http://bancroft.berkeley.edu/ROHO/projects/aa_faculty /edwards_harry.html.

Chapter 4: The Resisters

Shortly after arriving in California: Smith with Steele, *Silent Gesture*, 54.

James Richard Smith saw sports as a waste of time: Smith with Steele, 62.

Winter taught navy pilots: "A Need for Speed: Inside Jamaica's Sprint Factory," National Public Radio, May 4, 2012, www.npr.org/2012/05/04/151956595 /a-need-for-speed-inside-jamaicas-sprint-factory.

Smith's first step toward the victory-stand protest: Smith with Steele, *Silent Gesture*, 103.

Evans remembers working the fields: *Fists of Freedom: The Story of the '68 Summer Games*, directed by George Roy, written by Steven Stern, aired Thursday, August 12, 1999, on HBO.

"The motives behind the boycott are all right": "More Boycott Reaction," *Track & Field News*, February II 1968, 21.

Chapter 5: The Boycott Campaign

Harry Edwards formed the United Black Students for Action: Edwards, *Revolt of the Black Athlete*, 41.

"All I hope": Johnathan Rodgers, "A Step to an Olympic Boycott," *Sports Illustrated*, December 4, 1967, 31.

When he returned to San Jose: Edwards, *Struggle That Must Be*, 168.

"As it became crystal clear": *Fists of Freedom*.

Restoration of Muhammad Ali's title: Wright, *Stan Wright*, 143.

"In my humble opinion": "For the Record," *Sports Illustrated*, October 16, 1967, 109.

"Coach, Tom and I dig you": Wright, *Stan Wright*, 149.

"Avery Brundage was to this movement": *Fists of Freedom*.

"A racist down to his toes": *Fists of Freedom*.

"Many of the individuals and organizations": Guttman, *Games Must Go On*, 73.

"An erroneous report was": Associated Press, "Mistake of 1936 Olympic Games Not Forgotten," *Los Angeles Times*, March 29, 1998.

"I really respect the guys": Pete Axthelm, "Boycott Now or Boycott Later?" *Sports Illustrated*, February 26, 1968, 24.

"This new issue will force": Axthelm, "Boycott," 25.

Chapter 6: The Innovator

Today, every world-class jumper: Simon Turnbull, "Olympics: Four Decades Later, We're All Still Doing the Fosbury Flop," *Independent* (London), July 26, 2008, www.independent.co.uk/sport/olympics/olympics-four -decades-later-were-all-still-doing-the-fosbury-flop-878314.html.

Fosbury cleared 7 feet or higher: Jon Hendershott, "That Fosbury Flop," *Track & Field News*, July II 1968, 19.

Bill Bowerman, the acclaimed University of Oregon coach: Moore, *Men of Oregon*, 222.

Just because Fosbury's invention was deemed legal: Roy Blount Jr., "Being Backward Gets Results," *Sports Illustrated*, February 10, 1969, 27.

While browsing through the microfilm: Jon Hendershott, "HJ History Rewritten: The Fosbury Flop Turned the High Jump World Upside Down in the '60s, but Guess What—Dick Wasn't the First," *Track & Field News*, July 2000, 42.

"I wasn't there for the high jump": Hendershott, "HJ History Rewritten," 42.

"High jumping has always been": Brill with Lawton, *Jump*, 10.

"Fosbury and I were the first": Brill with Lawton, 19.

Chapter 7: The Cruelest Month

"long and bloody war": Clay Risen, "The Unmaking of the President," *Smithsonian Magazine*, April 2008, www.smithsonianmag.com/history/the-unmaking-of -the-president-31577203.

"King was the last prince of nonviolence": "McKissick Says Nonviolence Has Become Dead Philosophy," *New York Times*, April 5, 1968.

"No one looking at the six demands": Hartmann, *Race, Culture*, 96.

"Dr. King's assassination": Edwards, *Struggle That Must Be*, 189.

"to be carried out as solemn": Edwards, 81.

Chapter 8: Aftershocks

"For the first time since the talks": "Scorecard," *Sports Illustrated*, April 25, 1968, 21.

On the day King was killed: Wright, *Stan Wright*, 162.

"I think it would be a greater": John Underwood, "Winning Son of a Dedicated Loser," *Sports Illustrated*, June 6, 1966, 38.

Larry James's reservations about competing in Knoxville: Kenny Moore, "A Courageous Stand," *Sports Illustrated*, August 5, 1991, 76.

"American Nobel Peace Prize winner": Editor's Mailbag, "Sick US Society Needs Examining," *University of Tennessee Daily Beacon*, April 6, 1968.

"There were about a dozen reasons": Jack Olsen, "In an Alien World," *Sports Illustrated*, July 15, 1968, 41.

In 1968 there were fewer than 250 black students: Olsen, "Alien World," 30.

"If a Negro looks for help": Olsen, 32.

"I thought Jamaica High": Schaap, *Perfect Jump*, 53.

Graduating 1,093rd in a class of 1,182: Schaap, 66.

"You fellows should consider yourself lucky": Schaap, 78–79.

"We did not want that chap from California": Henry Giniger, "Mexican President's Aides and Students Confer," *New York Times*, October 5, 1968.

Chapter 9: Bumpy Road to Summit

"conservatives swallow hard": Bob Brachman, "Trojan Spikemen Win—Barely," *San Francisco Chronicle*, June 16, 1968.

"I just remembered why I was a runner": Kenny Moore, "A Life on the Run," *Sports Illustrated*, May 18, 1987, 60.

"They cheated Ryun from his deserved record": Frank Litsky, "Lindgren Wins National Collegiate 10,000-Meter Run in 29:41 in Berkeley," *New York Times*, June 14, 1968.

In its meet coverage: Associated Press, "Echo Summit Set to Host Olympians," *San Francisco Chronicle*, June 16, 1968.

"You have to go down to nine or ten": Dwight Chapin, "Specter of Edwards Shrouds US Trials," *Los Angeles Times*, July 1, 1968.

Chapter 10: Magic Mountain

"I am hopeful the example set": "Olympic High Altitude Training Site Dedicated," *Tahoe Daily Tribune*, June 17, 1968.

Blood samples showed: Associated Press, "Altitude Is Big Factor in the Olympics," *Kalispell (MT) Daily Inter Lake*, September 1, 1968.

Barometric pressure and the oxygen content: Noakes, *Lore of Running*, 42.

The effects of altitude on the distance events: Daniels, *Daniels' Running Formula*, 132–33.

At the 1967 NCAA indoor meet: Ryun with Phillips, *Quest of Gold*, 79–80.

Chapter 11: Melting Pot

George Frenn, a rambunctious hammer thrower: Matthews with Amdur, *My Race Be Won*, 178.

"The true losers at Lake Tahoe": Smit, *Sneaker Wars*, 69.

"We voted on the boycott": Associated Press, "Evans: Boycott Is Off; Edwards Stalls," *Sacramento Bee*, July 31, 1968.

"We—as individuals": Robert Lipsyte, "The Spirit of the Olympics," *New York Times*, August 1, 1968.

"I don't think it is possible": Hunt, *Drug Games*, 21.

Bowerman called a meeting: Moore, *Men of Oregon*, 228.

Chapter 12: Take Your Marks

"a casual atmosphere": Don Bloom, "Olympic Hopefuls Get Down to Serious Work at Echo Summit Training Site," *Sacramento Bee*, July 25, 1968.

"There was a street light": George Woods interview, "1968 Olympic Team Oral History Project," H. J. Lutcher Stark Center for Physical Culture and Sports, University of Texas at Austin, March 13, 2014, https://archives .starkcenter.org/1968ohp.

"Some pigeon droppings hit me": Charlie Laughtland, "Former Shoreline Star Among NWAACC Hall of Fame Class," HeraldNet, February 29, 2008, www.heraldnet.com/uncategorized/former-shoreline-star-among-nwaacc -hall-of-fame-class.

"The first day I tied the school record": Laughtland, "Former Shoreline Star."

Chapter 13: Out of This World

"I pinched a nerve in one of my vertebrae": Bob Seagren interview, "1968 Olympic Team Oral History Project," November 1, 2013.

"I was fortunate in that": Seagren, "Oral History Project."

"I found out it was a congenital defect": Seagren, "Oral History Project."

"You saw it, and you'll write it": John Underwood, "Triumph and Tragedy at Tahoe," *Sports Illustrated*, September 23, 1968, 19.

"The hammer throw is a foolish event": Matthews with Amdur, *My Race Be Won*, 181.

"If the hammer is good enough": Matthews with Amdur, 182.

Clarke agreed to pace Mills: Cordner Nelson, "Four Global Marks Fall," *Track & Field News*, September 1968, 36.

Chapter 14: Highs and Lows

"Who will get second and third?": ABC's *Wide World of Sports*, September 16, 1968, www.youtube.com/watch?v=DDo7qQsWOhA.

When he won the California state title: Reynaldo Brown interview, "1968 Olympic Team Oral History Project," April 1, 2011.

His teammate at Texas Southern: Jerome Solomon, "Hartfield's Feats Had to Be Seen to Be Believed," *Houston Chronicle*, January 29, 2012, www .chron.com/sports/solomon/article/Solomon-Hartfield-s-feats-had-to-be -seen-to-be-2794722.php.

Chapter 15: Interlude

"We were riding pretty high": Seagren, "Oral History Project."

Both relay teams took test runs: Wright, *Stan Wright*, 191.

the "A" team led the runoff: Wright, 192.

"I don't think any of those boys": Wright, 188.

"We couldn't dye our shoes": *Fists of Freedom*.

"We'd heard there had been": Randy Matson interview, "1968 Olympic Team Oral History Project," June 21, 2011.

"The Games of the 19th Olympiad": Guttman, *Games Must Go On*, 242.

Chapter 16: Mexico City

"It was exciting to meet": Reynaldo Brown interview, "1968 Olympic Team Oral History Project," April 1, 2011.

"I think Mexico City was": Seagren, "Oral History Project."

Just one athlete in Mexico City was disqualified: Goldblatt, *The Games*, 269.

"Two days later, we got a message": Matson, "Oral History Project."

"They called you in": Jarvis Scott interview, "1968 Olympic Team Oral History Project," October 14, 2011.

"He was never one": Watman, *All-Time Greats*, 22.

"My best friend literally": Seagren, "Oral History Project."

He'd spent the night with his girlfriend: Schaap, *Perfect Jump*, 24.

Beamon's flip-flop between Puma and Adidas: Smit, *Sneaker Wars*, 71.

"I didn't come here to talk about black power": Neil Amdur, "Davenport Gaines Seventh Track Gold Medal for US in Winning Hurdles," *New York Times*, October 18, 1968.

"Only a triple somersault": Jon Hendershott, "Fosbury Flop Loosens Crowd," *Track & Field News*, November 1968, 26.

"It is my honest opinion": *Tahoe Daily Tribune*, February–March special section, 1970, 3.

Chapter 17: Legacies

"The pressure of Mexico City had taken my mother": Smith with Steele, *Silent Gesture*, 193.

Carlos wrote in his autobiography that he intentionally let Smith win in Mexico City: Carlos with Zirin, *John Carlos Story*, 115.

"The establishment has changed": Robert Lipsyte, "An Outsider Joins the Team," *New York Times Magazine*, May 22, 1988, 34.

"I'd been drafted by the Miami Dolphins": Kenny Moore, "The Eye of the Storm," part 2, *Sports Illustrated*, August 12, 1991, www.si.com/vault /1991/08/12/124682/the-1968-olympians-the-eye-of-the-storm-the-lives -of-the-us-olympians-who-protested-racism-in-1968-were-changed-forever.

"There is no distance too far": Walt Murphy, "A Tribute to Larry James," CSTV .com, December 8, 2007, www.cstv.com/sports/c-track/stories/121807aaa .html.

BIBLIOGRAPHY

Books

Ali, Tariq, and Susan Watkins. *1968: Marching in the Streets*. New York: Free Press, 1998.

Bass, Amy. *Not the Triumph but the Struggle: The 1968 Olympics and the Making of the Black Athlete*. Minneapolis: University of Minnesota Press, 2002.

Branch, Taylor. *At Canaan's Edge: America in the King Years 1965–68*. New York: Simon & Schuster, 2006.

Brill, Debbie, with James Lawton. *Jump*. British Columbia: Douglas & McIntyre, 1986.

Carlos, John, with Dave Zirin. *The John Carlos Story: The Sports Moment That Changed the World*. Chicago: Haymarket Books, 2011.

Connolly, Olga. *The Rings of Destiny*. New York: David McKay, 1968.

Daniels, Jack. *Daniels' Running Formula*. 3rd ed. Champaign, IL: Human Kinetics, 2014.

DeWitt, Paul, and Dorothy De Mare. *Images of America: Echo Summit*. Charleston, SC: Arcadia, 2014.

Edwards, Harry. *The Revolt of the Black Athlete*. 50th anniversary ed. Urbana: University of Illinois Press, 2017.

———. *The Struggle That Must Be: An Autobiography*. New York: Macmillan, 1980.

Goldblatt, David. *The Games: A Global History of the Olympics*. New York: W. W. Norton, 2016.

Gotaas, Thor. *Running: A Global History*. London: Reaktion Books, 2012.

Guttman, Allen. *The Games Must Go On: Avery Brundage and the Olympic Movement*. New York: Columbia University Press, 1984.

Hartmann, Douglas. *Race, Culture, and the Revolt of the Black Athlete*. Chicago: University of Chicago Press, 2003.

Hoffer, Richard. *Something in the Air: American Passion and Defiance in the 1968 Mexico City Olympics*. New York: Free Press, 2009.

Howard, Thomas Frederick. *Sierra Crossing: First Roads to California*. Berkeley: University of California Press, 1998.

Hunt, Thomas M. *Drug Games: The International Olympic Committee and the Politics of Doping, 1960–2008*. Austin: University of Texas Press, 2011.

Hymans, Richard. *The History of the United States Olympic Trials: Track & Field 1908–2000*. Indianapolis: USA Track & Field, 2004.

Johnson, William Oscar Jr. *All That Glitters Is Not Gold: An Irreverent Look at the Olympic Games*. New York: G. P. Putnam's Sons, 1972.

Kurlansky, Mark. *1968: The Year That Rocked the World*. New York: Ballantine Books, 2004.

Lake, John. *Jim Ryun: Master of the Mile*. New York: Random House, 1968.

Lekisch, Barbara. *Tahoe Place Names: The Origin and History of Names in the Lake Tahoe Basin*. Lafayette, CA: Great West Books, 1988.

Matthews, Vincent, with Neil Amdur. *My Race Be Won*. New York: Charterhouse, 1974.

Miller, David. *Athens to Athens: The Official History of the Olympic Games and IOC, 1894–2004*. Edinburgh: Mainstream, 2003.

Moore, Kenny. *Bowerman and the Men of Oregon: The Story of Oregon's Legendary Coach and Nike's Cofounder*. New York: Rodale, 2006.

Murphy, Frank. *The Last Protest: Lee Evans in Mexico City*. Kansas City, MO: Windsprint, 2006.

Noakes, Tim. *Lore of Running*. Cape Town: Oxford University Press South Africa, 1985.

Ryun, Jim, with Mike Phillips. *In Quest of Gold: The Jim Ryun Story*. San Francisco: Harper & Row, 1984.

Schapp, Dick. *The Perfect Jump: The Rise and Fall of an American Athlete*. New York: Signet, 1976.

Smit, Barbara. *Sneaker Wars: The Enemy Brothers Who Founded Adidas and Puma and the Family Feud That Forever Changed the Business of Sport*. New York: Ecco, 2008.

Smith, Tommie, with David Steele. *Silent Gesture: The Autobiography of Tommie Smith*. Philadelphia: Temple University Press, 2007.

Stewart, George. *The California Trail*. New York: McGraw-Hill, 1962.

Stowers, Carlton. *The Randy Matson Story*. Los Altos, CA: Tafnews, 1971.

Strasser, J. B., and Laurie Becklund. *Swoosh: The Story of Nike and the Men Who Played There*. New York: Harcourt Brace Jovanovich, 1991.

Twain, Mark. *Roughing It*. 1872. Mark Twain Library edition edited by Harriet Elinor Smith, Edgar Marquess Branch, Lin Salamo, and Robert Pack Browning. Berkeley: University of California Press, 1993.

Waddell, Tom, and Dick Schaap. *Gay Olympian: The Life and Death of Dr. Tom Waddell*. New York: Alfred A. Knopf, 1906.

Watman, Mel. *All-Time Greats of British Athletics*. Cheltenham, UK: SportsBooks, 2006.

Witherspoon, Kevin. *Before the Eyes of the World: Mexico and the 1968 Olympic Games*. DeKalb: Northern Illinois University Press, 2014.

Wright, Stan, as told to George Wright. *Stan Wright, Track Coach: Forty Years in the "Good Old Boy Network."* San Francisco: Pacifica Sports Research Publications, 2005.

Zarnowski, Frank. *Olympic Glory Denied and a Final Opportunity for Glory Restored*. Glendale, CA: Griffin, 1996.

Video

Roy, George, dir. *Fists of Freedom: The Story of the '68 Summer Games*. Written by Steven Stern. Aired Thursday, August 12, 1999, on HBO.

ABC's Wide World of Sports, Jim McKay and Jim Beatty announcing the 1,500-meter final at Echo Summit, September 16, 1968, www.youtube.com /watch?v=DDo7qQsWOhA.

Oral Histories

Edwards, Harry. "Harry Edwards: An Oral History." Interviews by Nadine Wilmot. Transcript. University of California Regional Oral History Office, Bancroft Library, Berkeley, 2005. http://bancroft.berkeley.edu/ROHO /projects/aa_faculty/edwards_harry.html.

1968 Olympic Team Oral History Project. H. J. Lutcher Stark Center for Physical Culture and Sports, University of Texas at Austin. https://archives .starkcenter.org/1968ohp.

Journals

Wrynn, Alison M. "'A Debt Was Paid Off in Tears': Science, IOC Politics and the Debate About High Altitude in the 1968 Mexico City Olympics." *International Journal of the History of Sport* 23, no. 7 (November 2006): 1152–72.

Newspapers

Houston Chronicle
Independent (London)
Kalispell (MT) Daily Inter Lake
Los Angeles Times
New York Times
Sacramento Bee
San Francisco Chronicle
Spokesman-Review
Tahoe Daily Tribune
University of Tennessee Daily Beacon

Magazines

Life
Overland Journal
Smithsonian Magazine
Sports Illustrated
Time
Track & Field News

INDEX

Page numbers in italics refer to images.

AAU Championships, *xi*, 79–83, *81*, 119, 219–220

Abdul-Jabbar, Kareem. *See* Alcindor, Lew

Adidas, 50, 103–104, 151, 187–188

Agnew, Spiro, 198

Alamosa, Colorado, 13, 19, 153

Alcindor, Lew, 39

Ali, Muhammad, xx

altitude, 2–5, 7, 90

altitude training, 7–8, 89, 90–91, 95, 105, *117*

Amateur Athletic Union (AAU), 8, 77–79
See also AAU Championships

Angell, Austin, xxiii, *xxiii*, 113

Anti-Defamation League, 213

apartheid, 44

Arden, Alice, 119

Art of the Olympians, 209

Astrand, Per-Olaf, 2–3

Bacheler, Jack, 93, 96–97, 145, 182, 211

Baden-Baden, 1

Baeta, Al, 82

Balke, Bruno, 2, 3, 4

Bambuck, Roger, 79, 80

Bank, Dick, 103, 111–112

Bannister, Roger, 5–6, 7

Beamon, Bob, 69, 70–73, 82, 146–148, *147*, 185–187, 194

Beer, Klaus, 187

Beethoven's "Ode to Joy," 189

Bell, Andy, 126

Bell, Sam, 103

Bell, Wade, 84, 101, 129, 178, 189, 203

Bendlin, Kurt, 118, 189

Bigler, John, 12

Bikila, Abebe, 6, 190

Biwott, Amos, 191

Black Athletes of the University of California, 75–76

Black Power, 42

Black Youth Conference (Los Angeles), 39

Blue Ribbon Sports, 114

Boston, Ralph "the Master," 37, 61–62, 87, 97, 162, 168, 171, 221
at Echo Summit trials, 146–149
on golfing at high altitude, 102
Los Angeles Olympic trials and, 82, 84
at Mexico City Olympics, 185–187
on Stan Wright and OPHR, 42–43

Bowerman, Bill, 7–9, 13, 16, 18, 35, 52, 104, 113–114, 116, 141–142, 202–203

Bragg, Don, 65

Brasher, Chris, 174

Bright, Jerry, 136

Brill, Debbie, 54–55

British Empire and Commonwealth Games. *See* Commonwealth Games

Brown, Paul, 168

Brown, Reynaldo, xiv, *xv*, 153, 159–160, 173–174, 206

Brumel, Valeriy, 51

Brundage, Avery, xx, 2, 30, 44–46, 112, 167, 170, 176, 188, 204

See also International Olympic Committee (IOC)
brush spikes (Puma 68s), 136, *138*, 151
Bryant, Paul "Bear," 66
Bud Winter Field, 204
Burghley, Lord David, 176
Burke, Ed, xiv, *xv*, 101, 109, 142, 173, 189–190, 205, *205*
Burrell, Otis, 39, 153, 159
Byrd, Robert, 58

California Department of Transportation (Caltrans), 18, 21, 87
Caracalla (Roman emperor), 1
Carl Stough Institute of Breathing Coordination, 93
Carlos, John, xvii, xx–xxiv, *xxi*, 37–38, 85, 97, 102, 179–180, 215
  in 200-meter final at Echo Summit, 136–137, *137*
  expulsion from Olympic Village, 182–184, 196
  at Indian Summer Games, 217
  at L.A. trials, 84–85
  post–Mexico City legacy, 199
  with Puma brush spikes, *138*
  in relay runoff, 166
  on the victory stand in Mexico City, 180, *181*
Carlsen, Gary, 130
Carrigan, Casey "Spacey Casey," 83, 104, 134–135, 138–140, 190, 206
Carrigan, Paul, 83, 139–140
Carson, Kit, 17
Carson Pass, 17
Caruthers, Ed, xiv, *xv*, xv–xvi, 48, 89, 158–160, 167, 193, 194, *205*, 213
Cawley, Rex, 128
Chaplin, John, 52
civil rights protests, 33, 40–41
Clark, Bill, 158
Clark, Robert, 39
Clarke, Don, 86
Clarke, Ron, 4, 5, 6–7, 122–123, 145, 174
Clemente, Roberto, 62
Coleman, Leon, 144
Collett, Wayne, 198
Commonwealth Games, 6–7

Concert Against Hate, 213
Connolly, Harold "Hal," 105–108, *106*, 112, 141, 142, 172–173, 176, 205–206, 217
Connolly, Olga Fikotová, 106, *106*, 107, 204–205, 217
Connor, Bull, 45
Cooper, Carl, 13, 18
Copeland, Ron, 39
Cosby, Bill, 101
Cosell, Howard, 203
Covelli, Frank, 138
Crabtree, Laurence, xxi
Cuba, 165, 192
Culbreath, Josh, 3
Cummings, Rial, 53

Daily Beacon. See UT Daily Beacon
Daley, Arthur, 183
Dallas Morning News, 58
Danek, Ludvík, 209
Daniels, Jack, 3, *90*, 91–93
Dankworth, Richard, 15
Dassler, Horst, 151, 187
Dassler, Rudolf, 151
Davenport, Willie, 85, 142–144, 166, 188, 194
Davis, Preston, 14, 19, 187
Day, Bob, 145
de Klerk, Jan, 44
Delany, Ron, 65, 155
Díaz Ordaz, Gustavo, 169
Dickey, Doug, 66, 144
Divine, Roscoe, 114
Dooley, H. Kay, 112
Doubell, Ralph, 177, 178
drug testing, 50, 112, 175

Eastman, Julia, 67
Echo Lake, 94
Echo Summit, 20, *117*, 167, *218*, *220*, *221*
  airline ticket agents at, 140
  athlete selection process for, 83–84, 85
  bonding and rivalries at, 102, 104, 110
  California Historic Landmark marker at, xiv
  jobs held by athletes while at, 100–101

living accommodations, 87, *88*
opening of, 86, 89
previous names, 17–18
racial tensions, 108–109
recreational activities, 102
selection of, xvi, 17, 19
spectator accommodations, 116, 117
steeplechase pit at, *94*
training partners, 97
Echo Summit Ski Area, 16
Echo Summit track, xiv–xvii, *xvi*, 22,
    87–88, 217, 219–220
Echo Summit trials
    decathlon, 117–121
    hurdles, 121, 126–128, 143–144
    jumping events, 133–135, 141,
        147–149, 153, 158–163
    long distance, 123–124, 138,
        144–146
    middle distance, 128–130, 153,
        156–158
    relays, 165–166
    sprints, 121, 124–125, 136–137,
        149–152
    throwing events, 125–126, 130–132,
        138, 141–142
Eckert, William, 62
Edwards, Harry, xx, 24–33, *25*, 38,
    59–60, 84–85, 87, 109–110, 179,
    185, 206
    Avery Brundage and, 45–46
    Echo Summit and, 108
    Olympic Project for Human Rights
        and, 39–44, 47
    post–Mexico City legacy, 199–201
Eldorado National Forest, 20
Elliott, James "Jumbo," 63, 64–65, 104, 114
Ellis, Larry, 71
Enyart, Bill "Earthquake," 51
Evans, Lee, 33, 38, 64, 83, 84, 97, 102,
    165, 168, 182
    in 400-meter events, 74–75, 150–151,
        150, 183–185, 217
    announces no boycott in Mexico
        City, 108
    as auto mechanic, 101
    early life and college career, 34–37
    on learning breathing techniques, 93

OPHR and, xx, 24–25, 39–40
opinion of Avery Brundage, 45
personal bests and titles won, 82, 113
political inclinations, 43, 60
post–Mexico City legacy, 196,
    197–198
Ewry, Ray, 46

Farmer, Dixon, 127
Farrell, Chris, 130
Farrell, Tom, 14–15, 19, 129, 130, 178, 213
Figuerola, Enrique, 192
Fikotová, Olga. *See* Connolly, Olga
    Fikotová
Flagstaff, Arizona, 13
Flowers, Richmond, Jr., 47, 65–67, 68,
    85, 144
Flowers, Richmond, Sr., 65
foam pits, 53
Fosbury, Dick, *49*, 76, 85, 113, 140, 153,
    159, 160–163, *161*
    on being at Echo Summit, 221–222
    high school and college career, 48–53,
        55–56
    at Mexico City Olympics finals,
        193–194
    post–Mexico City legacy, 209–210
Fosbury Flop, 48, 49–50
400-meters event, 74
Free, Mickey, 18
Freeman, Ron, 97, 149, 151–152, 165,
    182, 184
Fremont, John C., 17
Frenn, George, 103, 141–142

Games Must Go On, The (Guttmann), 46
Gammoudi, Mohamed, 4, 5, 122, 190
Gay Games, 210
gender testing, 175
Gibson, Bob, 62
Gittins, Boyd, 126–128
Glickman, Marty, 46
Green, Jim, 80, 82
Greene, Charlie, 79–80, 82, 119, 121,
    125, 165, 166, 175–176, 192
Guttmann, Allen, 46

Hall, Al, 142

Hall, Erv, 66, 68, 103, 114, 144, 188, 194, 214
Hall, John, 183
Hamilton, Brutus, 99
hammer throw, origin of, 142
Hampton, Bob, 19
Hanley, Daniel, 5
Harrah, Bill, 14, 20
Hart, Eddie, 202, 203
Hartfield, John, 153, 159, 160–162, 203
Hartfield, Toni Wright, 160, 162
Harvard crew team, 109
Hay, Eduardo, 2
Heavenly Valley training site, 15
Hemery, Dave, 64, 76, 177
Herrerias, Rene, 75, 76
Higgins, Ralph, 13, 18, 154
high-altitude centers, 12–16, *13*, 19, 85
     See also Echo Summit
Highway 50. *See* US Highway 50 (Lincoln Highway)
Hill, Dick, 35, 143
Hines, Jim, 42, 79–82, *81*, 119, 121, 125, 160, 165, 166, 175–176, 192, 200, 201
Hodge, Russ, 118–121, *118*, 189, 219–220
Hoffman, Paul, 109
Hohne, Christoph, 189
Holdorf, Willi, 118
Humphrey, Hubert, 86

Indian Summer Games. *See* South Lake Tahoe Indian Summer Games
Inman, Stu, 28–29
International Amateur Athletic Federation (IAAF), 17, 82, 151, 175
International Olympic Committee (IOC), 1–2, 44–45, 47, 73, 112, 175, 182–183, 198
     See also Brundage, Avery
International Symposium on the Effects of Altitude on Physical Performance, 4
Irish Whales, 142

Jamaica, 165, 192
James, Larry J., Jr., 214

James, Larry "the Mighty Burner," 63–64, 67–69, 74–75, 79, 88–89, 97, 105, 149–152, *150*, 184, 193
     post–Mexico City legacy, 214–215
Jarvis, Bob, 117
Jenkins, Charlie, 65
Jipcho, Ben, 191, 192
Jochim, Al, 172
Johnson, John Calhoun "Cockeye," 16–17
Johnson, Lyndon Baines, 57, 59, 62
Johnson, Rafer, 32, 76
Johnson's Cutoff, 17
Jones, Jim, 9
Jones, Lou, 3–4
Jordan, Payton, 9–10, *10*, 19, 108, 117, 140, 149, 166, 186, 195, 212, 217
Jump (Brill), 54

Kaepernick, Colin, 199
Kaye, Danny, 101
Keino, Kipchoge "Kip," 6–7, 91, 191, 217
Kemp, Jim, 89, 150
Kennedy, John F., 78
Kennedy, Robert F., 76, 77, 78
Keys, Bob, 19
Killanin, Lord, 204
Killebrew, Bill, 15
King, Martin Luther, Jr., xx, 41, 57–60
Kiprugut, Wilson, 178
Klobukowska, Ewa, 175
Knight, Phil, 7, 114, 203
Knoxville News-Sentinel, 64, 67
Kutschinski, Ron, 129

La Noche Triste. See Tlatelolco massacre
Labetich, Ron, 29
Lake Tahoe, 12
Laris, Tom, 95, 123, 124
Laxalt, Paul, 15
Leatham, Victoria, 176
Leisz, Doug, 20–21
Lewis, Harley, 13, 18, 19
Lewis, Theron, 43, 152
Liljenwall, Hans-Gunnar, 175
Lincoln Highway (US Highway 50), 18, 21, 87

Lindgren, Gerry, 77–78, *77*, 83, 96–97, 101, 122–124, 145, 146, 202
Liquori, Marty, 45, 104, 114, 154, 156–158, *157*, 206–207
Little, Barbara, 11
Little, Bill, 11, 16, 218
Little, Richard, 11
Little, Vivian, 11
Little, Walt, III, xx, 11
Little, Walt, Jr., 9, 11, 15, 16, 218–219, *219*
Little, Walt, Sr., 10–11
Little Olympics, 5
Livingston, Cleve, 109
Lodge, Hilmer, 8, 84, 100
Loeb, Henry, 58
Lomax, Louis, 40, 179
Los Alamos, New Mexico, xxii, 13, 19, 85
Los Angeles Black Youth Conference, 39
Los Angeles Olympic trials, 83–85

MacArthur, Douglas, 78
Maggard, Dave, 97–98, 99–100, 102, 125–126, 173, 174, 176, 189, 212
Marshall, Gene, 19
Marshall, James, 14
Martinez, Juan, 95
Mathias, Bob, 9
Matson, Randy, 97–100, *98*, 112, 125–126, 167–168, 170, 173, 174–175, 194, 212
Matte, Harry, 116
Matthews, Vince, 97, 113, 149–152, 165, 182, 198, 214
Mays, Charles "Charlie," 87, 140–141, 148–149, 166, 187
McAlhaney, Hardee, 68
McCrary, Paddy, 126
McCullouch, Earl, 85, 142–143
McGuire, Edith, 44
McKay, Jim, 157
McKissick, Floyd, 41, 59
Memphis Commercial Appeal, 58
Mexico City, Mexico, selection of, 1–6
Mexico City Olympics (1968)
    call for boycott of, 24, 26, 38–44, 61–63, 84, 108, 168
    living accommodations, 173–174

South Africa and threat of boycott, 73
    student protests prior to, xix, 169–172
    US track and field medal count and world records set at, 192, 194
    women's events at, 178
Mexico City Olympics finals
    decathlon, 189
    hurdles, 177, 188
    jumping events, 185–187, 188, 190, 193–194
    long distance, 174, 190–191
    middle distance, 191–192
    racewalk, 189
    relays, 192–193
    sprints, 175–176, 179–180, 184–185
    throwing events, 174–175, 176–177, 189–190
Miller, Lennox, 76, 79, 80, 176
Mills, Billy, 4, 5, 74, 78, 121–124, 144–145, 213
Mills, Curtis, 196
Mills, Pat, 122
Montecito Country Club, 45
Moore, Kenny, 129, 194, 196, 202, 220
Moore, Tom, 80, 136
Morgan, Dave, 70
Morrow, Lance, xix
Mount Mitchell, North Carolina, 9
Munich Olympics, 197–198, 204, 212
Musburger, Brent, 183

Nam Seung-yong, 30
National Association of Intercollegiate Athletics (NAIA), 42
National Collegiate Athletic Association (NCAA), 77–78
National Collegiate Athletic Association (NCAA) Championships, *xi*, 75–76, 78, 83
National Museum of African American History and Culture, 199
National Track & Field Hall of Fame, 203, 204
Nelson, Van, 86–87, 94, 124
New York Athletic Club (NYAC), 40, 44, 46–47, 63

New York Times, 24, 58
Nieder, Bill, 22–23
Night of Sorrow. *See* Tlatelolco massacre
Night of Speed, 79
Nightingale, Conrad, 91
Nike, 7, 203
Nordwig, Wolfgang, 188
Norman, Peter, 179, 180, *181*, 182
Norpoth, Harald, 191

Obama, Barack, 199, 213
Oberlin College, 198
O'Brien, Parry, 50, 172
"Ode to Joy" (Beethoven), 189
Oerter, Al, 46, 75, 100, 112, 130–132,
     131, 170–171, 176–177, 183, 194,
     209
O'Hanlan, J. T., 52–53
Olimpia Battalion, 170
Olympic Project for Human Rights
     (OPHR), xx, xxii, xxv, 24, 26,
     41–44, 47, 63, 200–201
Olympic trials. *See* Echo Summit trials
Olympic Village, 173–174
Owens, Jesse, xx, 182, 187

Pan American Games, 3–4
Pan American Games (1955), 3–4
Patrick, Dave, 47, 63, 68–69, 76, 85, 104,
     113–115, 153–158, *157*, 211–212
Pender, Mel, xv, xix, *xxiii*, 80, *81*, 82,
     124–125, 165, 166, 168, 175–176,
     207–208, *208*
Pennel, John, 134, 190
Presley, Bob, 75
Press, Tamara and Irina, 175
Pryde, Jim, 97, 141
Puma, 50, 103–104, 187–188
Puma 68s (brush spikes), 136, *138*, 151

Quande, Bruce, 53–54
Questad, Larry, 80, 136, 137–138, *137*,
     166, 183, 192

race relations, 32, 45–47, 65–67, 85, 107–
     110, 130, 143, 145, 148, 167, 182,
     206–207
Randolph, Tom, 136

Reagan, Ronald, 15, 22, 39, 75
Return to the Summit, xiv–xxiv
Revolt of the Black Athlete, The (Edwards),
     185
Rice, Bob, 20–21, *21*
Riefenstahl, Leni, 45
Robinson, Jackie, xx
Robinson, Rey, 202
Roby, Douglas, 1, 184
Rogers, Russ, 89, 100, 102–103
Rohe, Chuck, 65, 66
Romary, Janice, 172, 173
Rose, Ralph, 172
Roughing It (Twain), 12
Royal, Darrell, 63
Rudolph, Wilma, 44
Running Strong for American Indian
     Youth, 213
Ryun, Jim, 13, 79, 91–92, 128–130,
     153–154, 156–158, *157*, 191–192,
     207

Saffold, S. T., 29, 31, 33, 34, 168–169
San Francisco Chronicle, 76, 79
San Jose, California ("Speed City"), 24
San Jose State, 39, 199, 204
San Jose State Spartans, 74, 196
Schiprowski, Claus, 188
Schroeder, Bill, 19
Schul, Bob, 4, 74
Scott, Jack, 198
Scott, Jarvis, 175
Scott, Lou, 93, 145–146
Seagren, Bob, 133–134, *135*, 165, 174,
     178, 188, 194, 212–213, 217
Shinnick, Phil, 111, 112, 148–149, 210–211
shoe wars, 50, 103–104, 186
     See also Adidas; Puma
Silvester, Jay, 75, 100, 101, 103–104, 108,
     130–131, 165, 173, 176–177, 209
Simburg, Art, 34, 103, 188, 198
Simmons, Steve, 214
Sloan, Rick, 88, 101, 102, 120, 141
Smit, Barbara, 103
Smith, Delois, xxiii
Smith, Denise, 84, 179
Smith, James Richard, 31, 32
Smith, John, 198

Smith, Ronnie Ray, 38, 80, 121, 125, 165, 166
Smith, Tommie, xiv, xx, xxiii, 39, 40, 82, 84–85, 110, 136, 166, 168
    on adjusting to Echo Summit track, 97
    on Bob Segren's pole vault, xvii
    childhood and adolescence, 31–32
    emerging activism, 33–34
    expulsion from Olympic Village, 182–184, 196
    Harry Edwards and, 24, 25–26, 200
    Lee Evans and, 35
    military service, xix, 33
    Olympic performances by, 179–180
    photographs, xv, xxii, 137, 139, 181, 197
    post–Mexico City legacy, 196–199
    at San Jose State, 32–34
    world records held, 34, 36
Smith, Tracy, xiv, xix, 95, 123–124, 174, 191
snake dance, 150
Sohn Kee-chung, 30
South Africa, 44–45, 47, 73
South Lake Tahoe, 9, 11–12, 13, 15–16, 18–20, 101, 219
South Lake Tahoe Indian Summer Games, 217
South Tahoe Intermediate School, xv, 15, 141
Soviet Union, 4, 7, 73
Sports Illustrated, 2, 3, 70, 91, 153, 206
Stageberg, Steve, 13
steroids, use of, 50, 110–111, 112
Stoller, Sam, 46
Stones, Dwight, 50, 55, 162–163
Stough, Carl "Dr. Breath," 93
student movements, xviii–xix, 169
Summer Olympics. *See* Mexico City Olympics
Summers, Frank, 28
"Superstars" (TV competition), 213

Tahoe Daily Tribune, 16
Tartan (brand) tracks, xxiii, 22–23, 50, 66, 116, 186, 217

Tate, Norm, *xv*, xviii, xxi, *xxiii*, 43, 100–102, 130, 140–141, 148, 167, 168, 209, 217–218
Tate, Ralph, 154
Temple, Ed, 43–44
Temu, Naftali, 7, 174
Tennessee State University, 43–44
Tennessee Volunteers, 68
Ter-Ovanesyan, Igor, 61
Texas Southern University Flying Tigers, 42
Texas Western Miners. *See* University of Texas at El Paso (UTEP) Miners
Thompson, John "Snowshoe," 17
3M Company, 22
Title IX (US Education Amendments of 1972), 107
Tlatelolco massacre, 170–171, 172
Tokyo Olympics (1964), 4, 44, 121–123
Toomey, Bill, xviii, 86, 89, 102, 118–120, 164–165, 167, 189, 194, 195, 213, 219
track and field, improvements in, 50
track meets map, *xi*
Tracy, Bob, 13, 15, 16, 18, 87
Tümmler, Bodo, 191
Twain, Mark, 12
Tyus, Wyomia, 44, 177, 178–179, 188

United Black Students for Action, 39
United States Track and Field Federation, 78
University of Tennessee Volunteers, 63, 67, 68
University of Texas at El Paso (UTEP) Miners, 69
US Department of Agriculture (USDA), 211
US Education Amendments of 1972 (Title IX), 107
US Forest Service, xiv, xvi, xx–xxi, 20
    See also Rice, Bob
US Highway 50 (Lincoln Highway), 18, 21, 87
US Men's Olympic Team, 222–223
US Olympic Committee (USOC), xvi, 4, 105, 167, 199, 202–203, 210
    Bill Bowerman and, 7–8

Echo Summit Olympic trials and, 79, 116

expulsion of Carlos and Smith by, 182–183

high-altitude training camp selection by, 12–16, 19

Los Angeles Olympic trials and, 83–85

oversight of medical testing by, 92–93

US Olympic women's team, xxii, 43–44, 85, 105, 167, 178, 193

UT Daily Beacon, 67

UTEP Miners, University of Texas at El Paso Miners

Vandenburg, Wayne, 69, 71–72

Vanderstock, Geoff, xiv, *xvii*, xviii, xxiv, 126–128, *127*, 149, 165, 177, 183, 212–213

victory stand statues, 199

Vietnam War, xviii, xix, 57, 164

Villanova Wildcats, 63, 68, 74–75

Villareal, Joe, 95

Von Ruden, Tom, *90*, 154–157

Waddell, Tom "Tommie the Commie," 110–112, 120, 210

Wagner, Berny, 52, 161–162

Walde, Hans-Joachim, 189

Walker, Art, 168, 182

Wallace, George, 65

Walnut, California, xxii, 85, 105

Walsh, Bill, 168

Warkentin, John, 220

West Coast Relays, 74–75

White, Willye, 105

Whitney, Ron, xiv, *xxiii*, 126–127, 128

Wieczorek, Larry, 13

Wilborn, Dave, *90*, 156, *157*

Williams, John, 9, 18–19, 20

Williams, Willie, 159

Wilson, Paul, 134

Winter, Lloyd "Bud," 24, 28, 33, 36, 37, 150, 196, 204

Winzenried, Mark, 129

Wolde, Mamo, 6, 122, 174, 202

women athletes. *See* US Olympic women's team

Woods, George, 125, 126

Woods, Norman, *219*

Wright, Stan, 41–43, 63, 84, 152, 160, 165–167, 180, 192, 202–203

Wright, Toni. *See* Hartfield, Toni Wright

Wyatt, Tom, 126–127

Young, George, 84, 90, 94, 108, 138, 190–191

Young, Larry, xiv, *xv*, 189

Zahn, Mel, 185–186